INHERITANCE

INHERITANCE

The Story of Knole and the Sackvilles

Robert Sackville-West

Walker & Company
New York

Extracts from *Orlando* by Virginia Woolf reproduced by kind permission of
The Society of Authors as the Literary Representative of the Estate of Virginia Woolf

Extracts from *Pepita* by Vita Sackville-West reproduced with permission
of Curtis Brown Ltd, London, on behalf of the Estate of Vita
Sackville-West. Copyright © Vita Sackville-West 1937

Extracts from *The Diary of Virginia Woolf* edited by Anne Olivier Bell, published
by Hogarth Press, used by permission of the Random House Group Ltd

Images are from the author's collection, except where credited otherwise.

Published by Walker Publishing Company, Inc., New York

All papers used by Walker & Company are natural, recyclable products made
from wood grown in well-managed forests. The manufacturing processes
conform to the environmental regulations of the country of origin.

Every reasonable effort has been made to contact copyright
holders of images reproduced in this book, but if any have been
inadvertently overlooked the publishers would be glad to hear from them and
to make good in future editions any errors or omissions brought to their attention.

LIBRARY OF CONGRESS CATALOGING-IN-PUBLICATION DATA

Sackville-West, Robert.
Inheritance : the story of Knole and the Sackvilles / Robert Sackville-West. — 1st U.S. ed.
p. cm.
Includes bibliographical references and index.
ISBN: 978-0-8027-7901-4
1. Knole (Sevenoaks, England) —History. 2. Sackville family. 3. Aristocracy (Social
class)—England—Biography. 4. Sevenoaks (England)—Genealogy. I. Title.
DA690.K7S28 2010
929.7′2—dc22
2010004253

Visit Walker & Company's Web site at www.walkerbooks.com

First U.S. edition 2010

1 3 5 7 9 10 8 6 4 2

Typeset by Hewer Text UK Ltd, Edinburgh
Printed in the United States of America by Worldcolor Fairfield

For Jane

Contents

PLAN OF THE HOUSE

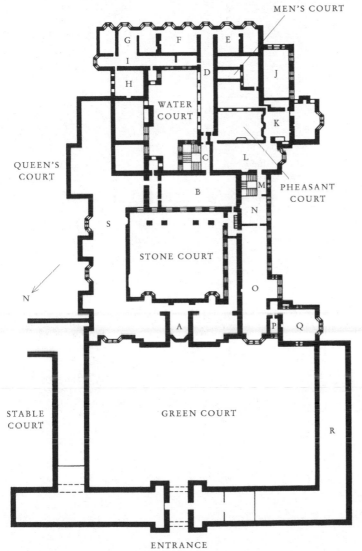

MEN'S COURT

G F E

I D

H J

WATER
COURT K

QUEEN'S
COURT C L

M

B N PHEASANT
COURT

S

STONE COURT O

N

A P Q

STABLE
COURT GREEN COURT

R

ENTRANCE

0   50   100
feet

KEY

A Inner Wicket
   (under Bourchier's
   Tower and Clock)

B Great Hall

C Great Staircase

D Brown Gallery

E Lady Betty Germain's
   Bedroom

F Spangle Bedroom

G Billiard Room

H Venetian Ambassador's
   Room

I Leicester Gallery

J Chapel

K Archbishop Bourchier's
   Great Chamber

L Ballroom (formerly
   Thomas Sackville's
   Great Chamber) on first
   floor; Poets' Parlour on
   ground floor

M Second Painted Staircase

N Reynolds Room

O Cartoon Gallery on first
   floor; Colonnade and
   Boudoir on ground floor

P King's Closet

Q King's Room on first
   floor; Library on ground
   floor

R Orangery

S North Wing

THE SACKVILLES OF KNOLE

Owners of Knole are in CAPITALS

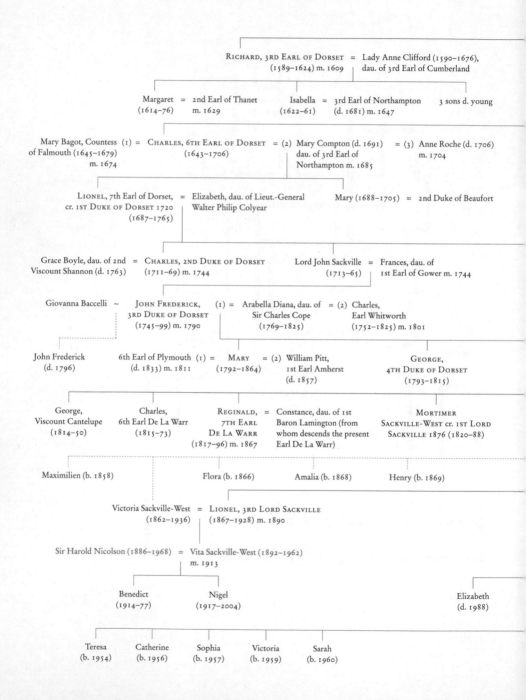

RICHARD, 3RD EARL OF DORSET = Lady Anne Clifford (1590–1676),
(1589–1624) m. 1609 | dau. of 3rd Earl of Cumberland

Margaret = 2nd Earl of Thanet
(1614–76) m. 1629

Isabella = 3rd Earl of Northampton
(1622–61) (d. 1681) m. 1647

3 sons d. young

Mary Bagot, Countess (1) = CHARLES, 6TH EARL OF DORSET = (2) Mary Compton (d. 1691) = (3) Anne Roche (d. 1706)
of Falmouth (1645–1679) (1643–1706) dau. of 3rd Earl of m. 1704
m. 1674 Northampton m. 1685

LIONEL, 7th Earl of Dorset, = Elizabeth, dau. of Lieut.-General
cr. 1ST DUKE OF DORSET 1720 | Walter Philip Colyear
(1687–1765)

Mary (1688–1705) = 2nd Duke of Beaufort

Grace Boyle, dau. of 2nd = CHARLES, 2ND DUKE OF DORSET
Viscount Shannon (d. 1763) (1711–69) m. 1744

Lord John Sackville = Frances, dau. of
(1713–65) | 1st Earl of Gower m. 1744

Giovanna Baccelli ~ JOHN FREDERICK, (1) = Arabella Diana, dau. of = (2) Charles,
3RD DUKE OF DORSET Sir Charles Cope Earl Whitworth
(1745–99) m. 1790 (1769–1825) (1752–1825) m. 1801

John Frederick
(d. 1796)

6th Earl of Plymouth (1) = MARY = (2) William Pitt,
(d. 1833) m. 1811 (1792–1864) 1st Earl Amherst
(d. 1857)

GEORGE,
4TH DUKE OF DORSET
(1793–1815)

George,
Viscount Cantelupe
(1814–50)

Charles,
6th Earl De La Warr
(1815–73)

REGINALD, = Constance, dau. of 1st
7TH EARL Baron Lamington (from
DE LA WARR whom descends the present
(1817–96) m. 1867 Earl De La Warr)

MORTIMER
SACKVILLE-WEST cr. 1ST LORD
SACKVILLE 1876 (1820–88)

Maximilien (b. 1858)

Flora (b. 1866)

Amalia (b. 1868)

Henry (b. 1869)

Victoria Sackville-West = LIONEL, 3RD LORD SACKVILLE
(1862–1936) | (1867–1928) m. 1890

Sir Harold Nicolson (1886–1968) = Vita Sackville-West (1892–1962)
m. 1913

Benedict
(1914–77)

Nigel
(1917–2004)

Elizabeth
(d. 1988)

Teresa
(b. 1954)

Catherine
(b. 1956)

Sophia
(b. 1957)

Victoria
(b. 1959)

Sarah
(b. 1960)

Sir Richard Sackville = Winifred, dau. of Sir John Bruges,
(d. 1566) | Lord Mayor of London

THOMAS SACKVILLE (1536–1608) = Cicely, dau. of Sir John Baker,
cr. Lord Buckhurst 1567 and 1ST EARL OF DORSET 1604 | of Sissinghurst (d. 1615)

Lady Margaret Howard (1), = ROBERT, 2ND EARL OF DORSET = (2) Anne, dau. of Sir
dau. of 4th Duke of Norfolk (d. 1591) | (1561–1609) | John Spencer of Althorp

EDWARD, 4TH EARL OF DORSET = Mary Curzon, dau. and heiress of Sir George
(1590–1652) m. 1612 | Curzon, of Croxhall, Derbyshire (d. 1645)

RICHARD, 5TH EARL OF DORSET (1) = Lady Frances Cranfield, dau. and heiress of = (2) Henry Powle
(1622–77) | Lionel Cranfield, Earl of Middlesex (d. 1687) | m. 1679

| Edward | Mary | Richard | Anne | Frances | Thomas |
| (1644–78) | (1648–1710) | (1649–1712) | (1650–1722) | (1655–1722) | (1663–1675) |

Lord George Sackville (assumed the name of Germain) = Diana, dau. of John
(1716–85) cr. 1st Viscount Sackville of Drayton 1782 | Sambrooke m. 1754

Charles Sackville-Germain, George (d. 1836) = Harriet Pearce
2nd Viscount Sackville,
5th and last Duke of Dorset (d. 1843)

ELIZABETH = George West, 5th Earl De La Warr   Caroline Harriet Sackville of Drayton = William Bruce Stopford
(1795–1870) | assumed name and arms of Sackville-   (assumed with her husband the name
m. 1813 | West 1843 (1791–1869)   of Stopford Sackville)

LIONEL, ~ Josefa Duran = Juan Antonio   Col. Hon. William = Georgina, dau. of   3 daughters
2ND LORD SACKVILLE : (Pepita) de Oliva   Edward Sackville- | George Dodwell
(1827–1908) (1830–71) (1831–89)   West (1830–1905) | m. 1860

Maud, dau. of (1) = MAJ.-GEN. SIR CHARLES = (2) Anne, widow of   Hon. Bertrand = Eva, dau. of
Capt. Matthew Bell | SACKVILLE-WEST, 4TH LORD | Stephen Bigelow   Sackville-West | Maj.-Gen. Inigo
(d. 1920) | SACKVILLE (1870–1962)   (d. 1959) | Richmond Jones

Edward, 5th Lord Sackville (1901–65)   Diana (d. 1975)

Jacobine, dau. of J. R. (1) = Lionel, 6th Lord = (3) Jean, widow of Sir Edward   Hugh Sackville- = Bridget, dau. of Capt.
Menzies-Wilson (d. 1971) | Sackville (1913–2004) | Imbert-Terry (d. 2009)   West (1919–2001) | Robert Cunliffe, RN

Jane, dau. of = Robert, 7th Lord Sackville   Mary   Elizabeth   Jane   William
Mark MacAndrew | (b. 1958)   (b. 1960)   (b. 1962)   (b. 1964)   (b. 1967)

| Freya (b. 1998) | Arthur (b. 2000) | Edie (b. 2003) |

Preface

In the side chapel of the parish church at Withyham in Sussex, a magnificent stained-glass window provides a genealogy of the Sackville family, with an inscription that reads '*Nobilis familia Sackville hic expectat resurrectionem*' – 'Here the noble Sackville family await the resurrection.'

Nothing in this ambitious claim is any indication of what lies below. A modest wooden door, barred to all but the family, opens onto a flight of steps leading down to the family vault. Here, on three-storey shelves that line the dusty whitewashed walls, are stacked the coffins. Those of the more recent dukes and earls are covered in red velvet, studded with gilt decoration, and crowned with coronets. But the older they are, the more frayed the velvet and the more tarnished, and lacking in lustre, the gilt. Even further back in time, and the wood of the coffins has begun to rot away, exposing the lead cases in which the bodies were entombed, including the heartbreakingly tiny ones, no more than eighteen inches long, of infant children; in some cases, even the lead itself has come unsealed, and a couple of skulls have spilled out, and are now tucked between the coffins on a shelf.

In the early nineteenth century, in his *Memoirs of Lord Viscount Sackville*, George Coventry described the vault, which has changed little to this day: 'You are surrounded on either side by . . . those who once figured on the stage of life, and who were justly ranked among the honourable of the earth.' Coventry found a brass commemorating the subject of his memoirs: 'There is nothing further to perpetuate his memory or to record the worth of this distinguished character. No encomium, no comment: there he lies in the sepulchre of his forefathers; a lesson to the survivors of the instability of all human greatness.'

Thomas Sackville, the first member of my family to live at Knole, chose to be buried at Withyham, a few hundred yards from the home of his birth, Buckhurst. With only one exception, every single incumbent of Knole from Thomas Sackville to the 4th Lord Sackville in the 1960s has followed: a procession of earls, dukes and barons making a final journey of twenty miles or so from their grand ancestral home at Knole, where they died, to their more humble, earthy roots in a village on the outskirts of Ashdown Forest. All the characters who people the pages of this book – the grave Elizabethan statesman, the good-for-nothing gadabout at the seedy court of King James I, the dashing Cavalier, the Restoration rake, that magnificent and melancholy representative of the ancien régime, the 3rd Duke, and so on – they all returned to Withyham because the place exercised an emotional hold on them almost as intense as Knole.

Vita Sackville-West's remains are here, too. Her ashes were placed in a small pink marble urn, which had previously rested on her old desk at her home, Sissinghurst, and taken to the family vault at Withyham, where she joined her father and her uncle Charlie, who had died a month before. The urn now rests on her father's coffin, beside another urn bearing the ashes of a recently departed dog, belonging to her De La Warr cousins (Vita would not have minded – she was a great dog lover). But conspicuous by his absence is her husband Harold Nicolson. When Harold once suggested that he might one day join Vita at Withyham, she replied that she would not have him there – for the simple reason that he was not a Sackville.

Vita's cousin, Eddy Sackville-West, the 5th Lord Sackville, had intended to be buried in the crypt at Withyham, 'amongst the velvet

palls and silver coroneted coffins of his eighteenth-century ancestors', according to his friend, James Lees-Milne. But he had fallen
in love with the small village of Clogheen in Ireland, where he had
settled, and was buried there instead. My uncle Lionel, the 6th Lord
Sackville, talked about it to the De La Warrs, but eventually chose
for his ashes to be buried near his first wife's, beneath the flagstones
of the chapel at Knole, the house he loved. Me? I haven't yet made
up my mind.

The cramped physical conditions in which they chose to spend
the afterlife – the coffins stacked condominium-style on shelves in
the bowels of a simple parish church, could not have been more
different from the house they had departed; for Knole, not his
tomb, was Thomas's monument to posterity. Thomas wanted the
house to tell the world that he and his family had finally arrived. In
the words of the seventeenth-century statesman and philosopher
Francis Bacon: 'when men sought to cure mortality by fame . . .
buildings were the only way'.

No one is quite sure what Knole looked like in the early
fifteenth century, a couple of hundred years before it was acquired
by Thomas. There are some remains of towers, stairs and curtain
walls in the south-east corner of the house, where my family
and I now live. These scattered fragments probably formed part
of a medieval manor house and subsequently became embedded
in later structures. In 1456, Thomas Bourchier, Archbishop of
Canterbury, bought the manor of Knole – and whatever survived
of the earlier manor house – from Sir William Fiennes, Lord
Saye and Sele, for £266 13s. 4d. He built a massive gatehouse,
Bourchier's Tower, at the west end of the house, opening onto
the Stone Court. At the far side of the Stone Court stood the
Great Hall and Bourchier's reception rooms in the great chamber
block. Beyond the Great Hall, Bourchier incorporated elements
of the earlier house around a second courtyard, the Water Court,
on the north side of which were his kitchen, offices and service
areas, and on the south side were his private apartments and his
chapel. Where we now live, therefore, was once the heart of an
archbishop's palace.

Bourchier died at Knole in 1486, bequeathing the house to the see of Canterbury, and his successors as Archbishop, John Morton and William Warham, enlarged and improved the building. They added another external layer or skin to the western side of the house, creating what is now the Green Court and adding a new main entrance. Ranged around the Green Court, rather like the quadrangle of an Oxbridge college of a similar date, were sets of rooms, each reached by individual stairways, to house the Archbishop's retinue. They also added a range to the east of the house, beside the chapel, connected to the Great Hall by galleries which gradually caused the sprawling house to coalesce. These galleries also provided a brief pause, a processional space, halfway between the public and the private rooms.

In 1538, Thomas Cranmer, who had succeeded Warham as Archbishop of Canterbury in 1532, was forced 'voluntarily' to give Knole to King Henry VIII. Henry did not spend much time, or money, at Knole – after all, he had acquired a total of sixty royal residences by the time of his death. His daughter, Queen Elizabeth, however, visited Knole – her property – on a royal progress in 1573, almost certainly spending the night in what is now our bedroom.

This book is not, however, about Knole's early history. My story begins with Thomas Sackville. When Thomas took possession of Knole in 1604, he remodelled it entirely, turning a draughty and ramshackle medieval mansion into a Renaissance palace: a great show house to celebrate his success. His Sackville successors added to the house, using it to display the unique Stuart furniture they had acquired as cast-offs from the royal palaces and, later, the Old Master paintings they had bought on Grand Tours as a symbol of their wealth, taste and status.

Knole was built and furnished to awe and impress; and it has been a show house ever since. It is precisely this that can make it so impenetrable, such a difficult place to understand. Some people are put off by its sheer size, overwhelmed by its superlatives. It is one of the largest private houses in England, a calendar house with – allegedly – 365 rooms, 52 staircases and 7 courtyards, spread over 4 acres.

'Knole is a conglomeration of buildings half as big as Cambridge I daresay,' Virginia Woolf recorded on her first visit to Knole in July 1924; 'but the extremities & indeed the inward parts are gone dead. Ropes fence off half the rooms; the chairs & the pictures look preserved; life has left them.' Knole is vast and labyrinthine. It takes a long time to walk from one end of the house to the other, and the main routes meander through a series of lobbies or come to sudden stops at dead ends. On the way, you encounter the most unexpected juxtapositions: an eighteenth-century fire engine here, a range of cobwebbed classical busts there; a faraway attic room where Victorian wash jugs jostle with Greek pottery; corridors where First World War military uniforms and cavalry boots tumble out of cupboards, phials of laudanum lurk in Victorian medicine chests, and love letters from another age curl on a windowsill. It is the junk, the bits and pieces that people could never bring themselves to throw away that reveal just as much about the past as Knole's unrivalled collection of Tudor and Stuart furniture.

All those portraits and all the stuff that the subjects of those portraits left behind – the old bills and swatches of fabric – are everyday reminders of particular moments in the past. The rocking horse, for example, belonging to the 4th Duke, who inherited the title at the age of six: it was his death, fifteen years later – his spine crushed by a falling horse in a hunting accident – that brought the name of Sackville to the verge of extinction. The tulip trees in the garden where Vita's mother Victoria surprised her husband with his lover, Olive Rubens, in May 1919, precipitating Victoria's departure from Knole; our dining room, where Virginia Woolf lunched that summer's day: 'His lordship lives in the kernel of a vast nut. You perambulate miles of galleries; skip endless treasures . . . & penetrate at length to a round shiny table with a cover laid for one.' All these places, and the objects that fill them, are freighted with emotional significance, the subject of stories that have been handed down from generation to generation, and reinterpreted in one great concentration of past and present.

Far from being an empty, lifeless shell, Knole is full of personal associations; and it is the people who have lived there who bring the house to life. This book focuses on one family, the Sackvilles, on the private life of a very public place. It is a saga, unashamedly, of aristocratic life.

How often have you wondered who else has looked out of the same windows in your house and onto the same view, moved perhaps by the same longings and losses as you? Who has made love, given birth, died in your house, and where? Made and broken promises, slammed doors in anger, sobbed with laughter or grief? The way in which places are cluttered with the echoes of other people's experiences can be a matter of remote, vicarious curiosity. At Knole, those other people who have lived there, and whose experiences animate the house and its collection, who make it live and breathe, are my ancestors. They've left their smells and spores behind: in the dust, the worn leather, the potpourri of faded rose petals, the musty whiff of the boot room, the woodsmoke, the polish.

Not only do they share a genetic history, but also a shared predicament, their experiences eerily identical across the centuries. From portraits on the walls, their flinty, watchful gaze continues to follow their descendants hundreds of years later. It is easy to imagine them, too, feeling fretful or fearful in the middle of a sleepless night, as the great house creaks and wheezes around them, and the grandfather clocks tick away the time till they die. This is the story, then, of a family, my family, described by Vita as 'a race too prodigal, too amorous, too weak, too indolent, and too melancholy'. In short, 'a rotten lot, and nearly all stark staring mad'.

So what are the ties that bind these members of my family? Is it a quirk of heredity or some specific characteristic of their home, such as its size? Knole has lured generations of heirs with the promise of an ancestral place, an aristocratic life, a sense of unearned esteem and belonging. Many of these Sackvilles have revelled in the opportunity and loved the place. But others, once seduced, have found the expectation actually to lead an aristocratic life, or to maintain such a huge inheritance, hard to manage. The place has ground them down, becoming a curse and a burden, rather than a glory. The hopes they had invested in that Renaissance palace, seen glittering in the summer sunshine, became entombed in a great, grey, ragstone sprawl, sodden in the winter rain.

Those members of the family for whom there was never a hope of inheriting – the daughters, the younger sons, the widows, and the bastards – have had even more mixed reactions to the place. Knole has pulled them in and then pushed them away, acquiring in the process a monstrous organic energy of its own, far greater than that of any individual, influencing the lives they led and their relationships.

In his will, Thomas Sackville directed that his legacy, Knole, should – like the diamond-studded gold ring he had received from King James I – be handed from 'heir male to heir male' in perpetuity. From then on, as in most English aristocratic families, the principle of primogeniture, whereby property is passed through the male line, has prevailed. It is a principle that has been pretty much extinct throughout the rest of Europe for the past century and a half, but in England it has kept inheritances such as Knole more or less intact, rather than split between a number of children, and eventually dispersed.

At Knole, the shifting sideways of the inheritance, as it has moved crablike from generation to generation, setting brothers against sisters, mothers against sons, has tended to repeat itself against an unchanging brooding backdrop. I, too, have a stake in this story as the beneficiary of primogeniture. In my teens, I became aware that I was likely to inherit what was left to the family of Knole, bypassing five girl cousins, and taking precedence over four siblings, who were also brought up at Knole; and in 2004 I succeeded my uncle.

Over the past 200 years, there has been only one direct father–son succession at Knole; and so, woven into the story of the place, is a sense of disappointment and disinheritance. This is first apparent in the diaries of Lady Anne Clifford, who lived at Knole in the early seventeenth century. Anne felt doubly disinherited, excluded from her father's Clifford estates in the north of England and from her husband's Sackville estates in the south. Three hundred years later, similar resentments resonate in the writings of Vita Sackville-West, who was also barred from Knole by virtue of her gender. Vita did, however, recognise the pressures Knole imposes on its heirs – its life tenants – as well as on its disinherited. In *The Edwardians*, the novel which recreates the lost world of her childhood before the First World War, she raises, but fails to resolve, the reactionary and the rebel strains that struggled within her soul. Her main character, Sebastian, is made aware that he is as much a slave to his inheritance as a free agent. 'A place like Chevron [Knole] is really a despot of the most sinister sort: it disguises its tyranny under the mask of love . . . Then there is another danger which you can scarcely hope to escape. It is the weight of the past . . . That is real atrophy of the soul.'

A feeling of merely passing through the place weighs heavily on many of the people who have lived at Knole, particularly the women. Lady Anne Clifford felt shut out of the running of her husband's household; Vita's mother, Victoria, complained that she had 'slaved away' at Knole for nothing, her management of the house wrested from her when her husband returned from the First World War with a 'new authority'.

Is it possible, then, to make a mark on a house you'll never own, to carve a space for yourself in the corner of a sixteenth-century mansion, to celebrate a present that is not overwhelmed by the past? As I write this book, builders are creating a new home for us in the South Wing at Knole – just as previous Sackvilles have embarked on refurbishments every generation or so. Floorboards have been lifted, and layers of the house stripped back, unpeeling centuries not just of architectural and decorative detail, but of its private life too, as the house and its former inhabitants give up their secrets. Surrounded by packing cases, trunks of old papers and by piles of writing on Knole, I have spent two years of total immersion in the place; and have come to realise that whatever you do, you have to respect, and not fight against, that feel Knole has of fading magnificence, that magic which smoulders rather than sparkles. As new layers are applied, the question I often ask myself – and cannot answer yet – is this: In time, will those layers of today reveal lives that revelled in a glorious opportunity or ones that were swallowed up in the sheer mass of the place? Will the Knole I inhabit be a glittering Renaissance palace or a great, grey, ragstone sprawl?

Chapter 1

An Ancient Pile (1604–1608)

Thomas Sackville, 1st Earl of Dorset

As you walk out of the woods by Shot Tavern Gate, the turf falls away and there, settling into the gentle slopes of a classic English park below, lies what looks like a small town. A flag flutters from one battlemented tower, and a clock and belfry glitter in the summer haze above another, like the campanile of a Renaissance village. This approach to Knole – for the buildings below belong not to a village but to one of the largest privately owned houses in England – gives the walker the feeling of having wandered into a lost domain.

The view from here has barely changed in centuries, creating a sense of enchantment not experienced on the three-mile drive from the M25. In and out of the shade of beech trees, the fallow deer step delicately, flicking their tails: descendants of the same flock that has been grazing the park for even longer than the family which owns it. For the past 400 years, Knole has been inhabited by thirteen generations of a single family, the Sackvilles. 'Here have lived, for more centuries than I can count, the obscure generations of my own obscure family,' observes the eponymous hero in *Orlando*, Virginia Woolf's elegiac novel about Knole.

Orlando, the great country-house novel of the interwar years, is part of a tradition that reaches back to the poems of Horace in the first century BC and survives well into the twentieth century: in the novels of Woolf's lover, Vita Sackville-West (in *The Edwardians*,

Chevron is Knole), of P. G. Wodehouse and Evelyn Waugh. The tradition was flourishing too in the first half of the seventeenth century, in a genre known as the country-house poem. Around 1612, four years after Knole had been rebuilt as the home of the Sackvilles, the dramatist and poet Ben Jonson wrote 'To Penshurst', a poem praising life in the Sidney family house, a mere eight miles from Knole. For some, the poem was an oblique criticism of Knole:

> *Thou art not, Penshurst, built to envious show,*
> *Of touch, or marble; nor canst boast a row*
> *Of polished pillars, or a roof of gold:*
> *Thou hast no lantern, whereof tales are told;*
> *Or stair, or courts: but standst an ancient pile,*
> *And these grudged at, art reverenced the while.*

Jonson, ruing the passing of an era, counterpoints the joys of life in the Sidney home with life in other less satisfactory houses, in particular those of the nouveaux riches – newly powerful noblemen such as Thomas Sackville who had made their money at court and now wanted a second home in the country to show it off. Penshurst was not 'built to envious show'; nearby Knole, on the other hand, had many of the features of which Jonson disapproved: a 'lantern', 'courts' (seven of them, in fact), pillars, a grand staircase (painted in the most fashionable way), and chimney pieces of 'touch' (a black stone) or marble, rather than the natural, local materials enjoyed by Penshurst – the 'better marks, of soil, of air,/Of wood, of water'.

On the ideal estate described by Jonson and his contemporaries, the hall assumed a great importance. For it was here that everyone got together: where tenants presented their lord with the fruits of their labours in the fields – 'a capon . . . a rural cake, some nuts, some apples' – and where the lord, in turn, dispensed hospitality and good cheer: 'Where the same beer and bread, and self-same wine,/That is his lordship's, shall also be mine.' At the time Jonson was writing, this style of life had long since disappeared, at least on a regular basis, as the family had gradually withdrawn from the hurly-burly of medieval communal life into more private spaces where they could entertain at leisure. But it was recalled with a nostalgia to which there was a politically conservative purpose. During the sixteenth century, fewer landowners tended to farm their estates directly, but received rents from tenants instead. Inevitably, a less personal relationship developed, with the country house becoming increasingly removed from its agricultural context. Jonson was implying, by contrast, that the older and more traditional manor estates were more socially cohesive, bound together by medieval customs and mutual obligations, and by a lord's hospitality and good housekeeping.

This implied criticism of Knole, in favour of Penshurst, is a little unfair. For Penshurst had passed into the Sidney family in 1552 – a head start of only half a century on their supposedly upstart neighbours, the Sackvilles. The Sidneys, too, had a taste for some of the fancy finishes applied to the interiors of Knole: although struggling financially, they borrowed one of the craftsmen from the Knole works to paint the imitation marble pillars in Lady Lisle's banqueting house. In his funeral oration, George Abbot, Archbishop of Canterbury, praised Thomas Sackville, claiming that: 'No nobleman was more given to hospitality, and keeping of a great house . . . for more than twenty years besides workmen and other hired, his number [of household at his various establishments] at the least hath been 220 daily, as appeared upon cheque-roll. A very rare example in this present age of ours, when housekeeping is so decayed.'

Knole, like Penshurst, had developed over time, with a core dating from the fourteenth or fifteenth century that had been added to and adapted in the sixteenth century. It, too, was an 'ancient pile', sprawling and settling comfortably into its landscape. In *Knole and the Sackvilles*, Vita Sackville-West described her ancestral home as 'above all, an English house . . . I make bold to say it stoops to nothing either pretentious or meretricious. There is here no flourish of architecture, no ornament but the leopards.' In the final paragraph of the first chapter, she concluded that, 'Knole was no mere excrescence, no alien fabrication, no startling stranger seen between the beeches and the oaks. No other country but England could have produced it, and into no other country would it settle with such harmony and such quiet . . . It is not an incongruity like Blenheim or Chatsworth, foreign to the spirit of England. It is, rather, the greater relation of those small manor houses which hide themselves away so innumerably among the counties.'

Vita imagined Knole growing organically from the soil of south-east England, and then melting 'into the green of the garden turf, into the tawnier green of the park beyond, into the blue of the pale English sky'. The Sackvilles, too, she saw as quintessentially English, like their home. But how does the relationship between a place and the people who live there start? And where do ideas about the changelessness of this relationship, about the 'home', originate?

There is a portrait, in the National Portrait Gallery, of Thomas Sackville in 1604, the year he acquired Knole. He is seated at one end of a table with delegates to a peace conference from England and Spain – eleven of the most senior statesmen from two of Europe's most powerful nations. A gentle breeze through the open window rustles the leaves of an indoor plant, bringing some relief during the eighteen conference sessions that took place in Somerset House that summer. The room in which they are sitting is luxuriantly furnished: walls hung with tapestries, the table covered with a rich 'Turkey' carpet, the chairs upholstered with silks and velvets. Could these have belonged to Thomas Sackville? When Robert Cecil, one of the five English delegates, had been searching around for suitably rich furnishings for the Somerset House conference, the Earl of Nottingham, another of the grandees in the portrait, told him that he had nothing suitable but that Thomas Sackville, now Earl of Dorset, owned the best chairs in London.

All of these men shared a taste for fine things, a love of luxury characteristic of the Renaissance magnate. There is, for example, a list of jewels, described almost sensuously in Thomas's will, in far greater detail than that applied to the estates he was bequeathing to his family. It was the buildings, though, that were to prove the greatest legacy of this group. There was a country-house building boom in the sixteenth and early seventeenth centuries, reaching such a peak of competitive activity during the reign of King James I that

Bishop Goodman observed that 'no kingdom in this world spent so much in building as we did in his time'. These houses – known sometimes as 'prodigy houses' – were built by a group of lawyers, landowners, privy councillors and merchants, many of whom were self-made men rather than of ancient aristocratic lineage. They owed their success to holding office at court rather than to great feudal estates. The trend had been promoted by Queen Elizabeth I, who was famously stingy and chose, on royal progresses in the summer accompanied by a retinue of 150 privy councillors and retainers, to be put up for free in the great houses that her courtiers had built, or extended, for her use. The courtiers, in turn, hoped that a successful visit would result in favours from the monarch.

Sir Christopher Hatton built Holdenby; William Cecil, Lord Treasurer to Queen Elizabeth, built Burghley first, and then – for its commutable convenience – Theobalds, just ten miles north of London, in Hertfordshire, which Elizabeth visited thirteen times and treated almost as her own. It was at this Renaissance chateau, with its five courtyards and its front a quarter of a mile long, that Thomas Sackville, Cecil's successor as Lord Treasurer, waited with Cecil's son, Robert, in May 1604 to welcome King James I on his journey south into his new kingdom. In turn, Robert Cecil, Earl of Salisbury, succeeded Thomas Sackville as Lord Treasurer and spent almost £40,000 on Hatfield between 1607 and 1612. He died the same year as his house was completed, having passed only a few nights in the building. And Thomas Howard, Earl of Suffolk, who became Lord Treasurer in 1614, built Audley End of which James I observed wryly, on his one visit to the house, that it was too big for a king but fitting for a Lord Treasurer.

As children, we used to crawl through the spaces under the eaves of Knole, the very interstices of the house, and out onto the roofs. Here, daring each other to go just that one step farther towards the edge, we would catch unexpectedly giddy views of the skyline of turrets and finials, and the complex of courtyards below; and we would come right up close to those status symbols that meant so much to Thomas Sackville, Earl of Dorset, the first member of my family to live at Knole. The story of Thomas's success is stamped on the lead drainpipes that directed rainwater into cisterns in the courtyards, in the form of an earl's coronet and the initials 'TD' for Thomas Dorset and a date (1605 or 1607). It is shouted from the tops of the gables by twenty-seven heraldic stone leopards carrying the family coat of arms. Thomas's tale is not exactly one of rags to riches, but a more typically Tudor one of country gentleman to aristocrat, of timber merchant and ironmaster in the Weald of Kent to courtier and statesman.

Like most ambitious families of the time, the Sackvilles claimed that they had come to England with William the Conqueror, before settling first in Buckinghamshire and then at Buckhurst in Withyham in Sussex. There's a seventeenth-century family tree at Knole that traces the lineage back to the early Middle Ages, one of the first stirrings of a cult of ancestor worship that permeates the history of Knole and the Sackvilles. Thomas's grandfather, John Sackville, had married Anne Boleyn's aunt, Margaret. This made Thomas, born in 1536 – the year in which Anne was executed – a second cousin, and therefore one of the closest relatives of Queen Elizabeth (she had few enough), on her accession to the throne in 1558. Thomas's father, Richard, had been a lawyer, businessman and courtier, exploiting the lucrative opportunities afforded by public office (as future generations of the family were to do). As Chancellor of the Court of Augmentations, which administered the estates of monasteries dissolved by Henry VIII, Richard could cherry-pick former Church lands. This earned him a fortune and – according to the writer Robert Naunton, whose *Fragmenta Regalia*, or *Observations on the late Queen Elizabeth, her Times and Favourites*, was published the following century – the nickname 'Fillsack'. Gradually the Sackvilles acquired larger estates. Many of these derived their income from the sale of timber to the Wealden iron works, which used charcoal to fuel the blast furnaces. Richard Sackville also invested directly in forges, and profited from the production of cast-iron guns.

Like his father, Thomas studied common law at the Inner Temple, which 'bred and trained up' generations of Tudor gentlemen for government and public life. Thomas was also an acclaimed poet. His published works include a contribution to *The Mirror for Magistrates*; and two acts of *Gorboduc*, the first blank-verse tragedy in English (his fellow lawyer Thomas Norton wrote the other three acts). The play was performed – complete with music and mimed fights – at the Inner Temple's Christmas revels and, a couple of weeks later, before Queen Elizabeth herself at Whitehall in January 1562. 'Full of stately speeches and well-sounding phrases,' according to Sir Philip Sidney, it is little read today, although scholars view it as a minor landmark in English literature and an influence on Spenser and Shakespeare.

With one exception, however – a poem about old age – he had more or less stopped writing poetry by the time he was thirty, and had turned his literary skills (some 400 letters in his own handwriting have survived) to politics. It was a change of direction for Thomas, the Renaissance man and consummate courtier – the author, appropriately, of a sonnet commending Sir Thomas Hoby's translation of Castiglione's *Il cortegiano* to the reader. The Queen herself noted that he was 'a scholar, and a traveller, and a Courtier of speciall estimation' whose discourse was 'judicious but yet wittie and delightfull'.

On his father's death, in April 1566, Thomas inherited a large fortune, a country house at Buckhurst, estates in Sussex and Kent, and in 1567 he was made Baron Buckhurst – one of only two completely new peerages created by Elizabeth. As he later recalled in his will, he had 'receyved from her Majestie many special graces and favoures, as: first, in my younger yeres, being by her particular choice and liking, selected to a contynewall private attendance upon her owne person, and ymediately after my father's decease, by calling me to be a Baron, and Piere of the realme'. His career as a courtier was taking off, and in 1570, at the age of thirty-four, he acquired a lease on Knole from John Dudley and William Lovelace for £1,000 each. It was his first, and short-lived, association with the house that was to become so inextricably linked with his name.

At this stage in his life, however, he was abroad a lot and did not have the money to make the improvements he would later make. In any case, he did not even own the house outright. When Elizabeth I visited Knole in 1573, the house was described by the chronicler, John Nichols, as 'her own house', and Thomas received her not at Knole but at Westernhanger, another of the homes in his keeping. Who knows, perhaps he didn't even like Knole that much, and in 1574 he assigned the lease to John Lennard, a local landowner, whose family would occupy the house for the next thirty years.

In March 1571, Thomas Sackville was chosen – for his charm and his rhetorical skills – as the Queen's special envoy to France, to secure for Elizabeth a proposal of marriage from the French king's younger brother, the Duc d'Anjou. It was thought that a marriage treaty with France would neutralise any threat to England from Spain, and might also resolve the question of the succession to the English throne after Elizabeth's death. Throughout the 1560s, the House of Commons had repeatedly asked the Virgin Queen to marry and have children, or at least to name a successor (civil war caused by a disputed succession had, incidentally, been the warning message of Thomas Sackville's *Gorboduc*). Although nothing came of the discussions Thomas had with Catherine de Medici, the duke's mother, he continued to be selected for delicate missions. In November 1586, it was Thomas Sackville who had to break the news to Mary, Queen of Scots, imprisoned in Fotheringhay Castle, that she had been sentenced to death. So gently and compassionately did he fulfil his task that she presented him – or so family tradition alleges – with a wood carving of the procession to Calvary that is still in the chapel at Knole. In the absence of any documentary evidence, one of Knole's many myths wraps itself around the place, like the ivy clinging to its walls.

Thomas Sackville's most challenging royal commission, and the one that was to prove the most damaging politically, was his visit to the Low Countries in March 1587. Elizabeth had sent troops to support the Netherlands in their war against Spain, and was now asking Thomas to look into options for peace. His report on the situation there, after the recall to England of the Governor General, the Queen's favourite, the Earl of Leicester, highlighted the mess that Leicester had made – and, in particular, the starving conditions of the English troops. Leicester kept up a stream of complaints against Thomas, with Elizabeth taking the side of her favourite. Thomas was banished from court and confined to his London home. 'Because my hart doth best know, with what grete faith and dutie I have in this negotiation served Her Majesty,' he wrote, 'my greif is the greater to be thus deprived from the sight and presens of Her Majesty. That after so mainy cares, travels, sorowes and afflictions as in this servis I have suffred, I may yet at lencth receave the comfort of her prinsly face and presens.'

Thomas obeyed the Queen's order so literally that he remained at home during his banishment, seeing no one, not even his wife and children: 'a rare example of obedience, and observance unto his Soveraigne', as the Queen herself observed. 'Thus rolleth my fortune upon the wheel of sorrows and uncertainties, and my comfort still upon protractions,' he wrote mournfully to Lord Burghley. He was fully restored to favour in 1588.

Thomas was rewarded for his years of loyal service to the Crown in national and local government by a string of offices, including as Privy Councillor (1586) and Chancellor of the University of Oxford (1591). But, most significantly of all, Elizabeth made him Lord Treasurer in 1599 (the equivalent of Chancellor of the Exchequer today), a post to which he was reappointed by James I in 1604. His anxious wait at Theobalds in May, and his attempts to win the confidence of the new monarch whose succession he had, with Robert Cecil, partly engineered, were also rewarded with an earldom – of Dorset.

Sandwiched between, and overshadowed by, William Cecil and his son Robert, Thomas was the archetypal Elizabethan statesman. As Robert Naunton later observed, in a somewhat backhanded compliment, the late Queen Elizabeth 'might have had more cunning instruments, but none of a more strong judgement and confidence in his ways, which are symptoms of magnanimity and fidelity'.

There is a portrait of him, towards the end of his life, in the Great Hall at Knole, holding his wand of office as Lord Treasurer. This 'grave Elizabethan, with the long, rather melancholy face', and the heavy-lidded, hooded Sackville eyes, always reminded Vita Sackville-West of her grandfather, Lionel. They both shared a tendency to pessimism, to view the world and its vanities with a certain detachment. There's a foxiness, too, in his fondness for furs. When, in 1600, one of his rivals, Lord Cobham, learned that Thomas's two daughters had smallpox, he maliciously advised Robert Cecil that Thomas might catch it from them: 'You know he doth ever wear furs. There is nothing that doth carry infection as much as furs doth.'

By the 1600s, Thomas Sackville's estates were yielding around £6,000 in rents a year, making him one of the five wealthiest landowners in England. On top of this, there were his other business interests, and a pension from the King of Spain of £1,000 a year for his contribution to the peace treaty between Spain and England in 1604. Senior courtiers also benefited, as Thomas and Cecil did, from the administration of monopolies for goods such as starch (one of the most profitable industrial monopolies of the early seventeenth century because of its great demand in stiffening ruffs). There were the fees from the office of Lord Treasurer itself, which were worth about £4,000 a year (many times the tiny annual stipend of £365). And there were plenty of opportunities for bribes and backhanders – the 'gleanings and purloinings of the Old Treasurer', as one contemporary described them. Sometimes these were effected directly: a gift of silver plate to Lord Burghley to secure a wardship, for example. At other times, the transactions were more discreet, using family members to act as intermediaries. Thomas's daughter, Anne, Lady Glemham, was occasionally used – taking a bribe of £100 here or there on behalf of her father to get a favour granted, a piece of business expedited.

A whiff of impropriety follows Thomas, the old fox, but there was nothing unusual about this. Accusations of corruption attached themselves to many Elizabethan and Jacobean grandees, and were inevitable when private gain and public profit were so enmeshed; when, in the words of Edmund Spenser, writing about a courtier in 1590: 'For to increase the common treasure's store;/But his own treasure he increased more . . .' Nevertheless, according to Bishop Goodman, 'the greatest gettings were in Treasurer Dorset's time'.

One of the features of the lord treasurership of Thomas Sackville's predecessor, William Cecil, was the contracting, or farming, out of many of the functions of government. The trend to combine private gain with public profit accelerated while Thomas was Treasurer during the reign of James I, as the new regime was more extravagant than Queen Elizabeth's. Even before his establishment of a unified customs system in 1604, Thomas had been slanderously accused before the Star Chamber of granting customs' offices only 'to those who will buy them from him', thereby defrauding the Queen of £90,000 a year in customs' revenue. In 1604, he established the Great Customs Farm, which collected much of the customs duty for the country in exchange for guaranteeing the Crown an annual rent of £112,400. It was awarded – for a substantial consideration – to a City syndicate run by two merchants, Sir William Garway and Francis Jones, who were, unsurprisingly, business associates of himself and Robert Cecil, Earl of Salisbury.

By 1604, Thomas was feeling his age. He was tired and in poor health, which might explain some of the criticisms made of him, by implication, in a report written by the Chancellor of the Exchequer, Sir Julius Caesar, in 1608. Sir Julius claimed that, in his 'first two months and twenty days' in office, Robert Cecil, Thomas's successor as Lord Treasurer, wrote more letters (2,884) and collected more money 'I dare confidently affirme' than was ever 'done by any Lord Treasurer of England in two yeares'. Thomas needed a country house near London, and he needed it to be suitably grand. And so he and his agents started to search for suitable properties.

The establishment of an inheritance, the link between a place and its people, acquires a dignity and an inevitability with the passing of the years: a sense somehow that the Sackvilles themselves sprung from the sandy soils of Kent, rather than the sodden clays of the Sussex Weald. And yet the story could have been very different, for the 400-year association of the Sackvilles with Knole rested on the most slender of circumstances.

The Sackville roots were in Sussex, rather than Kent. This is where most of the lands that were the source of their political power lay. Thomas had been elected as Member of Parliament for East Grinstead in 1558, was Lord Lieutenant of Sussex, and controlled many of the parliamentary seats in the county. In the 1570s and 1580s, he lived mostly at Lewes, using his park at Buckhurst for hunting. As he grew older, it was to Sussex that he still looked for his roots. Like other courtiers of the sixteenth and seventeenth centuries, who established buildings for the good of the community and the glory of their name, in or near their home towns, Thomas directed his own acts of charity to Sussex. He left £1,000 in his will to build a granary in Lewes, with £2,000 towards stocking it with wheat, against times of hardship, and £1,000 towards the chapel at Withyham. For similar reasons, his son Robert was to endow a charitable institution, to be known as Sackville College, in East Grinstead. Quite naturally, it was beneath Withyham church that Thomas chose to be buried, instructing in his will that he wished to be interred there 'amongst the rest of my Progenitors'. So deep was the Sackville attachment to Sussex that the Sackville crypt at Withyham remained the family burial place until the twentieth century, and possibly beyond.

It would have been equally natural, therefore, for Thomas to have chosen Sussex – and, in particular, Buckhurst – as the site of his show house. And, yes, there were plans for one. Among the papers of the surveyor John Thorpe, there exists a design, probably drafted between 1599 and 1603, for a huge house at Buckhurst. It was to be centred around a great courtyard, with two smaller ones (and a tennis court) flanking it: a house more than fitting for a Lord Treasurer. No such house was ever built, and all that remains of the Sackvilles' original ancestral seat in Sussex is a forlorn, forsaken Tudor gatehouse.

So why did Thomas plump for Knole rather than Buckhurst? During the course of long – and unsuccessful – negotiations with Sir Robert Sidney for the hunting park and lodge at Otford, four miles from Knole, and like Knole on the estate of a former archbishop's and then royal palace, Thomas explained that he had 'no place near London to retire unto'. As he grew richer, and began acquiring more land in Sussex and Kent, he had begun casting around for a country residence in addition to Dorset House in London, which he was renovating. The roads around Buckhurst were notoriously bad in the seventeenth century: low-lying and waterlogged in winter, in contrast to the higher, well-drained roads around Knole. The mess made by the steady churn of carts, carrying iron and transporting trees from the Sussex Weald to the dockyards at Woolwich and Chatham, was exacerbated by the particularly heavy rains of 1594–97, making the journey long and uncomfortable for an old man suffering from rheumatism. Since 1601, Thomas had been renting West Horsley Place in Surrey from his son-in-law and for the last seven years of his life this became his main residence – the place he retired to when he thought he was dying in 1607. But he didn't own this house, whereas from 1605 he did own Knole.

One of the consequences of choosing Knole, rather than Buckhurst, was a curious sense of dislocation. Knole was a magnificent house, but it was miles away from the Sackville heartlands on the edge of Ashdown Forest, and never had the estates to support it. The area around Buckhurst, on the other hand, lay at the centre of the Sackville powerbase from the sixteenth to the eighteenth century. Substantial additions were made to the house at Buckhurst in the eighteenth century and even when, in 1870, the last direct Sackville descendant died, and the estates were divided, Buckhurst passed to the elder son and Knole to the younger one. Knole, one of the greatest houses in the country, became the junior inheritance. The implications of this reverberated down the centuries: Thomas had sowed the seeds of future controversy and a great nineteenth-century inheritance battle.

Tradition has it that, in 1566, Elizabeth I gave Knole to her cousin and councillor, Thomas Sackville, 'to keep him near her court and councils, that he might repair thither, in any emergency'. Like so many other myths, this probably originated in the eighteenth century and then resurfaced in an early nineteenth-century guidebook. It has been scrupulously repeated ever since, buffed and burnished until it has almost begun to acquire the patina of truth. But there is no documentary evidence for such a gift. The maze of property negotiations leading to Thomas's ownership of Knole conceals a less romantic story, but one that is perhaps a truer reflection of his character and the politics of the age.

In 1604, Thomas bought the lease on Knole (which still had another sixty-one years to run) from John Lennard's son, Sampson, for £4,000. On 5 April 1605, the Crown, which still owned the freehold on the property, sold this to Rowland White and others for £220 6s. 8d., and two days later, Thomas bought it off them for £2,500. Thomas Sackville had become the freehold owner of Knole – without the encumbrance of any sitting tenants. What lay behind this labyrinth of property deals?

One of Thomas's responsibilities as Lord Treasurer was the sale of Crown lands. Had he negotiated the sale of the freehold of Knole directly to himself, he might have aroused the suspicions of the King and the envy of his colleagues. But by authorising the sale to Rowland White and others, and then buying it back off them, he covered the paper trail with a thin veil of propriety.

And so, at the age of almost seventy, Thomas Sackville embarked on a massive building programme. A set of accounts, from 2 July 1607 to 5 May 1608, survives – itemising expenditure at Knole and elsewhere of £4,107 11s. 9d. The building works lasted from 1605 to 1608, so expenditure during this ten-month window should be multiplied several times to get a clear idea of the amounts spent overall. What is remarkable about these accounts, though, is that we now know who the craftsmen and builders actually were: Thomas Bickford, Locksmyth (£80); Thomas Mefflyn, Glasier; William Halsey, Plommer; John Pasmar, Brasier; Andrew Kerwin for 11 tonnes of Oxfordshire stone; John Lewgar, Coffermaker; Robert Wright, ironmonger; Richard Singleton, Upholsterer; Henry Waller, Joyner; George White for '60 wainscottes'; Thomas Holmden for building charges; Martin van Benthem and Henry Holdernes for painting and gilding the pattern of a frame for a picture; and payments, of course, for soft furnishings, damask, linen, featherdressers. The references in the accounts that link these names to Knole, and to particular pieces of work there, animate the place in much the same way as the air bubbles trapped in a pane of glass in the house are relics of the breath of a long-dead glazier.

The names of one group of craftsmen crop up time and again. 'Richard Dungan, the Ks. Plaisterer ... for Fretts and plaistering worke at Knoll ... £140 os. od.'; 'William Portinton, the Ks. Carpenter in discharge of a bill for 300 of deale bordes at £5 10s. od. the Hundred, for Spruce deales at 4/- the peece and watercarriage and other things for Knoll ... £20 12s. 6d.'; 'Cornelius Cuer, Freemason, for stones for a chimney piece in the Withdrawing Chamber at Knoll'.

All of these were master craftsmen in the King's Works, the largest building organisation in the country. One of the great privileges of the Lord Treasurer's office was control of the King's Works' staff and access to its master craftsmen (although paid for on private business by the Treasurer himself). Cornelius Cure, for example, was Master Mason in the Office of Works, a man 'honest, erect and full of invention ... having sen muck worke in forrein places'. At his workshop in Southwark – an area of London where many of these craftsmen were based – he specialised in monumental sculpture, including fountains designed for Greenwich Palace and Hampton Court, and a tomb for Westminster Abbey, in memory of Mary Stuart (commissioned by Thomas Sackville on behalf of King James in 1606). William Portington, the Master Carpenter at Knole, enjoyed royal patronage too, as did Richard Dungan, who worked on the elaborate plasterwork ceilings in the great chambers and galleries at the house.

From 1605 these master craftsmen joined hundreds of painters and plasterers, woodcarvers and stonemasons at Knole. Working Monday to Saturday, dawn till dusk, the craftsmen (other than the very skilled masons and carpenters) earned around twelve pence a day and the labourers around eight pence. There was no architect in the modern sense of the term, as a person whose vision and grasp of three-dimensional space determined, in advance and in detail, how the building was to be shaped. Fairly elementary plans and elevations were prepared by a surveyor (often a former master craftsman), and these were adapted as they progressed to working drawings and full-size templates. Individual craftsmen would have made changes, and so would the owner – at the last minute – without much thought to the consequences of the alteration to the finished design. And so the building would have staggered towards completion, the sum of a mass of different parts – of chimneypieces, staircases, screens, colonnades, wainscots – rather than a necessarily coherent whole.

The estate resounded to the thud of pickaxes from the pits, or 'petts', opened up on the edge of the park, where Kentish ragstone for the house was quarried; to the rasp from the sawpits, dug in the woods, where timber was sawn into floorboards; to the clatter of horse-drawn carts bringing more valuable stone from Purbeck in Dorset, and lead for the roofs and guttering from the mines of Derbyshire or the Mendips; to the grinding of cranes and lifting gear as stone was hoisted onto precarious wooden scaffolds. Above all this activity floated little clouds of evil-smelling smoke from the temporary kilns, where lime was manufactured for use in mortar and plaster.

The focus of all these sounds and smells was Thomas's new home: a house that had grown from a manor house in the fourteenth century, to a mansion belonging to the Archbishops of Canterbury in the fifteenth century, to a royal palace in the sixteenth century. Thomas wanted to soften the massive severity of the house, to bring touches of the modern age to his medieval home. He wanted greater domestic comfort; but most of all, he wanted to proclaim to the world his personal wealth and status as a senior statesman.

Sixteenth-century ideas about the structure of the universe and the natural order of things were reflected in architecture in a respect for symmetry and proportion. To add an impression of symmetry and order to the west façade, which incorporated in rather ramshackle fashion Archbishop Bourchier's original gatehouse, Thomas Sackville added a two-storeyed bay, topped with a gable, on either side of Bourchier's Tower. He enclosed the timber galleries around the Stone Court and faced them with stone, and at the far end of the courtyard he added a Doric colonnade to disguise the fact that the passage leading to the Great Hall was – as with most medieval halls – off-centre. He extended the east front, and altered it, introducing a series of eight timber-framed gables at second-floor level. On the south front, he built a colonnade with seven marble arches, to create an elegant, ordered façade. This Renaissance aspect to the house contrasts strikingly with the simple severity of the west front and with the looming bulk of the north front, where the outbuildings – a barn, an old brewhouse, a granary, and workshops for carpenters, bricklayers and painters – cluster higgledy-piggledy beneath the main tower, like the yards and farm buildings of a medieval village. Along at least two fronts of the house, he added shaped gables topped with carved stone leopard finials. And he introduced windows throughout.

Having just completed a major refurbishment of one wing at Knole, I am sensitive to some of the challenges of a courtyard house, the spatial problems with which my ancestors wrestled and the solutions (or perhaps bodges) they devised. The biggest problem has always been the location of the staircases. Thomas would have found a number of spiral stairs at Knole, most of them set into the corners of courtyards, and to these he added at least two very fine new staircases. These were designed not just for circulation from the ground floor to the upper floors, and down again, in one continuous flow, but also with a grander social purpose in mind.

The more imposing of the two staircases led from the Great Hall to the Great Chamber, where Thomas would have intended to do most of his entertaining. This was the style of room described, in an exactly contemporary set of household regulations from 1604, as 'the place of state, where the lord keepeth his presence'. Here, the craftsmen of the King's Works installed a plasterwork ceiling (by Richard Dungan), carved panelling and a frieze around the walls (by William Portington), and a magnificent marble and alabaster chimneypiece (by Cornelius Cure). The carved musical instruments above the fireplace suggest that this was a room for music, dancing and masques, performed by members of the household, as well as for eating.

The lord and his family would usually have retired to the Withdrawing Room next door for meals and privacy. But on grander occasions, they would have escorted a particularly distinguished guest in a ceremonial procession along the main gallery (with its floorboards then covered in rush matting) to the principal bedchamber, the King's Room. As the name suggests, this was designed to accommodate James I, should he visit Knole.

In many ways, a visitor to Knole today follows the same route as a grandee of the early seventeenth century: sweeping along the main axis of the house through two apparently symmetrical courtyards, the Green Court and the Stone Court, into the Great Hall, before processing up the Great Staircase to the door of the Great Chamber and along a parade of withdrawing rooms and long galleries, with splendid vistas, to the principal bedroom suites.

The Great Staircase was a crucial feature in the stately progress around a house of the late sixteenth and early seventeenth century. Due to greater sophistication in joinery, the spiral staircase which had previously connected the Great Hall to the Great Chamber was replaced by an open-well wooden staircase, its walls inviting splendid painting. Every surface of the Great Staircase is covered in paintings, mostly by Paul Isaacson. In this scheme, climbing the stairs represents not just a social ascent – towards the splendour and exclusivity of the first floor – but a spiritual one as well: a metaphor for the journey through life.

On the ground floor, man's earthly existence is shown in scenes from *The Four Ages of Man*. This was a theme very familiar to Thomas and his contemporaries. Indeed, he had addressed it himself in the one poem that he is known to have written some time between 1566 and 1574, after he had forsaken the world of poetry for public life. In 'Sacvyles Olde Age', as the poem was titled by the person who transcribed it, Thomas muses on the transitoriness of life, mourning the end of his 'fresh grene yeres' and 'youthfull daies' (he was in his thirties and on his first tenancy of Knole when he wrote it), as he leaves the spring and summer of his youth for the autumn fruitfulness of his prime. In the conventional wisdom of the day, which ascribed different activities as appropriate for different ages, now was the time to put away 'youthfull toyes' and 'false deliygtes' (including reading poetry) and to focus on his public responsibilities.

The idea is that, as you mount the stairs, you acquire a literally heightened awareness, through experience (in this case, visual), of *The Five Senses*, and your understanding and wisdom increase in preparation for a life after death. Less earth-bound, you begin to appreciate an order where, in wall-painted scenes of the Virtues conquering the Vices, Peace overcomes War, Justice triumphs over Evil, and Wisdom treads Ignorance underfoot. It was the sort of improving allegory of which the Tudors and Jacobeans were inordinately fond. Old age and death are inevitable, but a virtuous life may be a route to salvation. In his own bid for immortality, Thomas piously ended his poem on old age, by dedicating his future to praising 'the hevenly kynge that lives for aye'.

The interior decoration at Knole was, if anything, more important than the outside changes. To imagine what the rooms actually looked like then, you simply have to strip them in your mind's eye of all the existing furniture, including the fussy eighteenth- and nineteenth-century furniture, the Old Master paintings, the eighteenth-century portraits, and to furnish them sparsely instead with a few pieces of furniture, and some wall hangings and tapestries here, or a brightly coloured Turkey rug there, for warmth and decoration. The elaborate screens, ceilings and friezes were all the decoration that Thomas Sackville needed to convey an impression of grandeur and refinement.

The oak screen at one end of the Great Hall, for example, is monstrously exuberant: a riot of weird creatures, caryatids and heraldic beasts carved by William Portington. The Elizabethans and Jacobeans loved ingenious devices, symbols, hieroglyphs – anything whose meaning took a little time to unravel, and consequently conferred on both the builder and his guest the self-congratulatory pat on the back of a puzzle well set and well solved. The lattice windows at the top of the screen conceal a musicians' gallery, where a small orchestra would have performed to the guests below. It was another statement of Thomas as a man of taste and refinement. In his will, he made extraordinary provision for his musicians, 'some for the voice and some for the Instrument', who had given him 'muche Recreation and Contentation with their delightfull harmonye' after his 'many longe laboures and paynefull travels of the daye'.

Just as specific pieces of handiwork can be traced, through the accounts, to individual craftsmen, the designs on which they were based can be traced quite precisely to treatises on architecture that were fashionable at the time. The motifs on the hall screen, for example, were based on plates in Jan Vredeman de Vries's *Architectura*, which was published in 1565 and had a great influence on architectural decoration in the late sixteenth and early seventeenth centuries. So too was the strapwork of the pilasters in the Great Chamber, and the decoration of scrollwork and hunting dogs that leap across the chimneypiece in our dining room. The scenes on the Great Staircase, such as *The Four Ages of Man* and the *Virtues*, came from the works of Maarten de Vos published in 1596.

These matches, and copies, show how the design scheme for Knole was assembled. They are also an example, more generally, of the Renaissance in action in England: of how ideas, or at least motifs, spread. Thomas Sackville had been on grand tours of France and Italy in the 1560s, where he must have seen many of the new Renaissance buildings. He and his master craftsmen would also have been familiar with the pattern books, newly printed in France, Italy or the Netherlands, which circulated amongst a small group of builders, like source books or design magazines today, providing inspiration and templates. Patrons swapped ideas, and recommended – and poached craftsmen – to and from each other. Designs were adapted and spread across England, site by site, gradually creating a distinctive national style. This did not mean that the English builders necessarily understood the philosophy and intellectual principles that underlay the Renaissance approach to architecture: merely that they liked some of the devices, which they could then graft, in a pick-and-mix way, on to a more homegrown tradition.

In 1624 the author and diplomat Sir Henry Wotton described the various roles of the country house: 'Every man's proper Mansion House, being the Theater of his Hospitality, the Seate of Self-fruition, the Comfortablest part of his owne life, the Noblest of his Sonnes Inheritance, a kind of private Princedome.' Knole was all these things to Thomas Sackville: a home, a status symbol in an age of great status anxiety, and an opportunity to display his learning and wit, in the classical references of its ornamentation and the ingenuity of its elaborate devices. Knole was also his bid for immortality, his attempt to outwit death. The profusion of initials and heraldic devices all over the house announced the final arrival of a family whose spectacular success over the past century had made it one of the most powerful in England.

Thomas had begun to work on his legacy. He was worn out by his job as Lord Treasurer, which was made all the more difficult by King James I's extravagance. He had failed to solve the fundamental financial problems of the realm, and by 1608, after five years of peace, the Crown's debts stood at almost £600,000 – six times the net debt left by Elizabeth. As early as July 1599, he had written to Sir Robert Cecil that his physicians had told him 'not to use reading or writing for a while'. He had been complaining about a cough for years, but in May 1607 this had got so bad that 'only time, aier and free from business, must help this rooted cold and cough of mine, so fast fixed in me'.

By June he was 'in such extremitie of sicknesse' that, prematurely, 'it was a common and constant report all over London, that I was dead'. King James had a gold ring, set with twenty diamonds, delivered to him on his sick bed at his Surrey home, with the hopes for 'a speedie and perfect recoverie' and a life 'as long as the diamonds in that ring did endure'. The present did the trick and, according to Thomas, 'restored a new life unto me'. But his near-death experience prepared him, perhaps, for death, and prompted him to write a will.

Dated August 1607, some eight months before he died, the will runs to fifty-one pages, and was written, according to George Abbot, by Thomas himself. In it, Thomas – the survivor of five reigns, the owner of much of Sussex, the Lord Treasurer – exhibits a strong sense of self, status and ancestry. He describes how his funeral is 'to be performed without unnecessary and superfluous pompe, and yet within that comelie order, honoure, and decencye,

as apperteynethe to the state and dignitie of so noble a degree, and
to so high a place, as in this most renowned common-wealth'. The
opening is a scene-setter, a reminder of the transitory nature of life.
'It is a trueth infallible,' writes Thomas,

> that we are borne to die; That nothing in this world more certaine
> than death, nothing more incertaine then the houre of death, and
> that no creature living knoweth, neither when, where, nor how it
> shall please Almighty God to call him out of this mortall life: So as
> here we live every houre, nay every instant a thousand waies subject
> to the sudden stroke of death, which ought to terrifie, teach and
> warne us to make our selves ready as well in the preparation of our
> soules to God, as by the disposition of all our earthly fortunes to the
> world, whensoever it shall please the heavenly power to call us from
> this miserable and transitory life unto that blessed and everlasting
> to come.

When he came to the disposition of his earthly fortunes, Thomas
had very precise instructions about the ring. This should pass as an
heirloom from 'heir male to heir male' in perpetuity, with a message,

> that I and mine may for ever and ever become more and more thank-
> full, (at least if it be possibly in me) for so great honours, graces
> and favours, as this most clement and renowned King hath thus
> most gratiously vouchsafed unto me; the remembrance of which,
> because it may never die but be perpetually recorded in the mindes
> of those, that by grace & goodnesse of almighty God, both now are,
> & hereafter shall be the lineall stripe and succession of my house and
> family, to serve both him & his . . . if ever occasion may or shall be
> offered to any of my posteritie to do his Majestie or any of his any
> acceptable service hereafter then let them hold & esteeme themselves
> most happie if with the expence of life, & of all the fortunes that this
> world shall give them, they may actually approve and witnesse with
> effect, that they are not onely most loyall and dutifull vassals to this
> Imperiall Crowne, but also the most humble, faithfull, and thankfull
> sonnes and sequell of such a servant . . .

The ring, held in almost sacred trust, was Thomas's attempt to bind his successors to the monarch: a physical memento to posterity of the rewards of loyalty to the Crown. Many of his successors took his advice to heart, to the greater glory of Knole which was first built and then furnished on the profits of public office (although they do appear to have mislaid the ring). Thomas's will was the first explicit reference to an inheritance of house and family in the history of Knole. It articulated some of the themes that would dominate the story of the Sackville inheritance over the following centuries, and the cares that would preoccupy future generations of the family.

For Thomas, the stroke of death was sudden indeed. On 19 April 1608 he dropped dead at a meeting of the Privy Council in Whitehall. At his funeral at Westminster Abbey on 26 May 1608, George Abbot, who had been Thomas's private chaplain and was now Archbishop of Canterbury, took as the text for his sermon Isaiah 40.6–7 'All flesh is grass, and all the grace thereof is as the flower of the field./The grass withereth, the flower fadeth, because the spirit of the Lord bloweth upon it.' Musings on mortality and an account of Sackville's life followed, structured around the ages of man. Abbot quoted no less an authority on Thomas Sackville than 'a witness beyond all exception; and that is the late Queene of everlasting memorie . . . [who had] been pleased to decipher out his life' by 'seven steps or degrees'. The first three steps concerned his time as 'a scholar, a traveller, and a Courtier'. The fourth step of his life, 'noted by her most sacred Maiestie, was his imployment of higher nature, in Embassies beyond the seas', that is, the mission to France in 1571 and to the Netherlands in 1587. Steps five, six and seven referred to his banishment from court in 1587, his role as a privy councillor, and his time as Lord High Treasurer, 'in which place . . . [the Queen] noted the continuall, and excessive paines, and care which his Lordship did take in her business, his fidelitie in his advices, his dexterity in advancing of her profit'.

Thomas had had very little time to enjoy for himself the transformation that he had initiated at Knole. His new home was not a new-build like Burghley or Hatfield. What he had done was to graft

a sense of order and elegance on to the late-medieval mansion that
had been there before. The result, close-up, is often quite awkward
and ungainly. At the time of his death in 1608, Thomas's remodelling of Knole was barely complete. James I never came to the house
in whose honour the works had been undertaken. The great irony
was that the house was already almost out of date, and certainly far
too big. Built to accommodate a household, whose exceptional size
was already an anachronism, Knole looked back to the late Middle
Ages rather than forward to embrace modern realities. What had
been intended as a monument to a new dynasty was in danger of
becoming a mausoleum for the hopes of generations of Sackvilles
to come.

Chapter 2

An Owl in the Desert (1608–1624)

*Richard Sackville, 3rd Earl of Dorset
and His Wife, Lady Anne Clifford*

That Knole is a love it or loathe it sort of place is partly explained by the many faces it presents on different days and at different times of the year. On a dull winter's day, as you ride the crest of the knoll in front of the house (from which Knole may have derived its name), and the north front looms into sight, its sprawling mass of sodden Kentish ragstone strikes a sombre and slightly depressing note. But on a sunny summer's day, the south front – with its Colonnade of seven lightly coloured marble arches – dances to a different tune.

One of the best places to view the sunny, south-eastern, side of the house is a secluded spot in the garden now known as the Duchess's Seat, but described in an early seventeenth-century diary as 'the Standing'. The sight of the house unfurled below has barely changed since 1616, when the Standing was a favourite retreat of the author of that diary, the young mistress of Knole, Lady Anne Clifford. It was here that she came, prayerbook in hand, to beseech God to help her in her troubles.

The places she describes in her diary are instantly recognisable from the same spot today: the 'marble pillars' of the Colonnade, built by her husband's grandfather less than ten years before, that had become for her 'but the gay arbour of anguish'; the Chapel where her eyes were so 'blubbered with weeping that [she] could scarce look up'; the bedchambers where she and her husband occasionally slept together, but more frequently slept apart after another 'great falling out'.

The overriding mood of her diary is one of melancholy, the time grown so tedious that she had started going to bed at eight in the evening and staying there till eight the next day. She had begun, at the age of twenty-six, to wear clothes so frumpy – in particular, an old gown of green flannel run up for her by her overseer, William Punn – that her appearance was beginning to attract attention and her dress 'found fault with'. Why had this former society beauty begun to let herself go? What had sapped the confidence of a woman who described with pride the 'exquisite shape' of her body, the luxuriant brown hair that fell to her calves, and 'though I say it, the perfections of my mind' which 'were much above my body: a strong and copious memory, a sound judgement, a discerning spirit'?

During the spring of 1616, Anne was on the verge of separating from her husband, Richard Sackville. On 1 May she had word from Richard that she was no longer to live at Knole. The following day she heard secondhand from the servants, who had been briefed by Richard's steward, that her husband would come down to see her once more, but that this would be the last time that she would ever see him. On 3 May she got a letter from Richard saying that their daughter, Margaret, should be taken away from her the next day to her father in London: Anne was not to see her child for another seven months. And on 29 May, Anne learned that her beloved mother had died.

Although there were many aristocratic couples at the time who lived fairly detached lives, for Anne separation would have meant relative penury – since her money had been handed over to her husband on marriage. Divorce was almost impossible, save through an Act of Parliament, and there was therefore very little possibility of remarriage and (this applied equally to Richard and Anne) the birth of a legitimate male heir. Most poignantly of all, Anne still loved her husband despite his cruelties.

The intimacies of their marriage were played out in public. Even today, when just thirty people live at Knole, the atmosphere is occasionally a little claustrophobic, as the curtains twitch around the courtyards, and comings and goings are noted. 'I think your mother must have gone to visit so-and-so; her car's not there,' one of your fellow residents will tell you. 'There's a letter for you in the Estate Office; it looks as if it might be from . . .; your cousins have had one just like it.' In the early seventeenth century, however, there were over a hundred people in the household and the hot-house atmosphere – brought so vividly to life in Anne's diary – was even more stifling. Servants slept all over the place, in dormitories in the attics or on pallet beds at the door to their master's or mistress's bedroom. There was precious little privacy, and you were never more than a few feet away from a close-stool or some other unwashed body. Yet there were few places where you could feel more lonely than in the midst of all this bustle and gossip.

A seating plan for the household survives, of more than 120 dependants at Knole between 1613 and 1624. Middle-ranking servants, including the clerks of the kitchen, the slaughterman, the baker and brewer, the head gardener and groom, and the yeoman of the buttery and pantry, sat at the Clerks' Table at the raised end of the hall. Ranged at right-angles to the Clerks' Table along the hall were three tables: the 'Long Table' (still in the Great Hall) for lower servants, such as footmen, a farrier and a falconer, a bird-catcher and a barber; a nursery table, and a laundrymaid's table. Finally, at the bottom of the hall, there was a table reserved for kitchen and scullery staff, for characters with names such as Diggory Dyer, Marfidy Snipt and John Morockoe, 'a Blackamor'. The twenty-one most senior servants dined in a separate parlour below the Great Chamber; these included the chaplain, the steward, the Gentlemen of the Horse and 'Mr Matthew Caldicott, my Lord's favourite'.

It was the presence of these senior officials that Anne found most oppressive. Constantly jockeying for position and preferment with their master, they were forever taking his side in any matrimonial dispute. Anne often fretted about their intrigues, worrying about what the servants really thought about her, reassured when she heard that 'all the men in the House loved [her] exceedingly', and never really forgiving her husband's favourite, Matthew. She suspected him of such non-stop stirring – 'Matthew continuing still to do me all the ill offices he could with my Lord' – that she was driven to write a letter of complaint to the Bishop of London. The letter has not survived, but it presumably denounced Matthew's intimacy, and influence, with her husband.

Her diary entry for 12 May captures the tone of this miserable month, when she was alone at Knole, without her daughter, without her mother who was dying, and without her husband who was in London. Here, 'he had all and infinite great resort coming to him. He went much abroad to Cocking, to Bowling Alleys, to Plays and Horse Races, & [was] commended by all the World.' She, on the other hand, 'stayed in the Countrey having many times a sorrowful & heavy Heart . . . so as I may truly say, I am like an Owl in the Desert'.

At the heart of Richard and Anne's marital discord, as at the heart of so many marriages of the time, were disagreements about property and inheritance. The issues at stake were those that have dominated not just Knole and the Sackvilles, but most aristocratic families from the sixteenth to the twentieth century: the principle of primogeniture, which has aimed to preserve inherited property intact through the continuity of the male line and has consequently determined the character and relationships of parents, children and siblings for generations; and the system of compensation which has aimed to provide, in that male world, for wives, daughters and widows. Brides were expected to bring a dowry to the marriage, a substantial cash sum known as a 'portion'; in return for this, an annuity, known as a 'jointure', was settled on her in case she survived her husband. Any number of the documents that used to moulder in the muniments rooms at Knole (now at the Centre for Kentish Studies in Maidstone) – the wills, the marriage settlements, the complicated life interest trusts and so on – all show that, as with the house itself, the legal instruments designed to preserve it and the inheritance intact have changed remarkably little over the centuries.

Marriage was a deal and, like all deals, subject to renegotiation. Throughout their marriage, one of Anne's complaints was the way in which Richard used money, and the promise of financial security for her in the event of his death, as a lever, making and unmaking the jointure he was to settle on her for her lifetime. To understand why he did so, we have to go back to the couple's wedding day.

Richard Sackville and Anne Clifford were married on 25 February 1609 in the bride's mother's house in what is now Austin Friars in London EC2. There had been no time to publish the wedding banns beforehand, and the haste with which the marriage had been arranged was so 'irregular' that the couple required absolution afterwards from the Archbishop of Canterbury to spare them a sentence of excommunication. Two days later, the groom's father, Robert Sackville, 2nd Earl of Dorset, was dead, and Richard Sackville became Earl of Dorset – the third earl within a year – and the owner of one of the greatest fortunes in England. It was precisely this inheritance that had precipitated the marriage. As an unmarried man of only nineteen, Richard would have become a royal ward on his father's death and at risk of having a predatory courtier appointed as his guardian – with the right to benefit from his estate and to act as a broker in the matter of his marriage. As Richard's father lay dying in Little Dorset House, one of the family's London townhouses, there had been attempts to prevent this happening. Richard had even prevailed upon his friend Henry, Prince of Wales, to propose himself to James I as his guardian ('desiring', in Henry's words, 'rather to fall into my hands than of another'). By marrying, Richard removed the risk of becoming a ward on his father's death.

Richard's bride, Anne, was from a family at least as noble, if not quite as wealthy, as his. As the only surviving child of George Clifford, the 3rd Earl of Cumberland, and his wife Margaret (two older brothers had died young), Anne might have hoped to inherit the great Clifford estates in Westmorland and Yorkshire. However, on his death in 1605, her father had left his land to his younger brother Francis, the new 4th Earl of Cumberland, in the belief that Francis would be better at rescuing the estate from the enormous debts with which his own privateering expeditions around the world had encumbered it. To Anne he had bequeathed a £15,000 marriage portion or dowry; and, as part of her marriage settlement, his widow Margaret was left with a life interest in the Westmorland estates – and its four castles of Appleby, Brough, Brougham and Pendragon. On George's death, however, Anne's mother Margaret had contested the legality of the will, claiming all her late husband's estates on behalf of her daughter.

Anne's portion and prospects, combined with good looks and a quick wit (the poet and divine John Donne later described her as discoursing of 'all things from Predestination to Slea Silk'), made her one of the most eligible young women at the court of King James I. Her marriage to Richard, then, was a perfect match between two great dynasties: one from the north, the other from the south of England. However, the gossip John Chamberlain may have spotted a source of future trouble when he observed, on the haste with which the couple had married, that 'the matter might have been better handled, and he [Richard] eased himself of a burthen he may peradventure feele hereafter'.

The marriage gave Anne and her mother some political leverage at court, which they needed for their claim to the Clifford lands; and it gave Richard the prospect of ready money. Richard was always strapped for cash. His own income was limited by the chunks taken out of the Sackville estates to support his elderly female relatives, the lands held by his stepmother, and the annuity paid to his grandmother. When he married Anne, both her dowry (at the very least) and her claims to the Clifford estates (a far greater fortune if he could get it) became his – although, as it happened, he would have to wait ten years for any Clifford money. He had no emotional attachment to the lands in the north, and was to use the twists and turns of the case to wrest the largest amount of cash from the situation at any opportunity. It was this difference of perspective that was to set him on a collision course with his wife.

One of the main sources for this story is a series of diaries, begun by Anne in 1603 and concluding shortly before her death in 1676. By that time, the redoubtable eighty-six-year-old had, through sheer tenacity and longevity, secured her father's inheritance and become possibly the wealthiest noblewoman of her day. The 'Knole diary' covers the years 1603 to 1619 and has survived as a late eighteenth-century transcript, originally at Knole. To an extent, the diary is a memorandum, intended for public consumption, of dates and conversations in an inheritance contest; but due to the poignancy of her particular story, the diary has also identified Anne for ever as one of the house's moving spirits.

As newlyweds, Richard and Anne were a glittering couple in an era that sparkled with promise and expectation after the parsimoniousness of Queen Elizabeth's reign. James's court was freer and easier than Elizabeth's stultified court had become. Observers described it as a more licentious place, including Anne herself who noted 'how all the ladies about the court had gotten such ill names that it was grown a scandalous place'. To prove the moral decline of the country, the critics simply pointed to the fashions of the day. Ladies' necklines plunged to expose large areas of breast. Layers of cosmetics were applied to create complexions of an unnatural pallor. Skirts and dresses were upholstered to create extravagant silhouettes with wires, padding and hoops made from whalebone. There was a culture of heavy drinking, promoted partly by the new King himself. And there were numerous scandals, involving infidelity, incest, pederasty and poisoning, among the small group of friends and family that constituted the peerage of England.

Around the year 1600 there were no more than fifty or sixty noble families in England and Wales. Their landed estates marched hundreds of miles across the country, but in London their houses were within a few paces of each other, concentrated on either side of Fleet Street and the Strand. Here, in a nexus of wealth and political power, these aristocratic homes, mostly destroyed in the Great Fire of 1666, each proclaimed the name of a great family: Arundel, Bedford, Dorset, Essex, Exeter, Northumberland. Many of these nobles had been privy councillors to Queen Elizabeth; they were interrelated (Richard, for example, was grandson of the 1st Earl of Bedford, and his wife Anne, the granddaughter of the 2nd Earl of

Bedford); they sat for the same painters; and they went to the same parties. It was an extraordinarily small world that Anne described, and one of great power and privilege – but such is the traditionalism and sheer resilience of the British aristocracy that, in dynastic terms at least, it was not that different from the one described by the young debutante Vita Sackville-West in the first decade of the twentieth century.

On the surface, the Jacobean court was a magnificent place, and Anne participated in all its elaborate ceremonial and entertainments: in the round of weddings and funerals, tournaments and masques, royal visits and official receptions that filled a noble's life and the pages of John Nichols's *Progresses*, a sort of 'court circular' of its day. Masques, scripted by leading contemporary writers such as Ben Jonson, were particularly popular with James I's wife, Queen Anne, and their son Prince Henry, the short-lived heir to the throne. Featuring moving scenery and special effects, as well as long speeches and involved allegory, these amateur but highly spectacular dramatics were performed by members of the royal family and court. Just two weeks before her marriage, Anne had performed in the Masque of Queens as Berenice of Egypt – a part for which she was chosen (as she reminded people) for the beauty of her hair – in a costume designed by the architect Inigo Jones. The following year, in June 1610, in a masque that formed part of the celebrations surrounding Prince Henry's creation as Prince of Wales, Anne was cast, like the other great ladies at court, as a river nymph – in her case, the Aire, which flows past her birthplace of Skipton Castle.

Richard performed in masques too, but also – in a late, faux flowering of medievalism – at jousts in the tiltyard where clothes, because they conveyed status for men just as they did for women, were equally sumptuous. At least two contemporary accounts draw particular attention to the clothes worn by Richard at the marriage of James I's daughter, Princess Elizabeth, to Frederick, Elector Palatine on 14 February 1613. 'It were long and tedious to tell you all the peculiarities of the excessive bravery both of men and women . . . but above all they speak of the Earl of Dorset,' wrote

John Chamberlain, before adding in a letter to Sir Dudley Carleton that 'this extreme cost and riches makes us all poor'.

The sartorial splendour of the Jacobean court is captured in the 'costume pieces' of the artist William Larkin. Larkin's fashion-conscious aristocratic clients included the 3rd Earl, his wife and his brother Edward. Lady Anne records sitting for him at Knole, and the resulting portrait is almost certainly the one hanging in our home today. The rendering of the lace around her décolletage is extraordinarily fine; a baroque pearl hangs on a black silk thread through her left ear; and her flinty, watchful glance follows you about the room. Vita Sackville-West noted the tightening of the mouth and saw it as a sign of her fortitude in the face of adversity, the mark of a strong-willed woman jibbing against the conventions of the time.

Richard himself projects a certain swagger in his portrait by Larkin at Knole, his left arm cocked at the elbow and his fist resting nonchalantly on his hip. He is good-looking, too, in a sharp sort of way, with an aquiline nose, pointy beard, widow's peak, and thin lips – the 'face of a mafioso', as it has been described. The clothes he wears are recorded in an inventory of more than a hundred items of clothing in the Sackville archives: the black velvet cloak, embroidered in gold and black silk; the shoe 'roses' of black ribbon with gold and silver lace; a hatband with embroidery and lace in gold and silver. The list of these sumptuous clothes is written up, ironically, in exactly the same type of exercise book used to record the lands sold by Richard towards the payment of his debts: debts to which the cost of all this finery contributed directly. Reports of her husband's gambling and gallivanting also recur throughout the Knole diaries. Richard was a very big spender.

Whatever Anne's later grievances, the young couple seemed happy at first. She took pleasure and pride in her husband, in his sporting accomplishments, in his noble connections, in his fine and 'beauteous' physique and, perhaps less plausibly, in his 'just mynde' and 'sweete Disposition'. It was not until 1615 that Anne's relationship with Richard began to change. Until then, Richard had supported the claims of Anne and her mother against Francis

Clifford, in the hope that they would generate enough money to fund his way of life. When negotiations between the Cliffords and the Sackvilles broke down in 1615, however, the Lord Chief Justice and his fellow judges proposed a compromise which prefigured the final settlement: Francis was to compensate Anne in cash for the loss of the lands, which were awarded to Francis. Richard and Francis accepted the deal, but Anne was the stumbling block. 'By the power of God I will continue resolute and constant,' she wrote to her mother in November. She was well aware that her opposition to the deal might cause her to 'break friendship and love' with her husband – in other words, a separation – and, as a result, 'lived in fear & terror daily'.

Whatever pressure Richard tried to apply, he could not get his wife to agree to the judges' settlement. He was exasperated by her stubbornness, complaining in a letter to Anne that she was a wife 'whom in all things I love and hold a sober woman, your land only excepted, which transports you beyond yourself and makes you devoid of reason'. It was not just her husband who was apply-ing the pressure. On 16 February 1616, her 'cousin Russell' 'told me of all my Faults & errors in this business' and made her cry. The following afternoon, streaming with a heavy cold, she was summoned to a family council consisting of 'a great Company of Men of note' in the Gallery at Dorset House. The Archbishop of Canterbury took her aside and talked with her privately for one and a half hours, persuading her 'both by Divine and human means' to sign the judges' settlement. 'Much persuasion was used by him & all the Company, sometimes terrifying me & sometimes flattering me,' but Anne did not give in.

It was decided that she should travel to Westmorland with a copy of the settlement to discuss with her mother, and send an answer back by 22 March. Anne was mightily relieved, because she had feared that her refusal would finally precipitate the threatened sepa-ration. Instead, she had more than a month's grace. For the first part of the journey north, Richard accompanied his wife – each in a coach drawn by four horses. At Lichfield, however, he turned back, leav-ing Anne and her party of ten to continue the journey 'with a heavy heart, considering how many things stood between my Lord and I'. Crossing the 'Dangerous Moors' between Derby and Manchester – the first time, she claimed, that a coach had ever made the journey – was particularly difficult in the spring rains. The horses had sometimes to be unharnessed and the coach manhandled down the hills; one of the escort horses, ridden by Rivers, her Gentleman Usher, fell off a bridge into the river. Nevertheless, the little party got to Manchester on the night of 1 March, and to Brougham on the 6th. Here, Anne spent several days with her mother, sending an answer back to London 'which was a direct denial to the Judges' award'. Richard was furious when the news was relayed back to him. He immediately sent a message asking for the return of his coach, horses and servants – but specifically not his wife. Was this, finally, a statement of separation?

There was an element of game-playing in Anne's reaction. To protect herself from any subsequent charge of desertion, she had a document drafted, and witnessed by those present, stating that she had wanted to return to London with the men and horses, and had only not done so on the express command of her husband. Despite this, she did then decide to return south. After a 'grievous & heavy Parting' from her mother on 2 April (it was the last time she saw Margaret), she rode sidesaddle until she caught up with her husband's servants who had gone ahead. On 11 April, she had 'but a cold welcome' from her husband at Knole. The fact that she had intentionally left the unsigned settlement documents behind at Brougham irritated Richard intensely.

Margaret died at Brougham Castle on 24 May 1616, and the inheritance dispute intensified immediately. Richard realised that if he did not side with his wife and act swiftly, the Cliffords would move in on the Westmorland estates, which had been occupied during her lifetime by Margaret as part of her marriage settlement. Richard stirred himself to such an extent that he was with Anne by seven o'clock on Saturday morning, having left Lewes at dawn. He lost little time, too, in persuading Anne to sign over any rights she might have in the estates to him. Anne set off for the north again on 1 July, to bury her mother at Appleby and to stake her claim to her mother's property. As their interests coincided, Richard and Anne were temporarily reconciled. 'My Lord & I were never greater friends than at this time,' she recorded in her diary. And in the middle of August, Richard joined her in Westmorland, to be seen in possession of their disputed property.

The dispute divided loyalties at court and at county level. There were fights and small disturbances between groups of retainers in Westmorland – Francis's stewards using force to enter Appleby Castle, and Richard's supporters taking possession of Brougham Castle. On 29 July, two of Francis's men interrupted Anne's people hay-making in the park at Brougham, and were wounded in the leg with pitchforks. On 27 August there was a 'great uproar', this time at Penrith, where blows were traded, swords drawn, and three or four people were hurt. Local antagonisms were getting out of hand, and when Richard challenged Francis to a duel, and news of this had spread, the only course for the contestants was to submit the case to the King himself. James I liked to think of himself as a latter-day King Solomon, judiciously resolving controversies amongst his subjects. This, in effect, meant applying further pressure on Anne to accede to the settlement.

On 18 January 1617, the King's favourite, George Villiers, Earl of Buckingham, ushered Richard and Anne into James's Drawing Chamber in Whitehall Palace. It was a private audience. The King asked them to kneel either side of his chair, and to entrust the matter wholly to him. Richard consented to this, but Anne made it clear that she would 'never part with Westmoreland while I lived upon any Condition whatsoever'. 'Sometimes,' she continued, '[the King] used fair means & persuasions, & sometimes foul means, but I was resolved before so as nothing would move me.'

The private audience ended in deadlock, and so, two days later, at 8 o'clock in the evening on the 20th, Anne and Richard assembled once again in the King's Drawing Chamber. This time, according to Anne's diary, the company included Francis and his son, Henry, with their lawyers, the judge and privy councillors. Once again the King asked the interested parties if they would submit to his Judgement, to which the Cliffords and Richard agreed. And once again Anne refused to agree to anything 'without Westmoreland'. Just as she had resisted the pressure of the Church a year before – in the person of the Archbishop of Canterbury – she was now, a woman of only twenty-six, defying the state. The King flew into 'a great Chaffe' – one of the temper tantrums for which he was renowned, and which would have been exacerbated by the generally low opinion he had of women's intelligence. It was agreed that if Anne would not be party to an agreement, an agreement should be made without her.

James gave his decision – the 'King's Award' – on 14 March 1617, and it was signed and sealed the same day by Francis, Henry and Richard. The award upheld the settlement proposed by the judges in 1615, with Francis keeping all the Clifford estates, including the Westmorland lands enjoyed by Anne's mother during her lifetime. These were to descend in the male line, first to Francis and then to Francis's son Henry. If there were no heirs, then the estates would revert to Anne and her heirs (which is what happened in 1643, after the deaths, within two years of each other, of both Francis and Henry, 4th and 5th Earls of Cumberland respectively). In return, Francis was to give Dorset £20,000 – £17,000 within two years, with £3,000 payable if and when Anne accepted the award.

She never did. Once again, Knole became the unchanging backdrop to her brooding melancholy and 'many wearisome days'. It was here, after the disappointment of the King's Award, that she fell into a routine of reading and needlework, deciding 'to set as merry a face as [she] could upon a discontented heart'. Condemned by public opinion for not accepting the award, and almost, but not quite, broken in spirit, Anne sought sanctuary, as she had done the spring before, in the Standing or in a wooded area of the garden known then, as now, as the Wilderness. To make matters worse, her two-year-old daughter, Margaret, back in her care at Knole, had the ague – a fever accompanied by fits and convulsions that could prove fatal. The emotionally and physically exhausted Anne spent 'most of her time . . . going up to see the Child'.

It is unclear why there are no surviving diary entries for the year 1618, although the opening words for 1619 – 'the 1st of this month

I began to have the curtain drawn in my chamber and to see light'
– hint at a preceding year of illness and withdrawal. Closeted for
months in the stuffy darkness of the sick room, Anne emerged
pale and far too weak even to sit upright in a jolting coach. On
the evening of Good Friday she 'fell in a great passion of weeping'
and declared that her mind was so troubled she was not fit to take
communion at Easter. Her husband decreed that there should be no
family communion in the chapel at Knole that year.

There was a further source of sadness in Anne's life at Knole.
According to John Aubrey, writing sixty or so years later, 'Venus
was not the least' among the pleasures enjoyed by Richard. Aubrey
is an unreliable source, occasionally confusing Richard with
his younger brother Edward, but he lists at least two women as
Richard's mistresses: Elizabeth Broughton, 'a most exquisite beau-
tie, as finely shaped as Nature could frame', who 'grew common
and infamous and gott the Pox, of which she died'; and, secondly,
the 'wondrous wanton' wife of Dean Overall, who was 'not more
beautiful than she was obliging and kind, and was so tender-hearted
that (truly) she could scarce denie any one'.

John Aubrey failed to mention Richard's mistress, Lady
Pennistone, but there are several strained, rather understated references in Anne's diaries. In a note on 27 July 1619, she describes how
Lady Pennistone's visit to Tunbridge Wells to take the waters 'was
much talked of abroad and my Lord was condemned for it'; and on
24 August she records how Sir Thomas Pennistone and his Lady
stayed all day at Knole, 'there being great Entertainment & much
stir about them'. It was a public affair, conducted mostly at Lady
Pennistone's mother's house in the Strand, and one which produced
two daughters. Nevertheless, Anne too conceived a second child
that summer. She reported herself 'quick with child' in August, and
by the middle of October was feeling so ill – and subject to fainting
fits – that she did not stir from her chamber until the end of March
the following year, a month after the birth of a son.

Over the centuries, Knole has been surprisingly bereft of children. With the exception of Vita Sackville-West's lonely childhood
there at the turn of the twentieth century, the only decades in the

last two hundred years when the house and grounds have been overrun by Sackville children were the 1960s and 1970s. Similarly, there were probably only two or three equivalent periods in the seventeenth and eighteenth centuries. So whenever children make a brief appearance, as they do in Anne's diaries, playing a form of 'tag' on the Bowling Green in front of the Colonnade, they brighten the place up, making it feel less like an old people's home.

Anne's daughters, Margaret (born in 1614) and Isabella (born in 1622), were a great source of comfort to her, and she was an attentive and affectionate mother. Margaret, in particular, features prominently in the Knole diaries: with anxiety, on Anne's part, whenever she has a fever; or with pride as new teeth emerge. Anne's relationship with her daughter Margaret was as close as the one she had had with her own mother Margaret, and she fought for her daughters just as her mother had fought for her, defying the authority of her husband, the Archbishop, the great 'company of men', the King. In doing so, she has become something of an icon not only for feminist historians of the family, but also for mothers bringing up daughters at Knole. By the time of her death in 1676, Anne was a matriarch survived by her daughter Margaret and by several grandchildren and great-grandchildren.

The daughters were a source of disappointment as well as comfort, for the Clifford estate was not the only inheritance at stake; there was the Sackville estate, too. In addition to Margaret and Isabella, who lived into adulthood, Richard and Anne had three sons who 'all dyed young at Knowle where they were born': the longest-lived of them, Thomas, the one who had been conceived at the height of her husband's affair with Lady Pennistone, was born on 2 February 1620 and survived until 26 July. The death of these three infant sons must have been devastating in a dynastic – as well as a domestic – sense, because as time passed it looked increasingly as if Edward, her husband's brother and male heir, would inherit the Sackville fortune. This partly explains Anne's great distrust of Edward. She often refers to his attempts 'to do me and my Child a great deal of Hurt' – in particular, by encouraging Richard to settle the Sackville estates on him (in exactly the same way that her father had settled his estates on his younger brother). 'By the cunningness of his wit,' she wrote, 'he was a great practiser against me ... but I, whose destiny was guided by a Mercifull and Divine Providence, escaped the subtlety of all his practises & ye evils he plotted against me.'

Abandoned by her husband, who spent much of his time at court or at his house at Buckhurst; humiliated by accounts of his affair with Lady Pennistone; and bored and frustrated by life at Knole: Anne's experience prefigured that of several future chatelaines of Knole. Here she was, shut out of the day-to-day running of this great house by her husband's stewards, acutely aware that one day her brother-in-law would inherit and her own children would be disinherited.

Richard ran up huge debts – around £60,000 (about £6 million in today's money) – by the time of his death in 1624. From 1617 he was being forced to sell swathes of his great inheritance each year. These sales – to the value of £80,615 – included estates in Kent and Sussex, as well as much of Fleet Street and the Manor of Holborn in London. In just sixteen years, he had spent what his forefathers had taken a century to acquire. He even sold Knole itself to one Henry Smith, commonly known as 'Dog Smith', leasing the house back at a rent of £100 a year for his own use.

Anne saw her husband for the last time on Ash Wednesday, 9 February 1624, when he kissed her and his daughters goodbye before leaving for Great Dorset House and a meeting of Parliament. Six weeks later he lay dying of 'a bloody flux' – probably dysentery – although John Chamberlain ascribed his final illness to 'a surfeit of [sweet] potatoes' (then considered a luxury and much in demand as an aphrodisiac). His wife and daughters were unable to visit him on his deathbed because they were ill with the smallpox that was to scar Anne's face for life. Richard died on 27 March at the age of thirty-four.

Who can tell how unhappy her marriage had really been? Difficult as it is to unravel the mysteries of other people's marriages in the present, it is almost impossible over the gulf of four centuries. As the passing years softened the memory of some of the greatest hurts, Anne concluded that she had been 'happy in many respects being his wife'; that Richard was 'a very kind, loving, and dear father' to their daughter Margaret. Even at the time, in the midst of her emotional rollercoaster, she was begging her mother to have a better opinion of 'the best, and most worthy man that ever breathed' and imploring her husband to stay on at Knole to celebrate their wedding anniversary. Was she simply observing the outward courtesies and conventions when she wrote all this – of a man who had done his utmost to spend her inheritance as well as his own, who had regularly made and unmade his financial provisions for her, who had cruelly used the custody of their child as a bargaining tool, and who had been routinely unfaithful? Or do the diaries reveal depths of genuine affection, tolerance and physical attraction?

On Richard's death, Anne achieved some financial independence for the first time. She had a jointure, or life interest, in part of Richard's estate, a house in London, and a dower house, Bolebrooke Place in Sussex. It was the size of her jointure – in relation to the scale of Richard's debts – that her brother-in-law Edward so begrudged. Anne even imputed a break-in attempt at Bolebrooke in the early years of her widowhood to him: 'plotted by a great man, then my extreame Enemy'. Edward, or so Anne believed, continued to nurture this 'malicious hatred' for her until his death in 1652 – twenty-four years before her own. By the time of his death, Edward would have restored some of his brother's lost inheritance, but never – and this would have pleased Anne greatly – to anything like the glory of her own.

In the short term, however, Anne was doubly disinherited, disappointed of both Clifford and Sackville estates. In her memoirs, there is a reference to the sense of grief, detachment and withdrawal that this caused: how she lived in her lord's great family at Knole as the River Rhône flows through 'the lake of Geneva, without mingling any part of its streams with that lake'. There is a sense of simply passing through.

This was the first of many times in the history of Knole and the Sackvilles that the succession shifted sideways. The feelings of disappointment and bitterness that subsequent generations of women felt, as they and their children were disinherited in favour of brothers-in-law, uncles, cousins or nephews, were first articulated by Anne. Echoes of the same emotions emerge in the writings of Vita Sackville-West's mother, Victoria, almost three centuries later. Victoria read Lady Anne's diary within days of arriving at Knole in 1889, and its impression must have lingered. Years later when her own marriage, which had begun with such promise, started to sour, her memoirs – with their maudlin accounts of promises broken, slights inflicted, money appropriated – could almost have been modelled, in the most melodramatic way, on the diaries of Lady Anne Clifford. Deserted by her feckless husband, and increasingly reliant on 'the Child' as she sometimes, like Anne, referred to Vita, Victoria found a historical precedent for her present troubles.

One of the reasons why Anne's experience has seeped into Knole, staining it so richly, is the immediacy with which she records the place itself. This affected Victoria at the turn of the twentieth century, but it also affected Vita, who published an edition of Lady Anne Clifford's diaries in 1923 as a spin-off to *Knole and the Sackvilles*. Vita's sense of identification with Anne was heightened by a shared feeling for the very fabric of Knole. She projects herself as a young girl into the character of Lady Anne, seeing Knole 'as Anne Clifford saw it, with its grey towers and wide lawns and glinting windows, and the flag floating high up in the cool empty blue'.

In her diary, Anne had described how she had ridden to Withyham to see her husband's grandfather, Thomas Sackville's, tomb, returning to Knole in floods of tears. Vita, who claimed a particular empathy with Anne, did not find this particularly surprising. She, too, had been down into that vault herself, and it had not been a cheerful expedition. But, as she continued in a passage of quite outstanding one-upmanship in *Knole and the Sackvilles*, 'of course, when Anne Clifford went there there were not so many [dead Sackvilles] as there are now . . . and their blood did not run in the veins of Lady Anne, so on the whole she had less reason to be impressed than I'.

In May 1928, prowling the gardens at dusk on one of her last visits to Knole, Vita imagined herself as the ghost of Lady Anne Clifford. The plaintive hoots of an owl would have been wafting over the Wilderness, as they still do, particularly in spring and early summer, evoking the spectre of a young woman, prayerbook in hand, seeking sanctuary in the spot she used to haunt.

Chapter 3

'A poore unsuccessfull Cavalier' (1624–1652)

Edward Sackville, 4th Earl of Dorset

A
s he left the local parish church on the morning of Sunday, 14
August 1642, Sir John Sackville, agent at Knole for his cousin
Edward, 4th Earl of Dorset, was apprehended by parliamentary
soldiers. There was a brief stand-off, but as soon as the Sackville
retainers, the congregation of St Nicholas's church and the gathering crowd of townsfolk realised that the parliamentary force
was stronger, they 'suffered them to carry him away . . . fearing to
endanger themselves in such a combustion'. The Sunday morning
disturbance in Sevenoaks took place towards the end of an edgy,
rumour-filled phoney war, as the positions of King and Parliament
began to harden and both parties started to prepare for battle. Just
over a week later, on 22 August, King Charles I raised his standard
at Nottingham, declaring war on Parliament.

The three troops of horse sent to arrest Sir John Sackville had
been dispatched from Westminster at midnight on the Saturday,
under the command of Colonel Sir John Seaton and Colonel Edwin
Sandys, and had ridden through the night. They were acting on the
suspicion that Sir John Sackville 'was Popishly inclined and ill-
affected to the Protestant Religion', and on a tip-off that Sackville
had stockpiled weapons 'in caves and cellars' at Knole to 'Arme a
great number of the malignant party of that County . . . to assist
his Maiestie'. Correspondence that had fallen into the hands of

Parliament revealed Sir John's role as official receiver for Kent of royalist contributions towards the King's cause, but hardly the imminence of a Cavalier coup.

Throughout the Civil War, Kent lay far from the line that ran north to south through the middle of England, dividing the west of the country which was mostly royalist from the east which was predominantly parliamentarian. This line, though, was too fuzzy ever to constitute a front. The war could happen anywhere, at any time: as the stained-glass window in a church was smashed, as a gang of deserters held up a travelling merchant with his train of pack animals, as a gunman opened fire from behind a hedge, or as a band of horsemen stole up on a troop of retreating soldiers and cut them down with their swords. Neither of the war's two chief protagonists, Charles nor Oliver Cromwell, set foot in the county during the conflict; there were no major battles fought there, no sieges of a city or manor house; and no armies 30,000-strong laid waste to Kent in the way they did to some other areas of the country. But it would be wrong to think that Kent and the eastern counties were unaffected by the war. The everyday rhythms of life were still dictated by the seasons, but every now and then, as it did that summer Sunday morning, as the deer grazed under the oak trees in Knole's ancient park, the war could erupt with sudden activity and the threat of violence.

From St Nicholas's, the parliamentary soldiers rode across the narrow, closely cropped valley that separates Sevenoaks from Knole – just half a mile away – and up the knoll towards the main house, scattering the clumps of fallow deer as they went. From a distance of a couple of hundred yards, the west front would have appeared austere, forbidding even – with its watch tower, its massive ragstone walls, and its battlements. Up close, however, it would have become clear that these features were designed for decorative, rather than defensive, purposes and that much of the house, self-consciously old before its time, was – in architectural terms at least – a sixteenth-century attempt to recreate the might of a bygone medieval age. Clattering across the Green Court and into the Stone Court, the horsemen would have passed through the central gatehouse with its four battlemented corner turrets. There would have been no need to watch out for boiling water or molten lead from the parapet above because the machicolations, or openings through which these would have been poured, were no more than a design feature – and completely useless in the event of an invasion.

On Monday, the parliamentary soldiers took away five wagon-loads of arms belonging to the Earl of Dorset, 'there being,' it was claimed, 'compleat armes for 500 or 600 men', along with ammunition and saddles, and horses which they found stabled in underground cellars. These 'were brought with much joyfull exultation through the City unto the Parliament'. Poor Sir John was carted off, rather less ceremoniously, 'bound in the Coach', for examination before the Committees of both Houses of Parliament before being committed to the Fleet prison.

When justifying the raid on Knole to the House of Lords, the parliamentarian Lord General, the Earl of Essex, explained that it had been necessary to keep the weapons from 'being made use of against the Parliament'. It was an acknowledgement of the Earl of Dorset's perceived importance as a provincial magnate. Until ordered to surrender his commission, after the passing of the Militia Ordinance in March 1642, Dorset had been Lord Lieutenant of Sussex and Middlesex, one of the armed noblemen responsible since Tudor times for maintaining law and order throughout the country. If you look at the weapons that were removed, however, their confiscation would appear an over-reaction to no more than a perception of military might. The House of Lords ordered that an inventory be taken of the arms, and money given to the Earl of Dorset 'in Satisfaction Thereof'. Edward duly forwarded to the House an inventory taken in January 1641, which listed saddles, pistols, swords, 151 pikes, 76 full muskets, 56 'bastard muskets', halberds, armour, three suits of tilting armour, and so on. In fact, many of the arms removed with such 'joyfull exultation' were rusty and broken – twelve 'old ruset saddles trimmed with red lether and furniture defettive', thirteen 'old French pistols whereof four have locks [and] the other nine have none'. They were museum pieces, really, rather like the motley collection of weapons that hang on the walls of the armoury at Knole today.

Colonel Sandys, a member of one of Kent's leading puritan families, exceeded his parliamentary commission. His soldiers indulged
in some gratuitous violence and petty theft, ransacking the house,
and cutting and slashing at the furniture. In an account by the steward at Knole of 'the hurtes done . . . by the companie of Horsemen
brought by Colonell Sandys', they broke open over forty locks,
and ripped gold thread from some embroidered cushions. The great
hurt done may have been exaggerated, but the sense of outrage was
not. The house that Thomas Sackville had acquired and refurbished
in the first decade of the seventeenth century had been invaded, and
was soon to be inhabited, by an enemy force. It was an example –
forty years on – of just how fragile a family's hold on its inheritance
could be; and a manifestation, on a domestic scale, of the most revolutionary decade in English history: as ancient institutions, from
the monarchy to the House of Lords, were abolished, and the hier-
archies that underpinned society itself were overturned.

Worse was to come. Knole and some of the Sackville estates
around Sevenoaks were sequestrated, and in 1643, a year after the
raid, the Central Committee for Kent, which administered the
county for Parliament, collecting taxes and sequestrating the estates
of royalists, was based at Knole itself. The outbuildings were used
as a prison, the grounds as a magazine; the county committee, it is
said, held their meetings in what has been the family dining room
for over three hundred years now. Chairman of the committee was
the splenetic and dictatorial Sir Anthony Weldon, whose career
was a mirror image of that of the Sackvilles. Weldon had outraged
James I, and lost his job as a result, when the King read an unpublished account by Weldon of a visit by James to his native Scotland
in 1617. 'The air,' wrote Weldon, 'might be wholesome but for
the stinking people that inhabit it. The ground might be fruit-
ful had they the wit to manure it. Their beasts be generally small,
women only excepted, of which sort there are none greater in the
whole world.' From then on, Weldon's career had been fuelled by
bitterness towards the Crown – he was the author of two critical
studies on the *Court and Character of King James* and the *Court
of King Charles* – just as, conversely, the Sackvilles' success had

been founded on their support for, and favour with, the early Stuart kings. As Weldon held court in the family dining room, you might wonder to what extent, in this world turned upside down, the old rivalries and grudges within provincial society were being played out through the prism of war.

In a letter, published in 1648, *a gentleman in Kent giving Satisfaction to a friend in London of the Beginning, Progresse, and Ende of the late great Action there*', described the county committeemen:

> Their obscure parentage and education . . . making them ignoble and ignorant . . . they grew to have no scantling of any rule but such as proceeded from their own unlimited proud thoughts and passions. Hence they exercised their cruelty more than once over the lives and fortunes of their poor Countrymen . . . Hence also they erected to themselves a seraglio at Knole, and after at Aylesford, maintaining their state and princely economy at the sad charges of the county; living at the height of pride and luxury, till in the terror of their own consciences they broke up, when the devil himself came to appear amongst them (which is most true) as a committeeman.

Whether the charges of extravagance levelled at the committee's housekeeping were fully justified, and whether the devil really did appear amongst them, there is no doubt that the headquartering at Knole of the committee, a sort of Kent County Council, was quite an enterprise. The committee's bodyguard alone numbered over a hundred soldiers at Knole. Rooms in the house were converted into lodgings, with money spent on extras to complement the existing furnishings: £153 on sheets, table linen and carpets; and £22 on silverware, candlesticks, glasses and jugs. Large quantities of hay, oats, malt, wheat and hops were brought in, and beer was brewed in the brewhouse at Knole. Fruit was bought from the Sackvilles' gardener and wood, cut in the park, was bought from Sir John's wife, Lady Sackville. The committee did not pay any rent for the house itself – it had been sequestrated – but it did rent some of the neighbouring fields.

The Sackvilles' own servants waited on the committee, as records of payments and the odd gratuity show: £39 'for cleaning the chambers, light fires etc.', £69 and a nag for the chaplain, £1 to William Sparks 'for his pains in helping the cook at general Committees'. Most poignantly of all, there was the sum of £1 17s. 4d. paid to the 'carpenter and others employed in taking away the rails and levelling the ground in the chapel at Knole'. Throughout the country, altar rails and raised Communion tables were being removed in a direct reaction to Archbishop Laud's much-hated reforms. Laud's attempt to introduce more ceremonial into the Church of England, in particular into the sacrament of the Eucharist, smacked of popery; and his elevation of the altar to 'the greatest place of God's residence on Earth' created, many felt, an artificial hierarchy, separating the priest from his congregation. It was these religious developments that were as much a cause of popular distrust for Charles, and his Catholic wife Henrietta Maria, as his treatment of Parliament.

The chapel at Knole that the 'carpenter and others' were adapting on the committee's instructions had, in the mid-fifteenth century, lain at the heart of Archbishop Bourchier's palace. It was a pre-Reformation chapel, therefore, now being prepared for a style of worship simpler and sparser than it had ever hosted before – or was to host for most of its future. The fact that Edward Sackville was described in his day as everything from a puritan to a papist suggests that he was fairly ecumenical in his faith; and his friends certainly ranged from Catholics such as Sir Kenelm Digby to Puritans such as Richard Amherst. He was an enthusiastic reader of Sir Thomas Browne's *Religio Medici* (published in 1642, the year the Civil War started), which defends the doctrine of the Church of England and stresses the importance of reason in religious experience. Like Browne, Edward favoured the 'Jacobethan' Church of Elizabeth I and James I, which had tolerated different strands of opinion within a broad national framework. Like Dorset, subsequent generations of Sackvilles have generally been fairly conformist too. With the exception of a few years in the 1960s when my uncle's resident 'pet priest' Father Squire, in biretta and chasuble, and waving a censer, introduced an incense-laden waft of High Anglican pomp to Knole, Dorset's Sackville descendants have tended to avoid religious extremes and to float somewhere between a restrained Anglicanism and agnosticism.

This is the chapel where Lady Anne Clifford prayed when her eyes were not too 'blubbered' with crying, where Vita Sackville-West got married, dressed in cloth of gold and veiled in Irish lace that her mother had worn at the coronation of the Czar, where my father's coffin rested the night before his funeral, where my children were christened. It now lies at the heart of our apartment at Knole. It is a chapel where, for centuries, the decidedly un-Puritan outward signs and symbols of worship have been celebrated as much as the inner epiphanies. For several months in 1643 and 1644, however, its walls resounded to sermons up to two hours long by visiting ministers, such as the one delivered by Joseph Bowden, minister of the church at Ashford, to the members of the committee at Knole on 13 June 1644: 'Here is the model and line of your work,' preached Bowden: 'Suspension for suspension, degradation for degradation, deprivation for deprivation, imprisonment for imprisonment, banishment for banishment, sequestration for sequestration, spoiling for spoiling, blood for blood, . . . double unto her according to her works . . . If they have cut off God's people's ears, . . . we may warrantably cut off their heads.'

Published later as *A Alarme beat up in Sion, to War against Babylon*, this tirade was a call to arms against Anglicans, as well as Catholics, rather than a sermon, and stressed the impossibility of ending the quarrel between Sion and Babylon any way but by the sword. The barbarity of the tit-for-tat punishments demanded may have referred to Edward's earlier support for the punishment of the Puritan polemicist William Prynne. In 1634, William Prynne had been tried for libel on the basis of an attack in his book *Histriomastix* on female actors (an entry in the index, for example, read 'Women actors notorious whores'). Many people, including Edward, the Queen's Lord Chamberlain, saw this as an attack on the fun-loving Henrietta Maria herself, who was a great patron of such entertainments. Edward was as outspoken in his defence of the

Queen's virtues as he was in his attack on Prynne, arguing for his nose to be slit, his ears cut off, a £10,000 fine and life imprisonment. Prynne was subjected to some of these ordeals in May, with both of his ears being lopped.

The occupation of Knole by the county committee, and the celebration there of a style of religion so much at odds with the Sackvilles' characteristic lack of godly zeal, represented the failure of Edward on both a political and a personal level. In the Great Hall at Knole, there is a portrait from the studio of Sir Anthony van Dyck, Charles I's court painter, of Edward Sackville, 4th Earl of Dorset. The gleaming breastplate and helmet suggest a soldier, the scarlet doublet and embroidered ruffs a courtier. But what delighted us most as children was the key which dangles, in the portrait, from a blue ribbon at his waist and also, in real, three-dimensional form, from a corner of the picture frame.

This detail particularly entranced us, perhaps because we come from a family obsessed with keys. Generations of Sackvilles have hoarded them. 'You never know when this might come in useful,' they say to their children, as they squirrel away yet another rusty, unidentified key in a box, or hang it from a row of nails beside their bed (my uncle), or tie it to a string around their waist (my father): keys that might one day unlock no one knows which room, which chest or which moment in the house's secret history. The very mention of the word 'key' in a room of Sackvilles – 'key', 'what key?' – creates panic, as it is immediately assumed that someone has actually lost one. Little did we know, as children though, that it was, quite literally, keys that have unlocked the reserves of royal access, wealth and power on which the Sackvilles' success was based: for the key hanging from the corner of the picture frame is a symbol of Edward's office as Lord Chamberlain, gatekeeper first to Queen Henrietta Maria and then to King Charles I.

Here is a portrait, then, of a royalist at the time of the Civil War. It conforms to a number of the raffish stereotypes, or 'ridiculous Habits and apish Gestures' of the Cavalier described by a contemporary Puritan satirist. Edward is not wearing a 'hat in fashion like a close-stoolepan . . . set on the top of his noddle like a coxcombe'. But he does have 'long hair with ribands tied in it'; 'his sleeves unbuttoned'; 'in one hand a stick, playing with it, in the other side his cloke hanging out'; 'his belt about his hips'; 'his sword swapping between his legs like a Monkey's taile'.

Contemporary accounts also appear to confirm this portrait of a classic Cavalier. In his *History of the Rebellion and Civil Wars in England*, written in the 1660s although based on first-hand experience of Charles I's reign, Edward Hyde, Earl of Clarendon, described Dorset's

> person beautiful, and graceful, and vigorous; his wit pleasant, sparkling, and sublime; and his other parts of learning and language of that lustre that he could not miscarry in the world. The vices he had were of the age, which he was not stubborn enough to condemn or resist . . . [who] indulged to his appetite all the pleasures that season of his life (the fullest of jollity and riot of any that preceded or succeeded) could tempt or suggest to him. He had a very sharp, discerning spirit, and was a man of an obliging nature, much honour, of great generosity, and of most entire fidelity to the Crown.

For Vita Sackville-West, Edward was the 'embodiment of Cavalier romance', and she made him the hero of a lengthy romance, called 'The Tale of a Cavalier', which she wrote as a teenager.

To complete the swashbuckling image, there is Edward's account of a duel in which he fatally wounded Lord Bruce of Kinloss in 1613. No one is quite sure of the exact cause of the duel – had Sackville attempted to seduce one of Lord Bruce's sisters? – but it is clear that the quarrel had been going on for several months, before the two protagonists agreed to meet in August, ankle deep in the mud of a waterlogged meadow, at Bergen-op-Zoom, near Antwerp. Although wounded himself in three places, feeling faint – and with one of his fingers hanging simply by a flap of skin – Edward managed to run his rapier through Bruce's chest, just below his heart. Bruce died soon after of his wounds.

The duel put paid to any early success Edward had enjoyed at court. As the grandson – on his mother's side – of Thomas Howard, 4th Duke of Norfolk, and – on his father's side – of Thomas Sackville, 1st Earl of Dorset, Lord Treasurer to Elizabeth I and James I, Edward was the product of ancient nobility and new money. With such a distinguished ancestry, combined with natural ability, he had a lot going for him. The duel, however, greatly displeased James I, who had been trying to ban the practice, and it attracted death threats from the Bruce family. Edward was now effectively guilty of murder, and he embarked on a self-imposed exile in France and the Netherlands.

Just over a month after his return in September 1615, Edward was in trouble again. On 25 October, he was present at the execution at Tyburn of Richard Weston, the former warden of the Tower of London. Weston had confessed to feeding poisoned tarts to Sir Thomas Overbury to silence, for ever, Overbury's opposition to the marriage of Edward's cousin Lady Frances Howard and her lover Robert Carr, Earl of Somerset. As Weston stood on the scaffold, Edward was one of those who, in an attempt to clear Frances and Robert from any involvement in a plot, asked Weston whether he was really guilty or not, whether his confession had been forced out of him. When King James came to hear about this, Edward was thrown into prison for impugning the decision of the Court of the Star Chamber. His brief imprisonment did not prevent him from attending a dinner held by the Lord Mayor of London in November 1615. Some of the guests there were 'so rude and unruly', according to John Chamberlain, particularly in 'putting the citizens wives to the squeake, so far forth that one of the sheriffs brake open a doore upon Sir Edward Sackville, which gave such occasion of scandal' that they were sent away before the banquet began.

Edward had no expectations of inheriting (his brother Richard, the 3rd Earl, was just a year older), and his twenties are typical of the shiftless younger son in many aristocratic families, the 'spare' rather than the heir. Nevertheless, in all his portraits he projects a sense of energy and poise, and by the early 1620s it was beginning to look as if this urbane, affable young man might make his way on his wits alone. He had started on a slow rehabilitation, to becoming that 'great man at ye Court' whom his sister-in-law Lady Anne Clifford so feared. Edward had natural talent and ambition, and as member for Sussex in the Parliament of 1621, had started to attract notice as an eloquent parliamentary speaker. His support for the Crown in the key debates of the day – arguing for troops to be sent to recover the Palatinate for Frederick, James I's son-in-law, and contending that the King would be greatly, and rightly, offended by Parliament's interference in so delicate a matter as the proposed marriage of the Prince of Wales with the Infanta of Spain – failed, however, to secure him the position as ambassador to France he so wanted. Similarly disappointed in his efforts to find gainful 'home imployment', and without anything better to do, he petitioned in 1623 for a licence to travel in Europe.

What completely transformed his prospects was his surprise succession to the earldom. Edward was in Florence when he learnt that his brother Richard had died on 27 March 1624 and that he was now the 4th Earl of Dorset. Although the estates he inherited were encumbered with debts, the title and the sudden rise in status, if not wealth, gave his political career a boost. For a start, it made him more eligible for high office. As a Francophile, both by personal inclination and by politics, he was one of the noblemen chosen to accompany French ambassadors to audiences with the King, and was in the reception party at Dover in June 1625 to greet Charles's new bride, Henrietta Maria, to the country.

Edward inherited just a year before Charles I succeeded his father James I to the throne, so it was a new regime all round. In those days, when the King was the source of almost all patronage and power, the succession of a new monarch heralded a fundamental change in the political climate of the nation: in this case, from the chaotic, gossipy, unkempt court of James I to the stiff, ceremonial, well-ordered world of his son. Edward was installed as a Knight of the Garter in December 1625 – a sure sign of Charles's favour – one of just sixteen members, comprising the Prince of Wales, the Duke of York, six English earls, three Scottish noblemen and five foreigners.

Just as his grandfather, Thomas Sackville, had benefited from office as Lord Treasurer, Edward profited by proximity to the new

King. Edward's wife Mary, too, was at the heart of the court as governess to Charles I's sons. In 1626 he was appointed a Privy Councillor, and in 1628 he was made Lord Chamberlain to Queen Henrietta Maria. Here, he was responsible for organising the Queen's household and supervising her servants, for promoting the elaborate ritual and ceremony that were such a feature of the Caroline court, for hosting dinners for the King and Queen, and for pushing through cost-cutting reforms to the court. He also acted as spokesman for the Queen, as her agent in property transactions, and oversaw all her theatrical entertainments – it was this role that had made him particularly sensitive to William Prynne's criticisms. But, most important of all, he was the Queen's gatekeeper, controlling access to her person. At a time when Charles was trying to establish some privacy for himself and his family by withdrawing into increasingly closed areas of the court and by limiting the distribution of keys (just as, on a smaller scale, the Sackville family at Knole had begun to withdraw from the great state rooms to more private, domestic rooms), the holding of keys was crucial.

The royal household was like an aristocratic household writ large. If the aristocratic household was the basic unit of government in the counties, the royal household was the centre of power in the kingdom. Even in Stuart times, it was often difficult to distinguish between the private household of the monarch and the public business of the realm. The monarch's main residence was the Tudor palace of Whitehall: a rambling warren of more than two thousand rooms which, despite Charles's initial plans to replace it with a modern building designed by Inigo Jones, stayed Tudor. Its long galleries and back passages scurried with a household of some 1,800 people, from grooms and scullery maids to aristocratic advisers, all of them seeking favours and promotion – an anarchy on which Charles hoped to impose some order.

More important than the stipend of £100 a year, the eighteen-room apartment in Whitehall Palace (plus kitchen and cellar), and the right to enjoy a 'diet' of a ten-dish table that went with the Lord Chamberlain's job, was the direct personal access it gave Edward to the King and Queen – and the financial opportunities that flowed from this. Unlike his elder brother, Edward's entrepreneurial and political energies had not been terminally sapped by the expectation of an inheritance. His marriage to Mary, the daughter of Sir George Curzon, in 1612 had brought him estates in Derbyshire and Staffordshire; and, through his court contacts, he soon acquired a portfolio of business interests. Between 1629 and 1634 he was a commissioner for settling Virginia. The petition he wrote in 1637 to King Charles I, and for which – tantalisingly – there is no record of a response, is typical of the way in which the monarchy outsourced the functions of government to private contractors. It requested 'certain islands on the south of New England, viz. Long Island, Cole Island, Sandy point, Hell Gates', which 'were lately delivered by some of your Majesty's subjects, and are not yet inhabited by any Christians. Prays a grant thereof, with like powers of government as have been granted for other plantations in America.'

Closeness to the King gave Edward opportunities to exploit, not just in the New World but also at home. The right to collect the export tax on coal, for example, produced an annual income in the mid-1630s of over £1,000 a year – many times that yielded by his estates around Sevenoaks. Other public offices placed patronage at his disposal, which could be converted into cash in the form of bribes and backhanders. His role as a commissioner for the office of Lord Admiral, for example, enabled him to secure his petitioners appointments to ships, and to other lucrative posts – but always at a price. Edward's stance on the way business and politics operated was characteristic of the age. When, in November 1635, the Court of the Star Chamber was considering a case which involved a bribe that had gone astray, the privy councillors questioned whether bribery was acceptable in the first place. Edward was clear that he 'did not think it to be a crime for a courtier that comes up to court for his Majesty's service, and lives at great expense by his attendance, to receive a reward to get a business done by a great man in power'.

As a result, Edward could begin to pay off his brother's debts and to restore the estate that Richard had all but ruined. Entertainment at Knole recovered some of its former grandeur. A bill of fare for a banquet at Knole on 3 July 1636 begins with the instructions: 'To perfume the room often in the meal with orange flower water upon a hot pan. To have fresh bowls in every corner and flowers tied upon them, and sweet briar, stock, gilly-flowers, pinks, wallflowers and any other sweet flowers in glasses and pots in every window and chimney.' The menu that followed featured two courses of thirty-three dishes each, including barley broth, boiled teats, roast tongues, bream, perch, roast veal, mutton with anchovies, grilled pike, roast venison 'in blud', capons, wild duck, salmon, tench, crabs, venison pasty, swans, herons, custard, stewed potatoes, a whole pig, rabbits, and almond pudding.

During the 1620s and 1630s, Edward became heavily involved in national politics through his activities at court and in the Privy Council. His career blossomed and, even after the murder of his mentor (and the King's chief adviser), the Duke of Buckingham, in 1628, he managed to stay close to Charles. Between 1629 and 1640, he attended 538 of the 1,104 Privy Council meetings, and sat on numerous committees, proving himself an exceptionally hard-working member.

Edward was also an active provincial magnate, his political power residing with the heart of the Sackville estates in Sussex. The first five Earls of Dorset were all Lord Lieutenants of Sussex, holding the post almost continuously from 1569 to 1677; to this, from 1628 to 1642, Edward added the office of Lord Lieutenant of Middlesex. Lord Lieutenants were the link between the Privy Council and the provincial elites, the tentacles by which government stretched from the court to the counties. Their role had originally been mostly military, and with the country often at war in the late 1620s, they were increasingly active in conscripting and mobilising soldiers for military expeditions. They also commanded the local militia and were responsible for maintaining law and order.

For the Lord Lieutenant of Middlesex, Shrove Tuesday and May Day were particularly busy days, when riots of unruly apprentices and migrant workers broke out in London most years. As the country drifted towards civil war, the role of the Lord Lieutenant in preventing 'tumultuous assemblies' in the capital became more important. When, in November 1641, Edward ordered the militia

to fire over the heads of a crowd trying to block the entry of bishops into the House of Lords – an order that was, in fact, disobeyed
– he was doing his duty as a policeman rather than as a counter-
revolutionary. It was the military muscle of the Lord Lieutenants,
or at least a perception of it, that made Parliament so keen to disarm
them, and to order the raid on Knole, in 1642.

Edward was not, however, quite the hardliner he sometimes
appeared, and was a much subtler, more complicated character than
Vita's stereotype of the 'embodiment of Cavalier romance' suggests.
He was one of a group of people who would eventually, during
the Civil War, form a loose coalition of moderates described as the
Constitutional Royalists. The stirrings of their attempts in the 1640s
to seek peace can be seen in the politics of the 1620s and 1630s, as
they tried to negotiate a middle way between King and Parliament.
In 1626–27 he publicly supported the forced loan, which Charles
demanded, on pain of imprisonment, from his wealthier subjects,
arguing more lukewarmly in private that such policies 'in all *proba-
bility* tend to happiness'; by the Parliament of 1628, however, he had
come out against it. The same year, Parliament presented Charles
with the Petition of Right as a legal guarantee of their liberties,
demanding for example that taxes be levied only with Parliament's
consent, that martial law could never be imposed in peacetime, and
that there should be no arbitrary arrest or imprisonment. Edward
once again advocated a middle way between 'his Majesty's right'
and the 'people's liberties', dropping hints to the King in an attempt
to modify royal policy.

Edward believed passionately in monarchy, but in a monarchy
limited by the rule of law and by the obligation to work with the
Church and with Parliament. So finely tuned was the constitution
which he and his allies upheld that any monarch would necessarily,
and instinctively, seek to maintain a sense of harmony, generally by
asking consent for his actions. Edward's attitude to the Petition of
Right hardened to one of outright opposition because he believed
there was no need for Parliament to prescribe, and legislate for, this
delicate balance; and that any attempt to do so was as an unaccept-
able limitation on the King's prerogative and instinctive good sense.

As Charles's refusal to summon Parliament deprived him of the traditional income from import and export tax, he came to rely increasingly on a range of new financial expedients to raise money, or at least revivals of medieval taxes. Edward generally supported him – but within the limits of the law. His defence of the King's prerogative was based partly on his faith that the King exercised this prerogative for the good of his subjects, and that royal power and people's rights were therefore compatible. By the 1630s, however, the gulf between Charles's perception of his powers and Parliament's perception of them had widened to such an extent, and the bonds of trust between them become so broken, that attempts to mediate, such as Edward's, were prone to failure. By the late 1630s, Edward, who had been one of the most powerful privy council-lors in 1629, was well aware that his influence was on the wane, that he was excluded from the inner 'Cabinett Counseyll' and out of sympathy with Charles's key advisers, the Earl of Strafford and Archbishop Laud.

Much of the blame for this breakdown in trust can be laid on the King. The success of a personal monarchy depended to a large extent on the personality of the monarch. And, as Edward discovered, Charles was rigid and reserved, furtive and fickle in his treatment of those who were most loyal to him and who had the profoundest reverence for monarchy. It was Edward's misfortune to serve such a man. Although in public he was always deeply respectful, and horrified by any slight on the King and Queen, in private he was bewildered by Charles's behaviour, writing to the Earl of Middlesex in June 1642 that Charles was 'apt to take extempore resolutions upon the first impression'. The politics of consensus that people like Edward espoused were foundering on the personality of the King.

Edward agonised at the approach of war during the summer of 1642, imploring the Earl of Salisbury to 'study day and night, to keepe the more violent spirits from passing the Rubicon'. What he wanted was 'an easy and safe way' out of 'this darke and inextri-cable labyrinth': a hard task when 'there are too many hot-headed people both here and att London that advise and perswade desperate

wayes'. Edward's fear of an absolute victory for the hotheads or
hardliners of either side drove him in his increasingly desperate
search for 'an accommodation'. It was a failure to find this middle
way, this accommodation, that led Edward, along with two-thirds
of the English nobility, to join the King in 1642. Edward arrived in
York in May 1642 (his departure had been rumoured ever since the
passing of the Militia Ordinance in March) and signed the engagement to 'defend your Majestie's Person, Crown and Dignity, with
your just and legall prerogatives, against all persons and power
whatsoever . . . to defend the true Protestant Religion, established
by the laws of the land, the lawfull liberties of the subjects of
England, and the just priviledges of your Majestie and both Houses
of Parliament'. This was the balanced constitution that Edward had
supported throughout his life, and which he believed in the end had
been threatened more by Parliament's demands than by Charles's
personal rule. He also undertook to provide the King with sixty
horses for three months.

In August he wrote to the Countess of Middlesex (whose daughter, Frances, had married his eldest son Richard the previous year,
and who was one of his principal confidantes throughout the war
years):

> Behold into whatt a sad condition blind zeale, pride, ambition, envy,
> malice and avarice . . . hath plunged the honor, quiet, safety, peace,
> plenty, prosperity, piety of this late, very late, most happy king-
> dom . . . Wee are runninge headlong to destruction and like butchers
> one to quarter outt the other: Brother against brother, father against
> sonn, frend against frend and all for I know nott whatt: Religion to
> bee purified is the pretence of some, liberty to be preserved is the
> profession of others . . . Is Civill War the way to these happy ends?
> Oh noe! The Divell hath sett a fayre face on his fowle dressings:
> Atheisme wilbee brought in place of protestantisme; slavery will
> succeed this unbridld and ill coveted liberty . . .

In this letter of great anguish, he feared that 'wofull dayes are
att hand . . . All is lost, all is lost: soe lost, as I wowld I were quiet

in my grave.' Edward's characteristically neat and elegant script becomes more agitated as the ideas, passions and convictions which animate him take hold: the frenzied scrawl at the end of the letter evidence of a man in turmoil and despair. 'I wowld ... my children had never binn borne, to live under the dominion of soe many Cades and Ketts, as threaten by there multitudes and insurrections to drowne all memory of monarchy, nobility, gentry, in this land.' The dismissive reference to Jack Cade's Kentish rebellion of 1450 and Robert Kett's Norfolk revolt of 1549 are loaded with the patrician's defence of the established order and contempt for those who undermine it.

In December, Edward lamented to the Countess of Middlesex: 'I sigh to say itt, there is a shamble of mans flesh made, were there Canniballs to buy itt.' Was this a ghastly premonition of the murder, three years later, of his own son? Or simply an observation, born of first-hand experience, of the terrible damage that seventeenth-century ordnance could do: the single cannon ball which could take the heads off a file of men, six deep, or the soft lead bullets used by both sides which produced wounds far more extensive than those inflicted by swords, and which carried pieces of torn cloth into a wound, causing infection? He feared that the following year of civil war would witness 'more barbaratyes to bee committed, then ever yet any of our chronicles mention'd'; and observed how 'already, all suffer extremes in there goods, and will ere long, undergo all outrages and villanyes in there persons.' He simply wanted peace, for the sake of the 'publik weale, and the private sowle' – and, of course, for his own estates.

Within days of Charles raising his standard at Nottingham, royalist moderates had persuaded the King to send peace commissioners to Westminster, and Edward was soon pursuing informal peace initiatives with the leader of the parliamentary army, the Earl of Essex. Edward was to be involved in peace negotiations throughout the Civil War, his attempts constantly thwarted by Charles's failure to compromise. His role throughout the war was civilian rather than military, although in October 1642, he did attend the Battle of Edgehill, the first full-scale battle of the Civil War – indeed the first time since the Wars of the Roses, over 150 years before, that Englishmen had fought Englishmen. Here, his job was to look after the young Prince of Wales and the Duke of York. The story told by James, Duke of York, when writing to a Colonel Legge in 1679 is that the King ordered Dorset to take his two sons up the hill and out of the firing line, whereupon Dorset refused, claiming that 'he would not be thought a coward for never a King's sonne in Christendom'. As well as the two young princes, who would, as Charles II and James II, become Kings of England one day, there were on the field of battle that day fifteen soldiers who would one day sign Charles I's death warrant.

Edgehill would have been Edward's first experience of the war, and it informed his later writings: not just the battle itself, but the aftermath too, when the exhausted armies sat about stunned and silent in the dark, the only sound on the battlefield the cries of the wounded; the relatives arriving in search of loved ones, and the human scavengers stripping the bodies, and pulling rings from the fingers, of the dead who lay in their thousands on the ground. It was a vicious war and one in which, proportionally, as many English people died as in the First World War. Everyone knew someone who had lost a friend or family member, whose crops had been requisitioned, or whose house had been ransacked and burnt by marauding soldiers.

After the battle, Edward followed the King to Oxford, where the court and Cavalier high command were based from 1642 onwards. The university city became the King's new capital, a garrison town with defences and fieldworks stretching for miles in all directions. Charles was based at Christchurch, and Henrietta Maria with her spaniels, the familiar furniture from her London house, and with Edward as her Lord Chamberlain, set up home in the warden's lodgings at Merton. The city was overwhelmed by the number of its new residents, its streets piled with rubbish, its medieval drains overflowing, and its population succumbing to annual outbreaks of the plague. Nevertheless, some attempt was made to recreate, in Oxford, the normal patterns of domestic life at court, with its pastimes of playing cards and embroidery. In April 1644 the pregnant Queen left Oxford, never to see her husband again, and Edward was appointed Lord Chamberlain of the King's Household, a post held – in an example of the extraordinarily small world in which they all moved – from 1626 to 1641 by Philip Herbert, the second husband of Edward's sister-in-law Anne Clifford.

Edward suffered at the hands of Parliament for his loyalty to the King. Not only was Knole requisitioned as the headquarters for the county committee, but, on 5 June 1644 it was assessed that Edward should pay £5,000 to the committee for the Advance of Money for his failure to contribute voluntarily to Parliament's war effort. When he didn't pay, it was ordered that his estates and goods be seized and inventoried, although there are no records that any of the £5,000 was ever paid. The other parliamentary committee with the power to distrain the property of 'delinquents' was the same county Committee for Sequestrations, which sat at Knole in 1643–44. For contributing horses 'towards the maintenance of . . . forces raised against the Parliament', Edward was liable to have his 'estates as well reall as personal . . . seized and sequestered'.

There is evidence of two forced sales of goods during 1645–46. Records survive of chairs, tables, paintings and wall hangings, where they were at Knole, and what prices they fetched at auction – a total of £1,594 3s. 4½d. Several of the lots were bought by Edward's son Richard, and quite a few by a Colonel Boothby of Westerham and a Mr Beckwith of London, who could have been agents of the Sackvilles buying in goods for the family. Beyond these sales, there is no evidence that Edward's estates in Kent were severely affected. During the Civil War, Edward's London home, Dorset House, was protected from plundering by an order of the House of Lords, because two of the royal children, Henry, Duke of Gloucester, and Princess Elizabeth, were in the care of his wife, Mary. His lands in Sussex were similarly protected by an order of the Committee for the King's Children which allowed the countess – briefly, because she died in May 1645 – to enjoy the income of £2,000 a year from the Sussex estate by virtue of her royal employment.

Edward was to claim – in a letter to James Cranfield, 2nd Earl of Middlesex – that his fidelity to the King had cost him £40,000.

Although this was probably as much through the general wear and tear of war as through direct fines, Edward must have found the cost particularly galling when Charles questioned his loyalty. His commitment to peace, and his efforts to keep contact with parliamentarian peers throughout the war, opened him to accusations of treachery from the King. In the autumn of 1645, the royal fortunes sank to such a 'miserable state' that Edward and others tried to persuade the King to treat with Parliament. For his pains, Edward was accused by the King of having 'the voice of Jacob, but that his hands were those of Esau'. Charles even claimed that he 'would place his crown on his head, and preserve it with his sword, if the swords of his friends failed him'.

Edward was one of those who signed the articles of capitulation in June 1646, surrendering Oxford and bringing the first Civil War to an end. He asked to compound for his delinquency under the Oxford Articles; his petition described how he had 'voluntarily left his usuall place of habitacon he hath resided at Oxford and other places within His Majesties quarters, and hath adhered to His Majesties [cause] during this unhappy warre, and was at the surrender thereof, and is comprised within the articles then made. That his estate being sequestered for his delinquency against the Parliament, he humblie prayes that he may be admitted to a favourable composition for the same according to the sayd articles.' His original sequestration was duly suspended and, on 7 December 1646, he was fined £4,360, or one-tenth the value of his estates: this was lower than the standard rate of a third, and recognised the fact that the delinquent had surrendered. Negotiations to reduce this sum continued for several years, with Dorset eventually securing his discharge from the Committee for Compounding in May 1650. After eight years, he was back in full possession of his estates.

He was never free, however, of the money worries that had begun with the inheritance of his brother's debts and then been exacerbated by the war. In 1641 he had negotiated a dowry of £10,000 on the marriage of Frances Cranfield, daughter of the Earl and Countess of Middlesex, to his son Richard, but the Cranfields had been slow to pay. In a letter to Frances's mother in 1645, he expressed the wish that Richard would be able to buy back the estates around Knole with Frances's dowry, but in early 1647 there was still £4,000 outstanding, almost enough to cover his fine. He asked Frances's brother James, the 2nd Earl of Middlesex, for the speedy payment of £2,000 of this (and received it), 'for that bee the foundation whereon I must begin to build my owne freedome and your sisters future happynes, soe as hereafter they may live like themselves, and you bee comforted in seeing them contentedly provided for'. It is characteristic of the subtleties of the Civil War, and the intricate web of family ties within the peerage, that here was a so-called royalist delinquent – Edward – requesting money to help pay a fine from a parliamentarian, Middlesex: a fine for which Middlesex, as a member of the Committee for Compounding, was responsible.

Edward would continue to press anxiously for the final £2,000 into the 1650s, and even resorted to a legal action which lapsed. It was not until the 1670s that the Cranfield fortune would be the salvation of the Sackvilles, when the 3rd Earl of Middlesex died childless, and Edward's grandson Charles inherited the Cranfield estate. The procession of wagons that travelled from the Cranfield family seat at Copt Hall in Essex to Knole half a century later was loaded with treasures far more valuable than the ragbag of weapons that left Knole on Monday 15 August 1642.

The personal cost of the Civil War was every bit as painful as the financial. In November 1642, Edward's elder son Richard was captured by parliamentary soldiers after the battle of Turnham Green and briefly imprisoned; the following year, his younger son Edward was wounded at Newbury, the battle where, after twelve hours of fighting in filthy weather, 3,500 men lay dead. There was the constant fear for members of the family, both in life and death. In a letter of condolence, written in May 1645, Edward urged the Countess of Middlesex not to have her husband, Lionel Cranfield, buried in Gloucester Cathedral because the parliamentarians had a habit of exhuming and desecrating the remains of royalists. 'We live in sad times,' he concluded – a statement confirmed by the sorry tales that circulated, particularly after sieges, of soldiers breaking open burial vaults and dismembering corpses.

In the same month, Edward learned that his wife Mary had died. But the cruellest blow was yet to fall. A portrait of Edward's younger son, Edward, a beautiful young man with ringleted, fair hair, graces the first edition of Virginia Woolf's *Orlando*. It is part of a double portrait, with his older brother, painted five years before the outbreak of war. Hand on hip, the thirteen-year-old Edward gazes at the world with confidence and an innocence that startles you as you pass him in the hall that leads to our sitting room. In October 1645, Edward was taken prisoner by parliamentary soldiers just outside Oxford and then stabbed to death in cold blood by one of his captors near Abingdon. David Lloyd, the author of a memorial, published in 1668, described the murder and the loss of the 'Honorable Mr Edward Sackvile (the Earl of Dorset's son, a person of great hopes that having overcome those rosie nets, the flattering vanities of youth and greatness strewed in his way) distinguished himself not by Birth (his Mother's labour not his) from the common throng, but worth; (a Jewel come into the world with its own light and glory) and studies which cutting the untrod Alpes of Knowledge, with the Vinegar only of an eager and smart spirit to all that he was born to know'.

It was yet another instance of the war's everyday brutality, a war in which prisoners were routinely stripped, beaten and – sometimes, in fits of rage – murdered, their brains knocked out with the butt end of muskets (as in one account by the parliamentarian sergeant, Henry Foster, of an incident near Aldermaston). The poet Aurelian Townsend commemorated Edward's untimely death, ruing a new age in which acts of vengeful, vainglorious violence, broke the traditional bonds of society. He castigated the 'wretch' who killed Edward:

> *Unurg'd he did it; that his bloody Hand,*
> *Might both increase the sorrows of the Land,*
> *And the sinnes too: And get himselfe the name,*
> *Of an Arch Fyrebrand, in his Countryes Flame . . .*

After the fall of Oxford, Edward was offered a pass by Sir Thomas Fairfax 'to repaire unto London or elsewhere upon his necessary occasions . . . and to have full liberty at any time within six months to goe to any convenient port, and to transporte him selfe beyond the seas'. Edward chose to stay in England, but he withdrew from politics – apart from an episode in October 1647, when he was one of several peers summoned by Charles to Hampton Court to consider the army's Heads of the Proposals for a negotiated settlement. He played no part in the second English Civil War, a last-ditch royalist rebellion, which spread to Kent in 1648, and was so shocked by the execution of Charles I in 1649 that he vowed, it was said, never to stir from his house in London again except in a coffin. In this, his behaviour was similar, albeit in extreme form, to that of his political allies, who survived the Commonwealth and Protectorate by with-drawing to their country estates to live peacefully and with little chance of being called to cooperate with the new – and they hoped only provisional – regime. They wanted nothing to compromise them at the restoration of the monarchy.

After the death of his wife and son, Edward began to lose his grip. His estates were neglected and run down, victim to the local lawlessness of the war years. His steward told him that the woods on Seal Chart had been uprooted by soldiers who had been based there, and 'the poor of Senoke [Sevenoaks] are grown so insolent'. In February 1652, a few months before his death, Edward wrote despondently to his bailiff at Knole: 'I am neither Thomas Earle of Dorset Lord High Treasurer of England nor Richard Earle of Dorsett . . . nor Edward Earle of Dorsett L[ord] Chamberlayne not longe agoe to the Kinge, but a poore unsuccessfull Cavalier. I had never thought of sendinge for you nor I pray give unto any that is (so curiously impertinent) as to aske you any questions any answer. But bidd them goe looke and meddle with what they have to doe withal.'

'A poore unsuccessfull Cavalier', sad and broken in spirit, he was mourning the loss of that glorious noble inheritance, represented by his grandfather Thomas, his older brother Richard and, until not long ago, himself. But he was also mourning the passing of an age, in which nobles such as himself believed that, as the King's advisers, they had a natural right to rule. The glory days of high office for the Sackville family were over, at least for the time being – and with them their self-image as great men.

Edward was a man of the early seventeenth century, his vision of the world characterised by unity, harmony and order. The vision was hierarchical and unequal, yet it depended on consent between king and subjects, between lord and tenant, and it was precisely this consent that was now no longer being sought nor granted. The rules, and silent agreements, that bound society, and promoted a common wealth and wellbeing, were being broken. In the process, Edward was torn between a personal loyalty to his anointed sovereign and a commitment to a balanced constitution. In an age of increasing polarisation, his even-handedness, and his amphibian ability to stay friends with people of very different religious and political opinions, was put to the test as he was forced, like so many others, to make agonising personal choices.

For what? In an *Elegy upon the Most Accomplish'd and Heroic Lord Edward Earl of Dorset*, published two years after his death, the royalist writer James Howell described as perfect a man as ever 'Nature in one frame did span':

> *Such Highborn Thoughts, a Soul so large and free,*
> *So clear a Judgment, and vast Memory,*
> *So princely Hospitable and Brave Mind*
> *We must not think in hast on earth to find . . .*

But no fine words could conceal the fact that Edward had died a recluse, in debt, 'a poore, unsuccessfull Cavalier'.

Chapter 4

Restoration (1652–1677)

Richard Sackville, 5th Earl of Dorset

After the death of the 4th Earl in 1652, the Sackville inheritance was, for a second generation in succession, encumbered with debt. In the aftermath of the Civil War, the strains that such an inheritance can exert on individuals and their relationships became acute.

Knole itself was still owned by the executors of Henry 'Dog' Smith who had purchased it from the 3rd Earl thirty years before, and leased it back to the Sackvilles for £100 a year. Smith was a charitable man – as the monument to his memory on the east wall of Wandsworth parish church records. After his death in 1628, the income from his lands, including the rent from Knole, was to be assigned by his executors to good works such as redeeming 'poor captives and prisoners from the Turkish tyranny', the marriage of poor maidens, repairing highways, and helping the aged, orphans and persons with large families. On the 4th Earl's death, Smith's executors immediately 'did enter into and upon the Manor house and Parke of Knoll' – repossessing the property less than fifty years after Thomas Sackville had acquired it. This could so easily have been the end of the story of Knole and the Sackvilles, but in March 1653 a new lease was granted to Edward's son Richard, the 5th Earl, for eighty-two years.

Richard's claim on Knole was doubly tenuous, however. Because his father Edward had died in debt and intestate, the administration of his estate was granted to one of his major creditors, Nathaniel Thorold. Richard and Thorold were at loggerheads throughout the 1650s over who should pay for Edward's funeral expenses, and over who owned the lease of Knole itself – Thorold claiming that the lease should pass to him as a creditor. Richard and his wife, Frances, continued to live at Knole throughout these years of uncertainty. As late as 1657 Frances was writing to her husband that Knole still 'canot yet gett desided', although she was 'assured it will be yours at last'. The same year, Richard was bemoaning the fact in a letter to his cousin, the Countess of Northampton, that he was 'one of the poorest Earls in England'. Indebtedness did not appear to cramp his style, however. In 1652, he paid off £280 of debt, but he also spent £136 on 'clothes', £476 on 'household stuffe', £440 on 'general' expenses, £70 on 'spending money', and £216 on horses, his particular passion. In November 1653 he paid £30 for a 'bay mare with a white starre on her forehead', and just a month later pawned his wife's jewels for £340.

To escape his creditors, Richard left the country in 1656, although as his wife hints, there may have been other – emotional – reasons for his departure. 'I will not trouble you with my malin-coly and solitary condition for want of your company,' she wrote; 'I confesse if you had the desire [to come home] it would please me very much . . . some say you are so much in debt you could not stay in ingland others say you have a great desire in hand and last of all they have found out that you and I are parted.' While he was away, it was she who managed the estates. 'I have not yet received your rents,' she wrote to her husband; '. . .when all this halfe yeares rent comes together it will not pay what you lefte me to pay, there is great arrears upon Knoll which I must presently pay'. The legal costs, incurred by the earl's many disputes, were 'very greate' – in particular, the battle to gain control of Knole.

Frances was urging her husband to return: there was 'an absolute necessity of your being heare', since some things will be 'utterly lost if you do not speedily repare heather and I assure my selfe you will never all together forgete me and your pore babies your son Richard has had the smalle pox and now hee is almost well.' But she was also warning him that when he did, he must 'spare it in horse flech [spend less on horses] ... for indeede you must Concider to cutt your Coate according to your Cloath for monies are very scarce heare with me'.

It was a hand-to-mouth existence, based entirely on expectations of his Clifford inheritance. Throughout the 1650s, Richard insisted on deferring payment for many of his purchases until 'six months immediately ensuing the decease of Anne Clifford, Countess Dowager of Pembroke'. In one particular deal, he agreed to £66 for some black beaver cloth within six months of Anne Clifford's death, but only £61 – a £5 discount – if she died within the next two years. Despite Richard's expectations – and even a rumour of her death in 1668 – Anne lived until 1676.

The restoration of King Charles II in 1660 coincided with the restoration of Knole. In 1661 the manor of Knole, with its mansion and park, along with some neighbouring manors in the county of Kent, were settled upon the Earl of Dorset and his heirs, while in exchange other Sackville estates in Sussex were charged in perpetuity with a rent of £130, to be applied to the purposes of the Henry Smith charity. Thus, at last, was the issue of the ownership of Knole resolved; and from then until 1946, when the house was handed to the National Trust, the manor and estate have continued in the uninterrupted possession of the Sackville family.

How you capture the mood and concerns of a particular patch of the past depends entirely on what is left behind – the archives, portraits and monuments. But to a large extent, the survival of these scraps is a matter of chance. Some would have been destroyed by fire (the Great Fire of London destroyed Dorset House and its family papers in 1666); others by ancestors in one of the great once-in-a-generation clear-outs. As a result, our vision of the past is skewed by the type of material that has been retained.

Happily, a complete sequence of account books survive from 1652 to 1677, and from these emerge a sense of day-to-day life at Knole. Inside the house, there was expenditure on linen and livery for the servants, on cloth for the dining-room curtains, repairs to the glass in the windows, gloves, and so on. For the grounds outside, the picture the accounts reveal is of a working estate, slightly rough around the edges. Knole in the mid-seventeenth century is a far remove from Thomas Sackville's noble establishment of the early 1600s, on the one hand, and from the elegant spaciousness of the eighteenth-century ducal park it would become, on the other. The Wilderness, the part of the pleasure gardens where Lady Anne Clifford had sought silence and sanctuary half a century before, and where mossy paths now meander through clumps of beech and chestnut and between banks of daffodil and bluebell, was given over to hay-making and the coppicing of wood for hop poles. Carp were kept in stew ponds in the garden, and the rabbits which still overrun the park were hunted with ferrets, and then sold. Cattle, as well as deer, grazed the park, and plots of land were leased to tenant farmers, ploughed and used for growing wheat, oats, barley, turnips, peas and beans. As with the garden, the relative impecuniousness of the Sackvilles in the decades after the Civil War demanded that the broad acres of the park be farmed for profit as much as for pleasure.

The archives for this period also include recipes for invisible ink and for cordial for 'treating stone', advertisements for Agards Pills for gout, and amongst all these scraps of family life, letters of jocular congratulation from relations: to Richard, for example, the Earl of Northampton wrote: 'I am glad to heare that "my fat Mrs" [Frances] as you call her, still continues her virtuous qualities of multiplying the world', continuing: 'I am extreamely glad to heare that still wee are likely to have more of ye breede by my most fertill mistress, to whom, and all your pretty little ones I desire my most humble service.'

Richard and Frances had thirteen children, of whom six reached maturity: Charles, Edward, Mary, Richard, Anne and Frances. Their group portraits – of the oldest three in a classical landscape and of the two youngest girls trailing a squirrel on a blue ribbon – bring a warm glow of family life to our walls, amongst the sombre portraits, the still lifes and the sporting pictures. Despite their oddly elderly, oversized faces, painted by a 'provincial follower of Sir Anthony van Dyck', they lower the average age of Knole's long-term inhabitants lining the walls of the house. These portraits, together with the surviving notes between members of the family in the archives, give this particular era at Knole its bustle, and its background sound of family argument or children's feet.

Richard recorded – and receipted – the strange little deals he struck with his children. In September 1663, for example, he agreed to pay Charles, Edward and Mary £100 each of 'lawfull money of England' (but only after the decease of Anne, Countess Dowager of Dorset and Pembroke), in exchange for which they were 'for ever to cease demanding, requesting or desiring any colts, woods or trees now standing, growing, grazing, abiding within the limits, bounds or precincts of the park', manors or parishes of Knole, Sevenoaks, Seal or Kemsing.

There are curious glimpses, too, of the idiosyncratic ways in which the family ran their household and its accounts. In old pocket books and ledgers, meticulously recorded in Richard's cursive script, are the routine expenses one might expect to find. We learn, for example, what some of the Sackville servants earned each year – £12 for the gardener John Jackman, £10 for the cook William Gambett, £4 for footman Peter Chenaleen, £3 for laundrymaid Frances Hulman. But there are also some more peculiar entries, such as the fines Richard docked from his servants' wages for misdemeanours: for getting drunk, for being absent for a whole day without leave, or 'for being absent when my Lord came home late, and making a headless excuse'. H. Mattocks, in particular, came in for a lot of censure: 'for scolding to extreamity', 6d; 'for prating impertinently', 2d; for 'prating nonsence', 'for giving advice unasked', 'for telling tales out of schoole', 'for lying at dinner time', 'for lying to my face'. A picture of a parallel universe is revealed, as the household at Knole begins to separate, with the family withdrawing to private apartments, and the staff occupying their own quarters. Servants now dined in the Servants' Hall, rather than in the Great Hall, as they had done half a century before, and slept in attic garrets, rather than hugger-mugger with the rest of the household.

Despite the fertility, it was a rather fractious marriage. Frances was an occasionally querulous and cantankerous wife. Throughout the marriage, there is some evidence of Richard's other affections: a letter to a Mrs Katherine Ireland in 1669, flirtatiously accusing her of infidelity, and to a Mrs Elizabeth Barnes in 1675. 'My dearest Betty,' it began, and went on to refer to 'that true and lasting love which will bring us together'. Matters had come to such a head by 1673 that, in September, Richard was proposing to live apart from his wife, and had drawn up particulars in his own handwriting 'of what my Wife is to be allowed if she live asunder from me', for household expenses, food, clothes, servants, maids, a coach and six horses: the total came to £773 10s. 10d.

There is another strange agreement countersigned by the countess on 30 July 1674 – although, beside her signature, she has crossed out the words 'by my husband's Command'. The document is titled an 'Engagement from my Wife to me upon the dismissing of a Servant of mine named Thomas Jones at her desire', and relates how a certain Lady Charnoche had (or so Frances had been 'credibly informed') wagered that Frances would die within the year. When a new servant previously employed by Lady Charnoche arrived at Knole, Frances was terrified that he would 'in all lykelyhood have some Instructions' to poison or shoot her 'upon this surmise'. In return for her husband dismissing this servant, Frances promised that she would never trouble him with such a request in the future. But his conditions went further: she would 'never molestt disquiet or disturbe him again in this or in any other thing namely in medling with any business of his'; she would not hinder him from going or being where and 'in whatt Company he pleases, without my running clamouring or hunting after him'; and she would not stir from Knole without his consent. If she broke any of these conditions, there was to be an 'absolute separation' of the couple.

There is no evidence that they actually separated, although Richard went abroad for several months in November 1674. In a letter to her husband in February 1675, Frances complained that her daughter-in-law had told her that the reason for his trip was that 'I leade you a very unquiet life at home'. 'I am sure,' she continued, 'you and I parted too kindly for you to give them so much ocation of being pleased and triumphing over me I am so well aquanted with your good nature that I can never feare your adding to my injuries but I will trouble you now noe more aboute this foulish falsehoude . . . I longe to heare of you returning heather which will be the welcomemost newes that can come to . . . your most affectionate and obedient wife. F. Dorsett.' There are echoes here of Lady Anne Clifford, half a century before: of a woman coping on her own at Knole, unsupported by an absent, and rather feckless, husband: defensive, even paranoid, her greatest pleasure the spiting of her enemies.

The couple were forced together in mourning by the death of their youngest, favourite son, Thomas. 'Little Tom', as his father's letters refer to the twelve-year-old, travelled to France in 1675 with a young companion and their tutor, Mr Stephenson. As they made their way from Dieppe, to Paris, to Blois, to Saumur on the river Loire, Mr Stephenson kept Tom's parents posted of his progress: how Mr Sackville was recovering from 'his melancholy on parting from his mother' or how he preferred 'his play to his study'. In August he fell ill, 'complaining a little of a pain in the right side of his body' and vomiting. Within days, he was dead. 'My affliction,' wrote Mr Stephenson, 'is too great to lett me write any thing.' Others testified to the terrible effect 'the sudden, and unhappy death of Mr Sackville' had on Mr Stephenson. According to Robert Clark, who was in Saumur at the time, 'never man was more tenderly carefull of his charge, than himselfe [Mr Stephenson], who never stirred from him one minute in his distemper, nor wanted the assistance of the most able physitions of this place, I assure your Lordship he is equally afflicted, as if he had binne his owne sonne, butt it was not in the power of art, to save his life.'

Dr Edmund King, in a letter to Lady Vane, agreed that the French doctors could have done nothing more: 'having considered [their] accounts . . . I doe positively assure your Ladyship I doe believe in my conscience it was not possible for all the Art in the world to have saved the Gentleman's life in this disease.' His only reservation was that they had not given a more anatomical account, of precisely where the 'ulcer' was. Nevertheless, Dr King assured Lady Vane that he had never seen anyone recover from such a sequence of symptoms as Little Tom had displayed:

'inflammation, gangrene, followed by a mortification of the parts', and putrefaction.

Richard left a 'briefe Note of observations upon the sicknesse, and death, of my deare sonne, Thomas deceased the 19th of August 1675', in which he speculated on the possible medical causes of the death. Analysing the post-mortem accounts of the French doctors who were present 'both in his sickness, and at the opening of his body', he wondered whether it was an inherited illness called 'the King's Evil Humour', or perhaps the result of a blow from 'an ill-conditioned footboy of mine, with whom he used to play and upon falling out with him one day strike him a blow, in the pitt of his stomach.' His agonisings are every parent's struggle to find a rational explanation for an irrational fate: answers to the questions 'why' and 'could things have been done differently?' In the archives, there is a copy, decorated with tiny hearts, of an epitaph that was fixed to Thomas's coffin, and invokes the Roman poet Martial, the chief of epigrammatists:

> *To the immoderate in love, brief is life and rare is old age*
> *Whatever you love wish that it may not please you too much.*

The death – quite possibly from appendicitis – of 'my deare Jewell here on earth; and now a blessed Angell saint in heaven' united his parents in grief. Around the same time, another source of marital tension was removed: for, in 1674, the financial troubles of the Sackvilles came to an end. Marriage was the single most important strategic decision a family made every generation, and the marriage of Richard to Frances Cranfield had promised much. Throughout the 1640s, however – and into the 1650s and 1660s – the Cranfields were unable to pay the amount contracted in the marriage settlement, with sums arriving only intermittently. It was not until 1674, on the death, without children, of Lionel, 3rd Earl of Middlesex, Frances's last surviving brother, that the Sackville family got their money – and more, succeeding to the large Cranfield estates around Copt Hall in Essex, and to manors in Warwickshire and Gloucestershire.

Two years later, on 22 March 1676, Anne Clifford, Countess of Dorset, Pembroke and Montgomery, died aged eighty-six – a death that the Sackvilles had been willing, and wagering on, for the previous twenty years or more. Richard now secured the reversion of Anne's jointure estates. As two long-running sagas were resolved and both inheritances – Clifford and Cranfield – came good, Richard was freed from the debts that had hampered him for the greater part of his life, though he lived only another year to enjoy his prosperity.

Richard died at Knole on 27 August 1677, and was buried in the Sackville vault at Withyham. Here, at the traditional heart of the Sackville estates, and of their local acts of charity and piety, Frances commissioned the sculptor Caius Gabriel Cibber to build a monument to her husband and their thirteen children. Richard and Frances kneel on either side of the plinth which bears the semi-prostrate form of their son, Thomas, clutching a skull. On either side of the plinth, in bas-relief, are the other children – six boys on one side, and six girls on the other. Like Thomas, those who had died young hold a skull. But it is Thomas who appears as the focus of his parents' grief. As the inscription on the west end of the tomb reads, he was 'the great hopes of all the Family',

> *He never to his parents was unkeind*
> *But in his early leaving them beheind*
> *And since h'ath left us and for e're is gone*
> *What Mother would not weep for such a Son . . .*
> *Here lyes the thirteenth child and seaventh son*
> *Who in his thirteenth Yeare his race had run.*

In its chilly marble magnificence, the tomb commemorates in death those children who had once – with their pet squirrels, their squabbles and their schoolwork – breathed life into Knole.

Chapter 5

The Perks of Office (1677–1706)

Charles Sackville, 6th Earl of Dorset

Within decades of Thomas Sackville's transformation of Knole, the family – overawed, perhaps, by the grandeur of the formal, state rooms on the first floor – had withdrawn to the privacy and snug of the lower-ceilinged rooms on the ground floor. It was around these rooms that family life now revolved, as it does today. At the heart of this suite of rooms lies a parlour with a huge seventeenth-century chimneypiece of plaster, rendered to look like marble: a cheap mimic of the marble chimneypiece in the Great Chamber above. This has been the family dining room for well over three hundred years, and many of the portraits on the walls have hung here for almost as long.

Visiting the house in August 1752, the antiquarian Horace Walpole described 'a chamber of poets and players, which is proper enough in that house; for the first Earl wrote a play, and the last Earl was a poet'. Half a century later, an inventory of 1799 lists many of the same portraits that hang in the room today: Restoration playwrights, such as Sir Charles Sedley, Thomas Otway, William Congreve, William Wycherley; and poets such as the Earl of Rochester, John Dryden, Matthew Prior and Alexander Pope. This unchanging cast of characters is unusual because paintings tend to migrate around the place, reflecting the taste and hangs of successive generations. However, in the Poets' Parlour, as the room has come to be known, the subsequent addition of portraits of earlier writers, such as William Shakespeare and Ben Jonson, and later writers, such as Edmund Burke and Walter Scott, has simply reinforced the literary theme of the collection. These late arrivals have coalesced around a core of late-seventeenth-century writers, so that the feel of the room is still fixed firmly, and for all time, during Charles Sackville's residence at Knole in the 1690s and early 1700s.

Gleaming in the light of the huge fire, in front of which he held court three centuries ago, is a portrait of Charles Sackville, 6th Earl of Dorset. Kneller's portrait of 1692 captures that combination of rakishness and refinement that was so typical of the Restoration era. It shows a heavy-jowled fleshy figure, red-faced and swathed in a sumptuous satin dressing gown. Here is a man in his pomp, a man grown fat on the hospitality he was dispensing at Knole: in six months of the previous year alone, this had accounted for '85 gallons of sherry, 72 gallons of Canary, 63 gallons of White Port, and 425 gallons of Red Port'; and household accounts for a single day in September 1696 itemise '40 stones of beef, 1 mutton, 1 goose, 30 chickens, 2 pigs, 2 pheasants, 1 tongue, 1 partridge, 1 calf's head, 105 fresh herring, oysters . . .' and so on, followed by a similar account just two days later. 'His Table was one of the Last that gave Us an example of the Old House-keeping of an English Nobleman,' concluded Matthew Prior; 'A Freedom reigned at it which made every one of his Guests think Himself at Home.'

Surrounding Charles on the walls of the Poets' Parlour are portraits of his cronies, poised as it were to step out of the shadows cast by the wood panelling and take part in a ribald Restoration episode of *This is Your Life*. Here, they take turns to testify to his abilities as a hell-raiser, a poet, a patron and a public figure, contributing a scurrilous anecdote, a bitter-sweet memory, a piece of outrageous flattery.

Take, for example, the man with the twinkling eyes and podgy face, framed by a wig of shiny black hair. This is Sir Charles Sedley, Charles Sackville's companion in youthful excess. On the evening of 16 June 1663, Charles Sackville (or Lord Buckhurst as he then was), Sedley and Sir Thomas Ogle met for dinner at the Cock Tavern, in

Bow Street, Covent Garden. Accounts vary as to precisely what happened next, because the chroniclers and their subsequent editors have toned down some of the group's more offensive antics. First, they were served dinner by six naked women, before going out onto the balcony overlooking the street. Sedley certainly, and in some accounts all three of them, stripped stark naked and, according to the diarist Samuel Pepys, acted 'all the postures of lust and buggery that could be imagined'. Sedley then preached a mock sermon, which he concluded by offering a powder for sale that would make all the women in town run after the purchaser. An angry crowd had begun to muster in the street below, their religious sensitivities offended by the blasphemous toast proposed on the balcony by the unholy trinity to 'the salvation of Judas and another to the Babe of Bethlehem'. The mob showered the young toffs with stones, shattering the first-floor windows, and tried to force the tavern door, as Charles and his companions flung wine bottles at them (accounts vary as to whether they had urinated into them first). Disapproval seemed to go beyond the merely human. By some spooky coincidence on exactly the same day, Withyham church in Sussex, the mausoleum of the Sackvilles, was struck by lightning and a large part burnt down.

Sedley, as ringleader, was summoned to appear before the Lord Chief Justice of the King's Bench, charged with 'several misdemeanours against the King's Peace', and was fined 2,000 marks. Charles probably made an appearance in court, too, but was let off with no more than a reprimand. Four years after the Cock Tavern incident, Sedley – or 'little Sid' as he was sometimes known – was sharing a house in Epsom with Charles and the former orange girl, turned actress, Nell Gwynne. Charles, it is said, had been captivated by the sight of Nell's shapely legs as she rolled, revealingly, from one side of the stage to the other in a comedy called *All Mistaken*, or *The Mad Couple*, by James Howard. In July 1667, Nell had returned her acting parts to the King's House theatre and, according to Pepys, was 'keeping merry house' with Sedley and Charles next door to the King's Head tavern in Epsom Wells. By August the affair was already coming to an end, and towards the end of August, Pepys reported gossip that Charles had left Nell, and that 'he makes sport of her, and swears she hath had all she would get of him'. Two years later, she became the mistress of King Charles II.

There was no more scabrous chronicler of the sexual merry-go-round of the Restoration court than Charles Sackville's crony, John Wilmot, Earl of Rochester. 'Much wine has passed, with grave discourse/Of who fucks who, and who does worse', is how *A Ramble in St James's Park* begins, and how many an evening's discussion in the Poets' Parlour probably ended. Rochester's face emerges from the panelling, wreathed in the faintly sulphurous glow of the great fireplace: on the back of his portrait, some pious Sackville a couple of hundred years later has commented: 'Died repentant after a profligate life.'

Like Charles, Rochester was a Gentleman of the King's Bedchamber, which is probably how they first met. They were both soon part of that fashionable coterie of 'wits' at the court of King Charles II, the 'merry gang' described by the poet Andrew Marvell. Charles Sackville stood in for King Charles as godfather to Rochester's only son at his christening in January 1671; the other godparent tasked with renouncing the world, the flesh and the devil on the child's behalf was the equally reprobate Sedley. The irony was not lost on Sackville, who as he began his campaign against the forces of evil, confessed in a letter to Rochester on 24 December 1670, that ''tis with some unwillingness, I begin a war against a prince [of darkness] I have so long serv'd'. They were still running around together four years later. Returning from a night out in 1675 with Charles and Charles's friend, Fleetwood Sheppard, Rochester smashed the great glass 'Pyramidical' sundial that reached phallically towards the heavens in the King's garden at Whitehall. 'What, does thou stand here to fuck time?' Rochester shouted, adding a metaphysical twist to his act of vandalism.

Charles was a minor poet himself, with a talent, as Rochester acknowledged, for biting contemporary satire: 'For pointed satyrs, I would B[uckhurst] choose:/The best good man with the worst-natur'd muse.' Many of Charles Sackville's works, however, are little more than faintly obscene doggerel, and it is hardly surprising that history has been less kind to his reputation as a poet than his contemporaries were. In his day Charles was considered on a par with Rochester, who would now be generally acknowledged as the superior writer. 'My Lord Rochester was always witty, and always very ill-natured ... My Lord Dorset [Charles Sackville] was as much his equal in learning and sense, as he was inferior to him in Ill-nature and Invectives,' remarked the satirist Tom Brown. But, he continued, Charles was 'the most generous patron of the Muses, and the most certain friends of good men in distress'. Brown had probably got to the heart of the matter: Charles was a more illustrious patron than he was a poet, and the flattery he received was due as much to his powers of patronage as to his literary ability.

Many of the beneficiaries of Charles's lavish hospitality were men of letters. No fewer than thirty-five dedications to Charles of published works have been traced, and there would be hundreds more if congratulatory poems and addresses by sycophantic poets and playwrights were included. Between 1660 and 1700, he is frequently referred to as the 'Maecenas' of his age; and the Poets' Parlour was doubtless the scene of many of those splendid dinners for which Charles was famous in his day, not least for leaving a banknote for £50 under the dinner plate of a favoured guest.

One of Charles's protégés was the poet and diplomat Matthew Prior whose portrait, thin, red-cheeked, and reedy-looking, hangs between Pope and Edmund Waller in the Poets' Parlour. Charles, or so the story goes, first spotted Prior reading Horace in his uncle's pub, The Rhenish tavern in Whitehall, in 1676, and was so impressed by the precocious, twelve-year-old that he eventually offered to pay his tuition fees at Westminster School. After Charles's death, Prior dedicated his 'Poems on Several Occasions' to Charles's son Lionel, repaying his debt of gratitude in the most elaborate terms. Charles, he wrote, had been 'universally Belov'd and Esteem'd', 'Strong, Proportionable, Beautiful' in Body, and 'Easie and Courteous to all'; 'His Wit was Abundant, Noble, Bold ... [and] the Manner in which He wrote, will hardly ever be Equalled. Every one of His Pieces is an Ingot of Gold, intrinsically and solidly Valuable ... His Thought was always New; and the Expression of it so particularly Happy.'

The poet John Dryden was another beneficiary of Charles's patronage. His portrait, too, hangs in the Poets' Parlour between Congreve and Abraham Cowley. Their friendship of twenty years survived Charles's role as Lord Chamberlain – effectively, arts minister. His first task in the post, in 1689, was to terminate Dryden's tenure as poet laureate, on the grounds that Dryden, as a Catholic, was unable to take the oath of allegiance to the new Protestant monarchs William and Mary. Charles compensated Dryden for this by subsidising his friend out of his own pocket; and Dryden, in turn, thanked Charles for this 'most bountiful Present' in his dedication to 'A Discourse concerning the Original and Progress of Satire'. It was, he wrote, 'an Action of pure disinteress'd Charity' by a man willing to 'lay aside all the Considerations of Factions and Parties'. But without this gift, would Dryden really have associated Charles's poetry with Shakespeare, Homer, Virgil and Donne, or claimed that 'I never attempted anything in satire wherein I have not studied your writings as the most perfect model'? 'There is not an English writer this day living,' Dryden continued, 'who is not perfectly convinced, that your lordship excels all others in all the several parts of poetry which you have undertaken to adorn.'

Although there is no direct contemporary evidence of a visit to Knole by Dryden – or, indeed, by Sedley, Rochester, Prior or Pope – a splendid early nineteenth-century account of Charles's generosity at Knole survives. One evening Charles suggested that he and his guests should each write a few lines in a competition to be judged by Dryden. After due deliberation, Dryden announced Charles's contribution the best: the winning entry read: 'I promise to pay Mr John Dryden five hundred pounds on demand. Signed, Dorset [Charles].' Dryden is said to have commented: 'I must confess that I am equally charmed with the style and the subject; and I flatter myself, gentlemen, that I stand in need of no arguments to induce you to join with me in opinion against yourselves. This kind of writing exceeds any other, whether ancient or modern. It is not the essence, but the quintessence of language; and is in fact, reason and argument surpassing everything.'

With time, it can be increasingly difficult to distinguish fact from fiction – particularly when dealing with an age so rich in rumour. The tales that accrete in layers around a core of truth, just as later portraits coalesce around the seventeenth-century core of the Poets' Parlour collection, get compressed into myth with the passage of time. It is a compelling myth. Charles's style, and the way it has been felt to represent the spirit of an age, have always found favour with his descendants. This is partly because subsequent generations have always liked to be identified with a tradition of hospitality and conviviality, even if their own capacity for those qualities has been less wholehearted.

We like the type of person described by Gilbert Burnet, Bishop of Salisbury, in his pen-portrait of Charles: 'a generous, good-natured and modest man . . . so much oppressed with phlegm that till he was a little heated with wine he scarce ever spoke, but was upon that exaltation a very lively man. Never was so much ill-nature in a pen as his, joined with so much goodness as is in himself.' Subsequent generations have also liked the way Charles established Knole as a seat of patronage, nurturing literary associations that continued into the twentieth century and became interwoven with the house's story. It is as if Charles's descendants hope that some of the literary discernment of the past will rub off on the present, and bolster, however spuriously, their own sense of self-esteem. In Virginia Woolf's *Orlando*, Orlando (Vita) strides into the 'dining room [the Poets' Parlour] where her old friends Dryden, Pope, Swift, Addison regarded her demurely at first as who should say Here's the prize winner! [Vita had just won the Hawthornden Prize for her poem *The Land*] but when they reflected that two hundred guineas was in question, they nodded their heads approvingly.' It is a dialogue between past and present that continues to this day.

But the main reason that subsequent generations have always warmed to Charles is that we love stories of our predecessors' bad behaviour, particularly if they confirm a notion about a particular period in the past, and particularly if they are accompanied by charm. His was the company you wanted to keep every now and then, despite yourself. It was the 'mad, bawdy talk' of Charles and his cronies that made Pepys's 'heart ache'. 'But Lord,' he continued, 'what loose cursed company was this, that I was in to-night, though full of wit, and worth a man's being in once, to know the nature of it, and their manner of talk, and lives.' He was the sort of man, for instance, who could make light of a dose of the clap, as in this gracious letter to a prostitute who, he claims, had given it to him:

> Madam,
>   I had obeyed your commands exactly; but that I was ashamed to send you so inconsiderable a sum immediately after receiving a greater favour than any of your Sex have bestowed on me this five yeare; the best return I can make you is good counsel; for I doubt not, considering your youth and strong constitution, but a Little advice and a great deale of Physick may in time restore you to that health I wish you had enjoyed a Sunday night instead of
>   your humble suffering,
>   Servant

Even at his grossest, Charles oozed charm; and he led a correspondingly charmed life. Pepys records, for example, the antics of Sedley and Charles on their return to London from a particularly drunken royal progress of East Anglia with King Charles II in 1668, how they 'ran up and down all night with their arses bare, through the streets; and at last fighting and being beat by the watch and clapped up all night'. The King, Pepys complained, took their side, pardoning them and having the constable who had arrested them imprisoned instead. Once again, Charles had got away scot-free. It was probably this episode that Rochester had in mind when he observed to King Charles that 'he did not know how it was, but my Lord [Charles Sackville] might do anything, yet was never to blame'.

The myths that are one of Charles's greatest legacies to Knole are complemented by a material contribution to the inheritance as significant as any Sackville's since Thomas, the 1st Earl. This was the result of his access, through attendance at court and his personal friendship with the Royal Family, to a whole range of rich pickings.

After the lean years of the Commonwealth and Protectorate, the Sackvilles were favoured once more with royal grants on the Restoration of King Charles II in 1660.

Rumour-mongers ascribed the favours showered on Charles Sackville to the good grace he had shown in ceding his 'play wench' Nell Gwynne to the King: his appointment in 1668 as a Groom of the King's Bedchamber, for example, or the grant in 1671 of a ninety-nine-year lease on very advantageous terms of land in Blackfriars. But it is equally likely that these gifts were the just deserts of a member of an aristocratic family which had long been loyal to the Crown. In December 1669, Charles was promoted to Gentleman of His Majesty's Bedchamber, with a salary of £1,000 a year. Here, his duties included personal attendance on the King for a week in every quarter, when he had to sleep on a pallet bed in the royal bedchamber and, if the Groom of the Stool was away, help the King with his toilet. Despite the upheavals of the 1640s and 1650s, government was still largely personal, reaching out from the fug of the royal bedchamber, and from the cabals of the court, into the country: into the boroughs, where Charles was an MP for East Grinstead; into the counties, where he was firstly a Deputy Lieutenant and later a Lord Lieutenant of Sussex; into the army, where he was a captain in the Duke of Buckingham's Regiment of Foot; and into the diplomatic service.

In July 1669, Charles Sackville was paid £300 by Charles II to go on a mission to the King and Queen of France, to express regret at the illness of their son, the dauphin. The following May he was sent to France on a second embassy, this time to get permission from Louis XIV for King Charles's sister Henrietta, who was married to the Duc d'Orleans, to be allowed to stay in England for more than three days so that she could act as a mediator in the secret Treaty of Dover. Charles Sackville received £1,000 from the English Exchequer for his role in facilitating the treaty, by which Charles II was to receive £200,000 a year from the French king in return for making war, jointly with Louis, against the Dutch. From the French king he received lavish praise, and a pair of candlesticks and a gilt table that are still at Knole: the fleur-de-lis, the armorial emblem of the kings of France, on each of the four corners of the table frame support the furniture's royal provenance. It was a foretaste of the way in which Charles Sackville was to acquire one of the finest collections of seventeenth-century furniture in the world.

Proximity to the King resulted in a constant stream of jobs and rewards: the grant of the estate of a Hackney suicide (the property of a person who had killed himself went first to the Crown); the right to forfeit the goods of English ships which had landed their cargoes illegally in Ireland; or, as on 14 January 1673, the free gift of £4,400 from Charles II because of 'our royal favour towards . . . Lord Buckhurst, and in consideration of his merit in our service'.

Charles's continuing success at court was complemented by his coming into two inheritances. The first of these, the Cranfield inheritance, precipitated a family quarrel that lasted almost ten years. In 1655 Charles's uncle, Lionel Cranfield, the 3rd Earl of Middlesex, had settled his estates, should he die without issue, in trust for his sister Frances, and after that to her oldest son, Charles. However, in 1673, less than a year before his death, Middlesex changed his mind and willed his estates directly to Charles, bypassing Frances. Richard and Frances, Buckhurst's father and mother, promptly filed a joint bill of complaint in Chancery against Charles, citing the settlement of 1655.

The row between parents and son was compounded by their disapproval of his attachment to Mary, widow of the Earl of Falmouth. Mary had captivated many at the Restoration court including, it is said, the King, and had a slightly unsavoury reputation. Richard wrote reprovingly to his son about the 'very disadvantageous reports made of her', and his mother Frances thought he was 'in ill hands'. Buckhurst, however, was smitten, admitting to 'the violentest passion that ever any body was capable of having'. A love letter, from Charles to Mary, survives, containing a lock of hair: 'I do from this moment give unto you all my pretences to freedome or any power over my selfe, and though you may justly thinke it below you, to bee ownd the soveraign of so mean a dominion, as my heart, I have yet confidence upon my knees to offer it to you.'

Charles married her in the summer of 1674, but waited until after his uncle's death in October – when he became 4th Earl of Middlesex

– to confirm openly that stories of his marriage were true. In 1675 he proceeded to prove the will and to answer his parents' bill of complaint, insisting that his uncle had been entitled to dispose of his estates as he wished, and claiming there had been no complicity whatsoever. Despite Frances's continued attempts to prove her brother's will forged or invalid, the case was eventually settled in Chancery in 1679. Adding insult to injury, her brother Lionel had left her 'the full sume of ten pounds' in his will.

On the death of Charles's father, Richard, in 1677, he became 6th Earl of Dorset, as well as Earl of Middlesex. The estates of two of King James I's Lord Treasurers were now united: those of Charles's great-great-grandfather, Thomas Sackville, and his grandfather, Lionel Cranfield. Years of high living and heavy drinking were beginning to take their toll, however. In June 1678 his former lover Nell Gwynne reported in a letter to Lawrence Hyde: 'My Loord of Dorset worse in thre munthe, for he drinkes aile with Shadwell and Mr Harris at the duke house all day long.' He was 'much troubled' by 'the pain of the gravel' (kidney stones) and, after the death of Mary in childbirth, in September 1679 – the child was stillborn – he was free to return to his bachelor ways, as John Sheffield, 3rd Earl of Mulgrave, described his bereavement:

> . . . *A teeming Widow, but a barren Wife.*
> *With tame submission to the will of Fate,*
> *He lugg'd about the Matrimonial Weight,*
> *Till Fortune, blindly kind as well as he,*
> *Has ill restor'd him to his Liberty;*
> *That is to live in his old idle way*
> *Smoaking all Night, and dozing all the Day . . .*

In March 1681, Charles was seized by a fit of apoplexy in the King's Bedchamber, and on 23 August he received a passport signed by the King, permitting him to go beyond the seas 'for recovery of his health'. He was allowed to take six servants, £40 in money, and all the 'baggage, utensils, carriages and necessaries' he wished. The crossing to Dieppe on 3 September was smooth, and the only one to suffer from seasickness was Mr Raphael, one of the servants, who 'was kind to ye fishes'. From here, the party proceeded to Paris, where the rest-cure included orders back to London for the best canary from the Pope's Head, a large shipment of sack, and some good cheeses. Charles was abroad for only a few months, and on his return to England, he continued to resist pressure from his mother to get married again. 'I doe passionately Long to see you fixte,' she wrote to him, claiming that his continued failure to get married and produce an heir for 'the Continuance of *my* Family' would break her heart, particularly after the death of her younger son Edward in 1678. But Charles simply procrastinated with what his mother described as 'so many Evasions and Excuses'.

Nevertheless, in 1685 – in the tradition of his forefathers – he married an heiress, Lady Mary Compton, the seventeen-year-old daughter of the Earl of Northampton. Many years later, his grandson described how Charles 'married three times: but only one of these Marriages contributed either to his Honour, or to his Felicity'. This, his second marriage, was it. He appears, at the age of forty-two, to have settled down to country life at the Cranfield ancestral home, Copt Hall (Knole itself was inhabited during her lifetime by his mother Frances) and to have become increasingly uxorious. His wife bore him a son, Lionel Cranfield Sackville, in 1687, and a daughter, Lady Mary Sackville, the following year. Only his old cronies were a little disappointed by his new sobriety. George Etherege, who had corresponded with Charles in the 1660s in obscene verse about their shared pleasure in prostitutes and its venereal complications, now regretted that 'my Lord Dorset has given over variety and shuts himself within my Lady's arms'.

Knole fell free on the death of Frances on 20 April 1687. She had lived to see her son well married, and the birth of the heir she had longed for, but she was generally as unhappy as ever. Characteristically, her legacy included one posthumous spanner in the works. Although there was no dispute about the Sackville estates, including the manors of Buckhurst and Knole, which reverted to her son on her death, there was the separate matter of her personal estate. In a will written in 1684, Frances had appointed Dorset heir to and executor of this estate, except for the furniture in her London house, which she left to her second – and much younger – husband, Henry Powle. Powle had agreed at the time of their marriage in 1679 not to 'intermeddle' with Frances's legal affairs, and to expect no advantage from her estate; but on her death, he filed a bill to recover his dead wife's estates, insisting that he had never consented to her making the will of 1684. In 1687, the Lord Chancellor upheld Powle's claim, and it was not until December 1690 that, on appeal, the House of Lords overturned the Chancery verdict.

Knole, meanwhile, was vacant and in need of attention. A house that had tended, with the passage of time, to assume prime importance for members of the family began to have the feel of a second home. In August 1688, Charles offered Catherine of Braganza, King Charles II's widow, the use of the house and park rent free. Fleetwood Sheppard, Charles's agent, showed her around and pointed out the repairs, estimated at £20,000, which she would need to undertake. A few days later, he wrote, exasperated, to his master from the Bull Tavern in Sevenoaks: 'The Queen hath made you a very long complement, no rat or weasel ever crept into so many holes . . . shee did not declare her acceptance of the house nor will not this four dayes, suddaine resolutions being contrary to . . . the crowne of Portugal.' The Queen Dowager did not take up the offer.

The steady stream of royal favours dried up on the death of King Charles II in 1685, although for the time being Charles kept his post as Lord Lieutenant of Sussex, and was paid the arrears of £2,333 owing on his salary as a Gentleman of the Bedchamber. On 23 April, he took part in James II's elaborate coronation procession, where he displayed, according to the writer Aphra Behn, his customary 'Careless Grandure, and a Generous Air'. But there was no disguising the fact that, between 1685 and 1688, Charles was out of sympathy with the new, Catholic king, and out of office at court. It was a period which coincided with his retirement to Copt Hall with his second wife. In January 1688, King James ordered all the Lord Lieutenants, in the event of his calling a Parliament, to secure the return of candidates pledged to the repeal of the Test Act, a law which had effectively disqualified Catholics from offices in Church or State. Charles refused to question his Sussex officials as to their voting intentions and, along with several other Lord Lieutenants who refused to comply, was dismissed from office.

A few nights later at supper at his mother-in-law, Lady Northampton's house, he received an anonymous letter with a menacing cross on the top: "Twere pity that one of the best of men should be lost for the worst of causes: Doe not sacrifice a life every body values, for a Religion yourself despise. Make your peace with your lawfull soveraign, or know that after this 27 January you have not long to live. Take this warning from a friend, and repent before repentance is in vaine.' Despite the death threat – and despite a profound indifference to religion – Charles was one of twenty-one peers who agreed to stand bail, if it were demanded, for the seven bishops charged with seditious libel: the bishops had signed a petition, which was then published, against the Declaration of Indulgence, James's attempt to establish some freedom of religion for Catholics. Dorset was also present at the King's Bench in Westminster Hall on 15 June, when the bishops were brought from their week's imprisonment in the Tower for a hearing.

Under the influence of his wife's uncle, Henry Compton, Bishop of London, Charles was beginning to ally himself with the cause of the Protestant William of Orange and his wife, Mary, the elder daughter of James II, although he (unlike Compton) did not actually sign the document requesting William to invade. William, Prince of Orange, landed at Torbay in early November 1688. Three weeks later, when King James visited his army at Salisbury, Prince George of Denmark, the husband of his younger daughter Anne, fled to William's camp. Dreading her father's displeasure, Anne left the Cockpit in Whitehall, where she had lodgings, under cover of darkness on the night of 25 November. Charles helped her escape and, so the story goes, when one of her shoes stuck in the mud of St James's Park, he removed a white glove from his hand and placed it on her foot, as he led her to the safety of a waiting carriage. He then took her to the house in London of Bishop Compton, and the next day to Copt Hall before escorting her, with the fully armed bishop, to the seat of his friend, the Earl of Northampton.

On the morning of 18 December 1688, James II woke to find Whitehall Palace surrounded by Dutch troops. He then slipped away on the royal barge to Rochester, and thence to France to spend the rest of his life in exile. After the flight of the Catholic king, Dorset was one of those who voted for William and Mary to be declared King and Queen. The new king was quick to fill those offices that were in the gift of the Crown with the Whig noblemen who had been influential in bringing him to the throne. On 14 February 1689, the day after William's accession, Charles was appointed Lord Chamberlain of the Royal Household, a position his grandfather Edward had held in the 1640s, and two days later he was made a privy councillor. On 12 March, he was reappointed Lord Lieutenant of Sussex.

For eight years, then, Charles was a member of England's first cabinet, responsible both to the King and to Parliament. For one so lazy, and lacking in ambition, he had come very close to the heart of government on connections and charm. As William prepared to take command of the army in Ireland in 1690, he summoned a council at Kensington Palace, where he introduced his Queen to the nine great noblemen, known as the Nine, who were to advise her during his absence. It is unlikely that Charles was particularly influential or dynamic on these councils for, as Queen Mary wrote to her husband, 'Lord Chamberlain is too lazy to give himself the trouble of business, so of little use . . . Lord Chamberlain comes as little as he can with decency, and seldom speaks; but he never visits the cabinet council.' An anonymous versifier put it more cruelly in a poem called *The Nine*, which caricatured each of them, including Charles, in turn:

> *A drowsy Withal drawn down to the last,*
> *Dead before's time for having lived too fast,*
> *Lives now upon the Wit that's long since gone,*
> *Nothing but Bull remains, the Soul is flown;*
> *The Little Good that's sometimes of him said,*
> *Is because Men will speak well of the Dead . . .*

Nevertheless, after the death of Queen Mary in 1694, Dorset was one of several regents appointed to govern the kingdom during William's absence in Holland or when engaged in war against the French. Charles's proximity to power may have had little impact on national events, but his personal connections with the Royal Family, and the access it gave him, had a lasting effect on Knole and its collection.

As Lord Chamberlain of the King's Household, Charles regulated etiquette at court, and supervised the domestic affairs of the monarch. He ordered new keys for Queen Mary's apartments in Whitehall, made sure that the Speaker's Chair in the House of Commons had a new velvet cushion, and arranged for the accommodation of the court on its visits to the various royal palaces. One of the traditional 'perquisites' – or perks – of office was to dispose of furniture from the royal palaces, particularly Whitehall, Hampton Court and Kensington, when it was felt to be out of date, on the death of a sovereign or on the change of a regime.

This is how Charles acquired, for Knole, one of the finest collections of Stuart furniture in the world. The bed in the King's Room, made to celebrate the marriage of the future King James II to Mary of Modena in 1673, was removed from Whitehall Palace after the death of Queen Mary in 1694: it is the bed described in an inventory of that year as 'of cloth of silver flowered with gold & lined with a silver fringe and feathers of red and white'. Also removed from Whitehall, in 1695, was the bed in the Venetian Ambassador's Room, together with its matching suite of armchairs and stools. Many other goods were acquired in the same way: the tapestries in the Spangle Bedroom and the Venetian Ambassador's Room; the brass locks in the Cartoon Gallery bearing William III's monogram (taken from Whitehall Palace after the fire of 1698); the X-framed chairs of state flanked by footstools in the Brown Gallery; the close stool in the King's Closet, its red velvet seat originally graced by royal bottoms in Whitehall Palace – indeed, almost all the carved and upholstered pieces of furniture at Knole. Stamped on the webbing beneath some of the chairs and stools are the initials, W.P. (Whitehall Palace) or H.C.

(Hampton Court), denoting the palace where the chair featured in its last royal inventory.

The rewards of high office were not confined to cast-off furniture. There were also opportunities for profit from the sale of public offices. On assuming the role of Lord Chamberlain, Charles was besieged by relatives, friends and acquaintances, begging for preferment and places at court. There were letters from the Bishop of Rochester, asking that one of his acquaintances be given the job of Charles's secretary, and that another who had been accused of fraud be granted a royal pardon. There was a letter from John Dryden asking that free lodging at Somerset House be made available to a friend of his, a Mr Munson; and one from Thomas Shadwell requesting a vacant parsonage in Surrey for his friend Nicholas Brady. Most pathetic of all, perhaps, was a letter from Charles's old mucker Sir Charles Sedley in October 1691, requesting he put in a good word with the King to secure Sedley a post as housekeeper at Whitehall (which Sedley didn't get). As one anonymous complainant wrote:

> If Papist, Jew or Infidel
>   Would buy a place at Court:
> Here Dorset lives, the Chamberlain,
>   To whom you may resort.
> Then come away, make no delay.
>   Bring coin to plead your cases;
> He'll turn the King's friends out of doors,
>   And put you in their places.

After years of retirement at Copt Hall, Charles was back at court, and life there was beginning to take its toll once more. He was approaching fifty, drinking heavily and ageing fast, complaining often about suffering from his 'spleen'. In August 1691, his second wife died of smallpox after six years of marriage. A Lady of the Bedchamber, she had become a great favourite with Queen Mary, although some courtiers were scathing in their references to her looks and her marriage. The Earl of Monmouth, for example, ascribed her 'wondrous yellow' colour to the incessant smoking of her husband, that 'fullsom dull Bedfellow' who:

> Smoaks her like Bacon every Night,
> A dainty Prelude to delight . . .
> 'Twas said in Rhime her Spouse was dead;
> I fear she finds him so in Bed.

Gradually, during the 1690s, Charles retired from court, but not before he had exacted, with the help of his friend and fixer, Fleetwood Sheppard, all possible spoils. In March 1697 he sold the Keepership of Greenwich Park to the Earl of Romney, and the following month he was paid a rumoured £10,000 to resign his office of Lord Chamberlain to make way for the Earl of Sunderland. One of Sunderland's first acts in his new role was to reclaim by royal warrant all the silver plate that had, on the instructions of his predecessor, been delivered from the Jewel House to prominent persons around the court. Dorset's name was second on this list with 1,126 ounces of silver, but by the end of May 1700, he had returned none of it, despite repeated threats.

The rich pickings of public office notwithstanding, Dorset was in debt throughout the 1690s, and in arrears with the wages of his own servants. In May 1701 he was forced to sell Copt Hall, which was already mortgaged and becoming a bit dilapidated, to Thomas Webster, a Turkey merchant, for £13,000. Wagon after wagon, at £2 5s. per journey, transferred furniture, pictures, tapestries – in fact, pretty much all of the moveable goods – from Copt Hall to Knole: the copies of the Raphael Cartoons by Mytens, now in the Cartoon Gallery; the portraits of the Cranfield family by Dobson and Van Dyck; those royal perquisites that had gone first to Copt Hall; even the large carved shield in stone, bearing the Cranfield arms, that now crowns the roof of the Great Hall. At last, the possessions, as well as the estates, of two Stuart Lord Treasurers, Thomas Sackville and Lionel Cranfield, were assembled in one place. The focus of Dorset's life, which had been shifting over the previous decade from Copt Hall to Knole, also settled for the time being in one place. It was at Knole that he would entertain the Prince of Denmark, Princess Anne and their son on their way to Windsor in 1697; and it was here that he hosted the wedding of his daughter Lady Mary Sackville to Henry Somerset, Duke of Beaufort, in July 1702.

Knole's fading magnificence dates from the 1690s and early 1700s. It is the atmosphere evoked by Vita Sackville-West in her description of the Venetian Ambassador's Room – 'I never saw a room that so had over it a bloom like the bloom on a bowl of grapes and figs ... greens and pinks originally bright, now dusted and tarnished over' – and echoed by Virginia Woolf in her description of the same room in *Orlando* – 'The room ... shone like a shell that has lain at the bottom of the sea for centuries and has been crusted over and painted a million tints by the water; it was rose and yellow, green and sand-coloured. It was frail as a shell, as iridescent and as empty.'

The house's lustre was established during the last fifteen years of Charles's life, around a hundred years after Thomas Sackville's refurbishment of Knole. It was then that the house, which had been ransacked by parliamentary troops in the 1640s and its contents dispersed, began to fill up again. The silver furniture, the glowing green-and-gold tapestries that swathe the walls, the russet velvets that cover the chairs of state (and the royal 'seat of easement' as the close stool was called) are contemporary with Thomas Sackville's Knole, giving the state rooms an all-of-a-piece integrity. But, in an irony that would have appealed to the irreverent Charles, the collection of the objects that create this sense of integrity was entirely happenstance: the chance pilferings and perks of a public servant.

On 14 August 1700, a report reached London that Charles had, in a drunken delirium at Knole, attempted to stab himself. Although other accounts dispute this, there is no doubt that, by 1703 or 1704, his mind was going. In October 1704 this lifelong 'Dupe of Women' married an Irishwoman 'of very obscure connections' called Anne Roche, with whom he lived at first in a house in Hampstead and then in Bath. There, according to the historian Nathaniel Wraxall who claimed to have heard the tale first-hand from Dorset's grandson, Anne 'held him in a sort of captivity ... She suffered few persons to approach him during his last illness, or rather decay, and was supposed to have converted his weakness of mind to her own objects of personal acquisition.' The family dispatched Matthew Prior to Bath to report on his state of mind and to advise on whether it was necessary to appoint guardians. Prior, having obtained access to the earl, found him 'greatly declined in his understanding' but reported that 'he drivels so much better sense even now than any other man can talk, that you must not call me into court as a witness to prove him an idiot'.

There was no need to take any action, however, because Charles died in Bath in January 1706; he was buried in the family vault in Withyham church. 'The end of a life which opened with such gaiety and éclat offers a very sordid picture,' wrote Vita Sackville-West reprovingly. 'From his portraits it is easy to see that he has grown heavy and apoplectic: his features are coarsened and swollen; his double chins hang in folds over his voluminous robes, his ruffles, and his ribbons. He could not hope to enjoy his life at both ends.' It was a fact of which Charles himself was well aware, telling Alexander Pope that the 'tenure' of a long life, if accompanied by pain, was 'not worth the fine'.

Charles had been living well beyond his means, and his estate was heavily mortgaged on his death, with the principal and interest totalling £34,687 10s. In March 1706, Spencer Compton wrote to his nephew Lionel, Charles's son, on the latter's return from a Grand Tour, where he had been sent by his mother's family to keep him away from his stepmother and his semi-imbecile father. The purpose of the letter was to prepare him for the disappointment of there being 'much less, I believe than what you imagine'. His allowance of £800 a year was almost ten times smaller than his father's income of £7,650 seven years before.

For hundreds of years, it has been a mantra of the British aristocracy that its members leave their individual inheritance in better shape than they entered it. This would not have been said of

Charles Sackville, 6th Earl of Dorset, at the time of his death. His son's threadbare inheritance, the household goods – linen, beds and furniture – that he left his widow Anne, the small bequests . . . what else did he leave behind? There were the two legitimate children, Lionel and Mary, stroking a deer prettily in a double portrait by Kneller, but after their mother's death they lived, for most of their childhood, with their grandmother in Northamptonshire, rather than with their father. Prior's description of Charles as a family man in his Dedication to *Poems on Several Occasions* seems strangely restrained: 'kind Husband He was, without Fondness; and an indulgent Father without Partiality'. It has the ring of truth, for the thrice-married Charles was, by temperament, a bachelor throughout his life.

In wills and private letters, yellowing and smelling slightly sour with age, there are references to several illegitimate children: two daughters by Mrs Philippa Waldegrave; and a son, for whom Philippa's brother asks for help in launching on a career as an attorney. There is another son, William Sackville, who asks for money, and a letter from a Mary, asking her father to 'bestow something on her this time that she may undergo her calamity with a little more cheerfulness and alacrity'.

These children joined the roll of the disinherited at Knole, their record eventually erased or consigned to the archives. Most pathetically of all there are letters of love and reproach, written in an uneven and painful scrawl by a certain Letitia Child, 'one who is for ever yours'. Letitia writes in the early 1680s from 'this melancholy place', where she has obviously been sent to keep her from the attentions of Charles, in the care of an aunt who won't let him near her. 'I am kept such a prisoner that I am weary of my life,' she tells him in a series of letters so faded that it is only just possible to tease out what is happening. There is a letter of remonstrance from Mrs Child to her daughter, warning her off the earl, and begging her 'not to let your foolishness make you miserable . . . I am not so vain as to think my Lord can love you honourably.' She was right. The lovesick Letitia complains to Charles of being 'as near . . . mad as ever poor creature was' and claims she never asked him for anything but for 'that poor little child' that 'is as much yours as mine'.

There's a similar lack of commitment about Charles's public career, although he certainly knew how to make the system work for him. For a politician, he was simply not that political, Matthew Prior concluding that 'in an Age when Pleasure was more in Fashion than Business, he turned his Parts rather to Books and Conversation than to Politicks'. But then there's a lack of commitment about Charles's writing, too. 'It is a general complaint against your lordship, and I must have leave to upbraid you with it, that, because you need not write, you will not,' chided Dryden. Those of Charles's poems that have survived generally did so at first in manuscript rather than printed form – like those of other aristocratic amateurs of his era – designed to be enjoyed in the present rather than by posterity. It was only many years later that they became a source of study, their attribution (because many of them were written anonymously) a matter for scholarly debate. Given that his writings were, in any case, less extensive than some of his contemporaries would have wished, it was for his conversation and verbal wit that he came to be renowned: qualities as fugitive as these are notoriously difficult to capture hundreds of years later, particularly in one so famously 'phlegmatic'. Jonathan Swift, for example, found him an excruciatingly dull companion with very little learning; and another contemporary source labelled him a 'Jealous Sot all Day, And an Empty Drone at Night'.

Dorset's talents lay, it seems, in his capacity for friendship. Most descriptions of him glow with accounts of his kindness and compassion, of a man so generous and good-natured that friends, acquaintances and servants frequently took advantage of him. And this is how he is remembered at Knole: as the relaxed, genial host dressed in a green-and-gold dressing gown in the Poets' Parlour.

He is also remembered for something rather more substantial than this. Although at the time of his death, Charles's legacy may have appeared rather meagre – a couple of children whom he viewed with a certain distance, a few loose ends, a house in which he had spent not much more than a decade, a mind half-gone, an inheritance heavily mortgaged, a talent wasted – it has grown with the passage of time. His legacy is, in fact, as substantial as that of any of my ancestors; for it is Charles's collection, which began as an almost casual acquisition of cast-off furniture displayed in the same rooms then as now, that has come to define the house today.

Chapter 6

Folly and Sense (1706–1769)

Lionel Sackville, 1st Duke of Dorset and His Sons

There's a watercolour of Knole by the English landscape painter Paul Sandby that shows a quintessentially eighteenth-century scene. Deer and horses graze the turf in front of the house; a party of riders return with their dogs from a hunt; and under the spreading branches of an oak tree a couple of gentlemen take their ease. There is a leisured elegance about this summer's afternoon, a spaciousness in the skies above and in the parkland stretching into the distance. Here is a country seat, set in the broad ancestral acres of an ancient family, a symbol of aristocratic power and prestige.

The first guidebook to Knole, written by John Bridgman and published in 1817, paints a similar picture. Lionel Sackville, who owned Knole for the first half of the eighteenth century, lived, according to Bridgman, 'in great hospitality all his life; and when at Knole, he was so beloved and respected, that on Sundays the front of the house was so crowded with horsemen and carriages, as to give it rather the appearance of a princely levee rather than the residence of a private Nobleman'. What is surprising though – and this is noted by Bridgman – is that Lionel, generally acknowledged to be 'the first man in Kent', started out 'without any landed property in the county'. How had he achieved this, from such relatively unpromising beginnings?

When Charles Sackville died in decrepitude in 1706, the eighteen-year-old Lionel succeeded him as 7th Earl of Dorset. First, he needed to position himself to advantage in the event of a change of regime. In May 1706, the year of his own succession, he accompanied the Earl of Halifax and the Duke of Marlborough on a mission to Hanover to present the Act for the Naturalisation of the House of Hanover to the future King George I and his wife, paving the way for his succession to the English throne. Eight years later, he was at Kensington Palace the weekend on which Queen Anne died, writing to his wife at Knole that 'Everything goes very smoothly, and I believe the great men of yesterday will submit very quietly.' Within a week of the Queen's death, he was in Hanover to congratulate George on his accession, and the following month he escorted the new king on his journey to England to assume the throne, sailing across the Channel on the royal yacht accompanied by a fleet of twenty-two men-of-war and four frigates. His immediate rewards were the Order of the Garter and his reappointment as Lord Warden of the Cinque Ports.

The Sackvilles, once again, hovered on the periphery of power, participating – just – in the making of history. In a story that had begun with Thomas Sackville and his father, the fortunes of the family continued to be closely linked with those of the Royal Family. Lionel, an outspoken champion of the Hanoverian succession during the last days of Queen Anne, now served the new dynasty in a variety of household and state offices. He was, in the dismissive description of Lord Shelburne, 'in all respects a perfect English courtier, and nothing else. A large grown, full person . . . He had the good fortune to come into the world with the Whigs, and partook of their good fortune to his death. He never had an opinion about public matters, which together with his qualifications as a Courtier and his being of an old Sussex family . . . kept him during his whole life in a continual succession of great places, such as Steward of the Household, twice Lord Lieutenant of Ireland, President of the Council, Warden of the Cinque Ports . . .'

On 24 September 1716, the Prince of Wales, the future King George II, stayed the night at Knole – the first visit by a once or future king since Thomas Sackville had remodelled the house precisely for that purpose over a hundred years before. The steward at Knole received advance notice of the royal requirements:

> H. R. Highness designs to dine at Knole on Monday come Sen. Night – I hear they are persuading the Prince to lay at Knole. I shall take care to provide good wine of the Severall Sorts. I shall send the people to lye at Seaven Oakes on Saturday night. Send 2 Waggons for the Plate, Linnen, Wine, etc. Provisions for the Princes Table I shall send from hence because of the Larding, etc., but I desire you'll send me word which fowl you can get as Pullets, Turkeys, Pidgeons, Partridges, for the other tables, which I believe is much cheaper there, and whether my Lord won't have a Brace of Bucks killed. I believe you must get half an Ox, 4 Sheep and a Calf killed, which most of it must be rosted by our own Cooks.

The total expenses for the stay came to £257 1s. 10d. Lionel Sackville was rewarded for his support of the new regime by a promotion in 1720 from 7th Earl to 1st Duke of Dorset – at a time when admission to the aristocracy was more tightly controlled than it had been under the Stuarts. Even though the sources of power and patronage were slowly shifting away from king and court, these personal links between noble families and the Royal Family were still important, and at the very least provided the duke and his sons with a stream of household appointments: as steward, equerry, Gentleman of the Bedchamber, Master of the Horse, and so on.

But in addition to this, noble families such as the Sackvilles dominated the Cabinet (Henry Pelham's 1744 cabinet included no less than seven dukes), the upper echelons of the armed forces (Lionel's youngest son, George, was a general) and the executive. During the eighteenth century, England was still run – just as it had been in Thomas Sackville's day – by a tiny group of aristocrats, a few hundred families perhaps, whose jaws were locked on the profits and perquisites of state.

Above the fireplace in the Great Hall at Knole, hangs a painting by John Wootton of the duke in ceremonial procession to

Dover Castle in 1728, on his reappointment as Lord Warden of the Cinque Ports. The Warden was responsible for administering the five – *cinque* – ports of Dover, Sandwich, Hythe, Romney and Hastings – and, in this capacity, there were many opportunities to promote family power and wealth through the use of patronage. He appointed, for example, the officers of the ports themselves, his son Charles as Governor of Walmer Castle and his son John as Lieutenant of Dover Castle. The duke's dominance of local government was further secured by the office of Lord Lieutenant of Kent, which he held for much of his life, appointing magistrates and commanding the militia.

But there was another arena in which aristocrats found it increasingly important to have influence, and that was Parliament. Lionel had argued in a debate in the House of Lords in September 1716 in favour of elections every seven years, rather than every three years, because the latter tended to 'destroy all family interest, and subject our excellent constitution to the caprice of the multitude'. Much of the Sackville family correspondence of the first half of the eighteenth century is devoted to sustaining this 'family interest', through placing sons or supporters in safe seats – the so-called 'pocket' boroughs – and through electioneering.

In 1733, Lionel's eldest son, Charles, Lord Middlesex, was put up as one of two Whig candidates for the county of Kent at the next election. The 'Treat' in honour of Charles and the other candidate, Sir George Oxenden, at Kippington consisted of a 'very noble . . . 80 stone of beef, a side of choice Veal, Six Venison Pasties, 6 Legs of Pork, 6 Turkeys, 18 large plum puddings, and Wine in great plenty at every table, besides an Innundation of Punch'. The total expenses of the election campaign, which the duke financed on behalf of his son, came to £2,353 2s. 8d. – more than a quarter of his annual rental income. The fact that Charles did not get elected in 1734 must have been a little galling – he had been abroad for much of the campaign – but the sums spent show just important it was, as power ebbed gradually from king and court to Parliament, for a family to have a seat or two in the House of Commons as well as one in the Lords. As it happened, Charles was elected Member of Parliament for the safe family seat of East Grinstead, which he held from 1734 to 1741; his middle brother John was MP for Tamworth from 1734 to 1741; and his youngest brother George was MP for Dover (a borough in his father's gift as Lord Warden of the Cinque Ports) from 1741, and for East Grinstead from 1768 to 1783.

As a prominent Whig grandee, and a deft political operator, the 1st Duke was seldom out of office during the reign of King George II, his political career distinguished by two spells in Dublin as Lord Lieutenant of Ireland. At the start of his first spell, which lasted from 1730 to 1737, he and his wife Elizabeth moved into magnificent new lodgings in Dublin Castle with their four children: Charles, John, George (who in 1733 entered Trinity College, Dublin) and Caroline. Once the Irish parliamentary season was over, they would return to England each year for the summer.

It was in Dublin that the Sackvilles came into contact with the satirist Jonathan Swift, Dean of St Patrick's and a friend of their long-term house-guest at Knole, Lady Betty Germain. She had written to Dean Swift, commending her friends, the Dorsets, to him: 'He is the most worthy, honest, good-natured, great-souled man that ever was born. As to my duchess, she is so reserved, that perhaps she may not be at first so much admired; but, upon knowledge, I will defy anybody upon earth, with sense, judgment and good nature, not only to admire her, but must love and esteem her as much as I do.' Swift, in turn, pestered the duke for Church appointments for his friends, and when these were not forthcoming, he complained to Lady Betty (in 1737): 'I now dismiss you, madam, for ever from your office of being a go-between upon any affair I might have with his grace [the duke]. I will never more trouble him, either with my visits or application. His business in this kingdom is to make himself easy; his lessons are all prescribed him from court; and he is sure, at a very cheap rate, to have a majority of most corrupt slaves and idiots at his devotion. The happiness of this kingdom is of no more consequence to him, than it would be to the great Mogul.'

Petitions for patronage and preferment came from all sorts of people. According to Horace Walpole, the duke was 'a man of dignity, caution and plausibility' in public, but 'in private the

greatest lover of low humour and buffoonery'. There are references in the archives to a relationship between the duke and the
Irish actress, Margaret 'Peg' Woffington, who often performed in
'breeches', wearing male dress specifically to display her elegant
legs. Humorous verses pastiched 'The humble Petition of Margt.
Woffington, Spinster' to the duke:

> *May it please your Grace with all Submission*
> *I humbly offer my Petition.*
> *Let others with as small pretensions,*
> *Tease you for places or for pensions;*
> *I scorn a pension or a place,*
> *My sole design's upon Your Grace,*
> *The sum of my petition this –*
> *I claim, my Lord, an annual kiss;*
> *A kiss, by Sacred Custom due*
> *To me, and to be pay'd by You . . .*

The flirtation is taken a stage further, in the form of a spoof application – purportedly written by 'Peg', but possibly penned by one of
the duke's sons – for a job at Dublin Castle: 'That your Memorialist
[Margaret Woffington] is a Woman of great merit . . . extremely well
qualified to discharge the Office of Housekeeper to his Majesty's
Castle as it does not require much greater abilities than the Rolls or
the Chancellorship of the Exchequer . . . That her personal attachment to your Grace is so well known that odd reports have been
raised in relation to some intimacies that have past between two
persons that shall be nameless, and which she defies her adversar-
ies to prove.' In a postscript, she adds that 'she is ready and willing
to act as first Chambermaid to your Grace, to warm your bed and
tuck you in, which, as she is advised and verily believes, the present
Housekeeper is in no manner qualified to do.'

The duke's second lord lieutenancy, from 1750 to 1755, was less
successful than his first. He was much under the influence of his
chief secretary, his son George, 'a man of very sound parts', according to Horace Walpole, 'but hot, haughty, ambitious, obstinate'.

Their administration antagonised the Irish, and parliamentary opposition to the Crown reached such a pitch that Dorset was replaced in 1755.

Back in England, the Sackvilles, like many aristocratic families, spent much of the year in their London home, managing their estates through a steward. But it was in their country home that they could show off as head of the local community, and receive the deference they felt was their due. Here they would spend the summer months, wooing the local gentry, entertaining tenants and building an 'interest' of political supporters with hospitality and job offers.

There were dinners, balls and assemblies, venison feasts at election times, and cricket matches in the summer, where votes could be canvassed. The Sackvilles were among the earliest patrons of the game. The 1st Duke kept a cricket ground at Knole regularly mown and rolled, and employed as a gardener one Valentine Romney, 'the best cricket player,' according to the *Kentish Gazette*, 'in the world'. Both the duke's older sons inherited their father's enthusiasm for the sport. Charles raised a Kent team to play a London and Middlesex team, sponsored by the Prince of Wales, in July 1735. At stake was a wager of £1,000 for the winning team – since gambling, as well as politics, was as intertwined with the game in its origins as it is today.

Two years later, also with the help of the Prince of Wales, his brother John arranged what the *London Evening Post* described as 'the greatest match at cricket that has ever been contested' at Kennington Common. Games such as this attracted crowds of up to 10,000 and could get rowdy. The crush outside the Prince of Wales's pavilion was such that 'a poor woman by the crowd bearing upon her unfortunately had her leg broke, which being related to His Royal Highness, he was pleased to order her ten guineas'. John was also the organiser of the first match for which a full scorecard has survived – England vs. Kent, on 18 June 1744, at the Artillery Ground. John took the match-winning catch, in the words of a contemporary versifier: 'Swift as the falcon, darting on its prey,/He springs elastick o'er the verdant way.'

There were lavish parties at Christmas, christenings, comings-of-age and weddings. Christmas 1728 at Knole was kept in grand style:

> . . . *See how bounteous the Master, the Cellars stand open,*
> *And out comes the Butler, and bids you all tope on,*
> *Here's a Health to their Graces, who duly each year,*
> *Bid you welcome to Knole, to taste their good cheer.*
> > *Brave boys drink about, for the weather is cold,*
> > *Let the new year begin, as we ended the old,*
> > *Let brisk Bumpers go round, we'll replenish the Bowl,*
> > *For who keeps a House, such as we keep at Knole.*

These verses, in the Knole archives, celebrate the great housekeeping tradition that was already almost out of fashion in Thomas Sackville's day.

As John Bridgman had noted, the Sackvilles had little land in Kent itself, with the bulk of their property clustered around their ancestral heartlands in Sussex. Land lay at the heart of the aristocrat's power and credibility, and their belief in the right to govern. The Sackvilles, therefore, like hundreds of other aristocratic families, regarded their estate as a trust to be passed from generation to generation. Landownership was, according to the political theorist Edmund Burke, 'a sacred partnership not only between those who are living, but between those who are living, those who are dead, and those who are to be born'. This partnership contributed to the stability of the state itself. In his will, Thomas Sackville had left very precise instructions about the ring given to him by King James I, that it should pass as an heirloom from 'heir male to heir male' in perpetuity. Thomas's will was the first explicit reference to an inheritance of house and family in the history of Knole, but by no means the last.

Woe betide any family member who, like the 3rd Earl or like the 1st Duke's father, the 6th Earl, or his son, the 2nd Duke, failed to keep this trust. Estates had to be maintained, if not increased, and there was a panoply of land laws, entails and family settlements, designed to hold estates, house, heirlooms, name and titles together in the male line through primogeniture. It was a system abolished in France at the time of the Revolution, and very rarely used in the rest of Europe from the first half of the nineteenth century. In the Knole archives, the greatest volume of parchment is represented over the centuries by wills and settlements, with instructions to trustees cropping up time and again, 'upon trust to preserve the contingent uses and Estates hereinafter limited from being defeated or destroyed'. All of them attempt to achieve similar objectives: principally, to preserve the patrimony for the eldest son, but also to provide for the widow, to guarantee enough cash to the daughters to enable them to marry, and to the younger sons to give them a start in life, through the sale every generation or so of some outlying properties. The settlements effectively involved three generations: the father and his widow, their children, and their unborn grand-children. Everyone knew where they stood and this, it was hoped, would minimise litigation later. It worked particularly if there were male heirs.

Although the 1st Duke had nothing like the acreages of the Dukes of Bedford and Devonshire, or the Earls of Warwick and Derby, he was wealthy enough, with a rent roll in 1738 of £9,181 7s. 2d. from estates in Sussex, London, Warwickshire and Staffordshire. He benefited from the increased efficiency and profitability that were a feature of aristocratic estates during the eighteenth century: partly as a result of enclosing common land and putting it into produc-tion, partly from the replacement of copyhold (with fixed rents on long leases) by fixed-term rack rents with rents reviewed on a much more regular basis, and partly due to rising prices.

Knole was, perhaps, at its most magnificent as a ducal residence during the eighteenth century. The consolidation of political and economic power in the hands of the landowning classes was reflected in a wave of competitive country-house construction and collecting. Three of the greatest houses of the eighteenth century, Blenheim, Castle Howard and Houghton Hall, were all started between 1700 and 1725, monuments to the triumph of the aristocracy. While the 1st Duke was not in this league of super rich, he did embark on a programme of improvement, placing his own stamp on the property.

When Lytton Strachey visited Eddy Sackville-West at Knole in August 1926, he described 'Knole as interesting – beautiful on the whole externally, with College-like courts and charming gardens and park, but the inside was disappointing – too much hole-and-corner Elizabethanism; one longed for the spaciousness of the eighteenth century; and the bad taste of countless generations of Sackvilles littered it all up. Eddy, it seemed to me, continued the tradition in his ladylike apartments.' Strachey had a point, although there are elements of this eighteenth-century spaciousness at Knole: not just in the park, as painted by Sandby, but in the house too.

Some of the patterns that have characterised life at Knole from the early seventeenth century to today were emerging: periods of affluence alternating with austerity, residence with absenteeism, bursts of redecoration with decades of neglect. When Lionel brought his young bride, Elizabeth Colyear, to Knole in 1709, he initiated the first improvements in a hundred years or so – just as we have done in the early years of the twenty-first century. But whereas we have attempted to fashion a Jacobean palace for modern family life, Lionel Sackville turned Knole into a place for a party.

Thomas Sackville's state rooms were adapted to suit the social requirements of the eighteenth-century assembly. His Great Chamber was turned into a Ballroom (and was referred to as such for the first time in an inventory of 1765); gilt sconces, bearing the duke's coronet and garter, graced the walls of the room and cast a flickering light on the dancers as they performed their minuets. Next door was a withdrawing room, where guests gambled at small tables, its walls swathed in crimson velvet that muffled the clack of the cards. As the party unravelled, the long galleries and reception rooms would have been infused with the light from a thousand candles: reflected off the polished wood floors and the gilt mirrors, smouldering in the fluttering décolletages of the women, and picking out the beauty spots and pox marks against the pallor of their powdered faces.

Lionel introduced fashionable elements of the classical style here and there: a Venetian window, with classical mouldings, was added to the Venetian Ambassador's Room; and the King's Room, originally designed for King James I, was redecorated with dado panelling painted in grisaille. But with a few exceptions such as these, the Jacobean state apartments on the first floor were too extensive for a makeover and were left mostly untouched. The changes were focused on the family rooms on the ground floor. The Colonnade was glazed, and its walls decorated with trompe l'oeil arches and niches containing giant urns. It now connected a suite of south-facing rooms: an 'Armoury' that, with its Ionic pilasters, was more decorative than defensive; a Boudoir, whose new bay window gave an even finer view of the garden; a Music Room, with a Queen Anne mantelpiece made around the time Lionel was moving into Knole with his young wife; and, of course, a Library, fitted out for the first time in the mid-eighteenth century, to display the duke's culture and refinement as well as his wealth and power.

In 1723–24 the artist Mark Antony Hauduroy was commissioned to decorate the second of Thomas Sackville's Jacobean staircases, connecting the Colonnade on the ground floor and the Ballroom on the first floor, with grisaille trophies of weapons and the duke's coat of arms. In 1745, a clock and belfry were placed above Bourchier's gatehouse, crowning Knole's ancient glories with a more fanciful ornament of the modern age. And in 1748 a balustrade, bearing the initials of the 1st Duke, was built above Thomas Sackville's Doric colonnade in the Stone Court.

The duke's remodelling did not impress Horace Walpole when he visited the house in 1752: 'The furniture throughout, ancient magnificence; loads of portraits, not good nor curious . . . The first little room you enter has sundry portraits of the times; but they seem to have been bespoke by the yard, and drawn all by the same painter . . . A visto cut through the wood has a delightful effect from the front; but there are some trumpery fragments of gardens that spoil the view from the state apartments.'

Spending on the park, as well as the mansion, was another visible sign of wealth and status. During the eighteenth century, many landowners decided to 'improve' their parks, employing designers such as CapabilityBrown or Humphry Repton to create self-consciously picturesque landscapes. Knole largely escaped this type of makeover – partly because the deer themselves already made the place look ornamental enough, and partly because of the same innate conservatism of the Sackville family (or simply the impossible scale of the endeavour) that has led to the house remaining relatively untouched, too, over the centuries.

Nevertheless, the 1st Duke did spend money on planting at Knole, in a way that reflected the taste and aspirations of the eighteenth century. In 1700, the park at Knole had changed little since Thomas Sackville's death in 1608. The clumps of hawthorn, oak, yew, hornbeam, silver birch, bird maple and ash that had dominated the woodlands of the Weald since the Middle Ages were still in evidence; and fallow deer grazed the sandy grasslands, as they had done since Tudor times. During the seventeenth century, there had been some attempt at generating revenue from the park, through the sale of timber to the shipyards at Chatham or from the coppicing of wood for hop poles. Some of the land had been ploughed for growing crops, but the soils were thin, and the park remained substantially unchanged. By the early eighteenth century, however – as topographical engravings of Knole by Jan Kip and Leonard Knyff show – changes were being made.

In 'prospects' and bird's-eye perspectives by these two artists, avenues of trees radiate from the house, the centre of power, across the park. Records for 1723 alone itemise the purchase of '2,000 small beeches in ye Park', to be planted in stands and in broad tree-lined avenues, in place of the old coppiced woodlands. These avenues have now come to define the park: the Chestnut Walk and the Broad Walk, of beech and oak, which converge on the Mast Head in the southern corner of the park, and the Duchess Walk of oak, which leads northwards away from the house.

When describing their hereditary responsibility for the land, Edmund Burke had referred to noble families as the 'great oaks that shade a country, and perpetuate . . . benefits from generation to generation'. What could say more about a family's dynastic confidence and its commitment to holding land in trust for future generations than the planting of trees themselves? It is a view to which Lionel Sackville, 1st Duke of Dorset, obviously subscribed, and which his namesake, my uncle, shared two centuries later. Uncle

Lionel loved Knole, I am sure of it, although he rarely articulated his love for the place, except in his passion for its trees.

For fifty years, at first at weekends only and then, after his retirement, every day of the week throughout the year, he would spend at least two hours in the plantations, slashing at the weeds, the birch and the bracken. As you were walking through some bluebell woods, or searching for ceps in the soggy, musty leaf mould beneath the beech trees, or simply stretching out under the shade of chestnut tree, a sprightly man of almost ninety might emerge from the undergrowth or from behind a clump of bracken brandishing a pair of clippers. Dressed in ill-fitting jeans, a tweed jacket, and a tie, was this a gamekeeper out ferreting, or a slightly deranged, and possibly dangerous, member of the public? No cause for alarm – it was my uncle out foresting. Lionel, like his great-great-great-great grandfather, believed in trees, not just for their beauty but also as an investment in the future, in shaping a landscape today for the enjoyment of generations to come. It was a profoundly conservative impulse, but a very generous one – and one for which I have many reasons (not just the trees) to be grateful.

As with the enfilades of rooms within the house, the avenues, *allées* and *claire-voies* in the park and garden gave a structure to the property and that eighteenth-century sense of spaciousness which Lytton Strachey craved. Parts of the garden wall were demolished to make way for railings where you could survey the park from the house and, in one place, for a sunken ha-ha that gave the impression that house and garden opened right onto the park. A Gothic Revival building, a folly and an artificial ruin were added to the landscape in the 1760s to give that 'whimsical air of novelty' that people found so pleasing.

When Horace Walpole visited in 1752, he may have been disappointed by the house – it was never as 'vast and venerable' as he remembered it or as 'extensive' as he expected – but the park, he wrote, 'is sweet, with much old beech, and an immense sycamore before the great gate'.

In their tastes and their passions (as well as their survival strategies), the Sackvilles represented many aspects of aristocratic life throughout the eighteenth century. But their experience, during this period of economic prosperity and political power, differed from that of many other noble families in that it coincided with an unprecedented era of family stability. Though the duke occasionally found his sons troublesome, the estate held together because the family did. The 1st Duke owned Knole for almost sixty years. For fifty-six of those years, until his death in 1765, he was happily married to Elizabeth Colyear – 'my dear Colly', or 'dear, dear, dear girl', as he refers to her in his letters, a positively effusive greeting in a family famous for its 'excessive reserve and silence'.

The duke's own inheritance was one in a sequence of five father-to-son successions, spanning a century and a half, that had begun with his great-grandfather the 4th Earl in 1624 and ended with his own son the 2nd Duke's succession in 1765. To put this dynastic continuity into context, the average span for aristocratic families of the period was just a hundred years; and there have only been two direct father-to-son Sackville successions since 1765: one, involving a minor, the 4th Duke in 1799, and the other in 1962.

The duke was sometimes disappointed by his sons – and, in particular, by the extravagance of his eldest, Charles. There is a full-length portrait of him in the Ballroom at Knole, painted in 1738 by Franz Ferdinand Richter to record the role played by Charles in a masque he and his friends put on in Florence: a spectacle, according to a contemporary account, that 'set all Italy talking'. The twenty-five-year-old Charles is dressed as a Roman consul returning in triumph from the wars. Less virile, or less ridiculous, is a delicate pastel by Rosalba Carriera, in which Charles, a fine-looking – almost effeminate – man, is dressed not for war but for the Venetian carnival. The light picks out the intricate patterns of his richly brocaded coat, his classical features and the carnival mask perched on his head.

Both portraits record the fact that, like many of his contemporaries, Charles went on the Grand Tour to Italy, first in 1731–33 with Joseph Spence, Professor of Poetry at Oxford as his tutor, and then again in 1736–38. On returning from his first trip he became a founding member of the Society of Dilettanti, whose origins and aims were later described by Robert Wood in the preface to a book published by the Society: 'In the year 1734, some gentlemen who had travelled in Italy, desirous of encouraging, *at home*, a taste for those objects which had contributed so much to their entertainment *abroad*, formed themselves into a Society, under the name of the DILETTANTI . . . It would be disingenuous to insinuate, that a serious plan for the promotion of Arts was the only motive for forming this Society: friendly and social intercourse was, undoubtedly, the first great object in view.'

Horace Walpole was more forthright. The Dilettanti were 'a club for which,' he wrote, 'the nominal qualification is having been in Italy and the real one, being drunk: the two chiefs are Lord Middlesex [Charles Sackville] and Sir Francis Dashwood, who were seldom sober the whole time they were in Italy.' While in Florence in 1733, Charles founded a masonic lodge there, his membership of both the Freemasons and the Dilettanti not as improbable as it may at first appear, since both societies revelled in arcane ritual and ceremonial, and shared a role as drinking clubs and an enthusiasm for music and theatre.

Charles was developing a passion for Italian opera – the portraits of Handel and Corelli at Knole all date from this period – and he spent large sums of his own money promoting the art form on his return to London in 1739. He also canvassed subscriptions from members, including fellow Dilettanti, to support the Italian opera company, of which he was the principal director and impresario, at the King's Theatre, Haymarket. Even though he became a subscriber, Horace Walpole was one of those to express his doubts, referring to 'the improbability of eight young thoughtless men of fashion understanding economy', and to the fact that the 'odious' Muscovita, Charles's mistress Lucia Panichi, who had followed him to England, was so well paid – not just for her singing – but 'for secret services' as well. Others complained, too, that his lordship's motives had been partial: 'to make his mistress, the Muscovita [who survives, topless, at Knole in a portrait by Rosalba], appear to great advantage on the stage. With this intent, say they, he has taken care to hire singers with voices inferior to hers; and hers is not worth a farthing.'

Operas were performed for three seasons between 1741 and 1744, closing for a year while the directors of the opera sued some of their supporters for subscription arrears and for a contribution towards the previous season's deficit (for which the subscribers did not believe themselves strictly liable), before reopening in 1745–46. Horace Walpole was one of those subscribers who paid up, but was embittered by the whole experience and by the fact that the exuberance and passion with which Charles got the whole project off the ground were let down by his obvious financial and managerial failings. This undoubtedly explains his constant sniping at Charles, who 'must ruin the House of Sackville by a course of these follies'. In his correspondence, he chronicled the court cases and fallings out of the opera company, the arrears, the bad debts, the unpaid performers and composers, blaming the mess on Charles and his partiality. In August 1746, Walpole was claiming that 'Lord Middlesex took the opportunity of a rivalship between his own mistress, the Nardi [who succeeded the Muscovita], and the Violetta, the finest and most admired dancer in the world, to involve the whole ménage of the Opera in the quarrel, and has paid nobody.' The duke was embarrassed by his son's extravagance – not just on his own pocket, but also on behalf of his many aristocratic friends who were disillusioned subscribers to the opera. He even asked the King not to subscribe again.

Not even marriage solved young Charles's money worries. In August 1744, Horace Walpole wrote excitedly to his crony, Sir Horace Mann: 'Lord Middlesex's match is determined, and the writings signed. She proves an immense fortune, they pretend £130,000 – what a fund for making operas!' On 30 October, he married Grace Boyle, the only daughter and heiress of Richard, 2nd Viscount Shannon, attracted more by her fortune, perhaps, than by her looks, for the new Lady Middlesex was, in one account: 'Short and dark as a winter's day,/And yellow as a November morning.'

Her sallow colouring was confirmed by Walpole, for whom Grace was 'very short, very plain, and very yellow: a vain girl, full of Greek and Latin and music and painting', and the wedding itself was rather low-key: 'Nothing happens ... but Lord Middlesex's wedding, which was over a week before it was known. I believe the bride told it then; for he and all his family are so silent, that they would never have mentioned it; she might have popped out a child, before a single Sackville would have been at the expense of a syllable to justify her.'

Grace was, however, a great favourite of the Prince of Wales (he was known to enjoy high-minded conversation with intelligent women) and was reputed – with no foundation – to have been his mistress. In her role as Mistress of the Robes to the Princess of Wales, she lived 'with them perpetually', according to Walpole, 'and sits up till five in the morning at their suppers'. Walpole claimed rather bitchily, when Lady Middlesex was pregnant in 1747 with a child she eventually miscarried, that the Sackville blood was the 'worst blood it is supposed to swell with' (the better blood being the royal blood), and when Lady Middlesex 'popped her child before its turn . . . my Lord loyally cries over it'.

Despite the marriage settlement which the duke had provided for Charles and his bride in 1744, comprising estates in Derbyshire, Staffordshire and Gloucestershire, Charles claimed that he was entitled to other properties under his grandfather's will, and even questioned his father's right to the lucrative Dorset Gardens estate in London. It was yet another saga in the squabbling between father and son that characterised many aristocratic estates (the duke's father, the 6th Earl, had fallen out fairly spectacularly with his own father and mother in the 1670s). By 1751 they were corresponding through their respective agents, and Charles was threatening legal action.

George Bubb Dodington, the politician and close friend of the Prince of Wales, kept a diary which describes in detail Charles's quarrels with his father. Charles had asked Dodington to broker a reconciliation with his father, and on 7 July 1752 he went to see the duke: 'I chose to put the question to him hypothetically; if his son should throw himself at his feet, and declare an unreserv'd submission and sorrow for what is past – what would he do? – He was much moved. I desir'd he would not answer me then, as I had no such commission – but consider of it.' Given this encouragement,

Dodington met the duke again, as go-between, on 2 October, and 'made his son's submissions to him, and endeavour'd to procure a full reconciliation. We had a long conference. He alleged the many, almost unpardonable provocations, which I know to be true, but did not absolutely refuse to forgive him. He boggled much at the freeing him [his son] from his debts.' By December a partial truce had been made, and the duke did apparently pay off some of his son's debts. But they were never close, and between 1743 and 1763 Charles was rarely, if ever, at Knole. Dodington records a conversation he had with the Princess of Wales in December 1752, in which she claimed that there was only one family more odd than the Sackvilles, and 'she would not name that family for the world', obviously meaning the Royal Family.

Money also strained relations between the eldest and youngest brother. When Charles's wife, Grace, was reduced to begging George for money, Lord George replied abruptly: 'I am sorry to say that my Ld. Middlesex's behaviour towards me for a Considerable time past has been such, as makes it impracticable for me to concern myself in his affairs.' The middle brother, John, kept his distance from these sibling rivalries, but only by default. From his teens, his life was blighted by bouts of severe depression. After his marriage in 1744 'under some very strange circumstances' (he had been forced to marry his mistress Frances two days after she had given birth to his child), he 'behaved still more strangely', according to Lord Shelburne, 'when he was embarking with his regiment upon some expedition, so that his family thought it most prudent that he should resign his commission and undergo a sort of family exile, under some sort of supervision, near Lausanne in Switzerland'. The precise nature of these embarrassing incidents unfortunately escapes us – although it is thought that he had been arrested for desertion on being ordered overseas – but they were enough to keep him on a tight leash. He had also been disappointed in not inheriting as anticipated the estates worth over £3,000 a year of his great-uncle, the Earl of Wilmington.

There is a series of heartbreaking letters, starting in April 1754, from John to his younger brother, in which he acknowledges his faults, and begs George to intercede for him with their father, the duke. All he wants is a 'last trial' at being his own master, 'that he may have some comfort in his life'. He rails against a Mr Villettes, who was in some way responsible for his financial affairs. 'Mr Villettes has taken the worst possible method to prevent my committing irregularities, as I have been obliged to furnish myself on credit, and borrow money where I could get it [driving him into debt] . . . He still continues to persecute me, and acts in regard to me in a most scrubby manner.' In his slightly paranoid way, John even accuses him of being a French spy. If only, however, he could be 'reinstated in my full income of 400 Pounds a year, I hope my future conduct would prove satisfactory to the Duke and Duchess and all my friends', and then his wife 'should come and live with me in this country, and bring master and miss along with her'.

In September 1754 he was complaining to his brother of another 'melancholy fit': 'It has been a pretty severe one and lasted a long time . . . I think if there be any difference the low fit does not last quite so long as it used to do, the good spirits two or three days longer; but while it does last, the low fit is more violent and the high fit less so.' A moving account of his sufferings has also survived in the form of a 'prayer' in French, made *'en sortant de sa melancholie, le 26 Juillet, 1759'*: from the lows when *'je suis plongé périodiquement dans une tristesse accablante, je suis rempli de crainte et de frayeur'* ['I plunged from time to time in an overwhelming sadness, full of fear'] to the highs when *'un mouvement vif des esprits animaux me font commetre mille désordres et folies qui ruinent ma santé et ternissent ma reputation, et me font passer bien amèrement les jours de tristesse qui ne manquent jamais d'arriver'*. [Here he described the animal spirits which drove him to a thousand acts of madness which destroyed his health and reputation before the days of depression returned.] 'O God,' he begged, *'aidez-moi de moderer ce feu qui m'entraine et me devore . . . adoucissez aussi ces violentes attaques'* ['help me temper the violence of these attacks'].

Lord Shelburne saw him in Switzerland in the winter of 1760, five years before his death, 'living upon a very poor allowance and but meanly looked after. He was very fond of coming among the young English at Lausanne, who suffered his company at times from motives of curiosity and sometimes from humanity. He was always dirtily clad, but it was easy to perceive something gentlemanlike in his manners, and a look of birth about him under all his disadvantages. His conversation was a mixture of weakness and shrewdness as is common in most madmen.' John's son, the 3rd Duke, also suffered from severe bouts of depression (as, indeed, had his grandfather): a pattern that was to be repeated into the nineteenth and twentieth centuries.

Lionel's favourite son was his youngest, George, who had been named after his godfather King George II. In family mythology, Lord George Sackville has tended to be ignored or even disowned. Vita Sackville-West, in *Knole and the Sackvilles*, finds him 'an incongruity among the Sackvilles, a departure from type'. She judged it 'best to leave him alone ... and to seek neither to blacken nor to whitewash his character. I scarcely regard him as one of the Sackvilles,' and concluded: 'for some reason Lord George never awakened my interest or my sense of relationship. He was a public character, not a relation.'

This distaste of hers may have had something to do with George's prickly, impatient character. According to Percival Stockdale, who had served in the army under Lord George's command at Chatham, there was 'a reserve and haughtiness in [his] manner, which depressed and darkened all that was agreeable and engaging in him ... His integrity commanded esteem, his abilities praise; but to attract the heart was not one of those abilities ... For want of this flexibility ... for want of a social gaiety, and affection, which one ought to cultivate, the public were not interested in his good fortune – his elevation gave them no pleasure; and they did not regret his fall.'

Portraits at Knole reveal a tall, heavy man – 'well formed', in the words of his admirers, or 'of a large make, though rather womanly', in the words of the ever-malicious Lord Shelburne. A bulbous nose and a fleshy, protruding lower lip lent themselves easily to caricature; as did some quirks of temperament (he was notorious for bearing grudges, for example) and of manner (he had a famously sharp tongue). But there was something else that isolated him from his fellows: the rumours of a 'private vice' that followed him for much of his career.

These first emerged when he accompanied his father to Ireland as the duke's chief secretary, for his second spell as Lord Lieutenant, in 1751 (two later Prime Ministers, the Duke of Wellington and Sir Robert Peel, were both to serve their political apprenticeship in this post). Stories started to circulate about homosexual relations between Lord George, the Primate of Ireland, George Stone, and a young army officer from Scotland called Robert Cunningham, whom Lord George had installed as aide-de-camp to the Primate. Horace Walpole reported that Lord George 'is supposed to have a seraglio, which is not at all in the style of a country that is famous for furnishing rich widows with second husbands. His friend the Primate . . . is accused of other cardinalesque dispositions too . . . Epigrams, ballads, pasquinades swarm. May I send you a very gross one that came to the Primate's hand . . . as he was at dinner at the Castle: "Religion is now become a mere farce/ Since the head of the Church is in Cunningham's arse."'

Nevertheless, in 1754, Lord George did settle into a long and apparently happy marriage, spurred on by his close friend Cunningham, who wrote to him just before the wedding: 'Before you receive this Letter I do suppose your Nuptials are consummated . . . We [Cunningham and his wife] can both easily imagine how you will be employed next Tuesday night, and shall certainly do what we can to imitate your example. I shall persuade Betty that what you have in size I have in vigour, that our wives, when they meet, may not dispute who are best served.'

Despite Vita's rather condescending lack of interest, Lord George was one of the ablest members the Sackville family has produced, and the one who came closest to achieving the highest office. 'I do not conceive,' wrote Lord Shelburne, 'that any but the checks which stopped his military career could have prevented his being Prime Minister.' He served as a soldier from 1737, fighting in Flanders during the War of the Austrian Succession and in Scotland during the bloody suppression of the Jacobite Rising of 1745. The fact that his commander had written of him, during this last campaign, as an officer who 'has not only shown his courage but a disposition to his trade, which I do not always find in those of higher rank' is particularly interesting in the light of later events.

The checks to Lord George's career began in 1759, when he was appointed commander-in-chief of the British troops in Germany, helping the Germans – under the supreme command of Prince Ferdinand of Brunswick – to defend Hanover against the French. At the Battle of Minden in 1759, the British cavalry failed to capitalise on the success of the allied artillery in breaking the French centre. What might have been a rout was merely a victory. Was this because, in the fog of battle, Lord George had been confused by three sets of conflicting orders from Prince Ferdinand? Was it simply because he was slow in manoeuvring his cavalry squadrons into the line of attack? Was it because he had actively disobeyed Prince Ferdinand? Or, worst of all, had his conduct been cowardly?

Prince Ferdinand blamed Sackville and was backed by King George II, who relieved Sackville of his command. Sackville was subjected to a vicious attack in the press and, in an attempt to clear his name, requested a court martial. There was a very real danger of a death sentence if found guilty, it being only a couple of years since Admiral Byng had been shot for failing to 'do his utmost' at the Battle of Minorca. Yet Sackville was adamant: 'I am conscious of neither neglect nor disobedience of orders, as I am certain I did my duty to the utmost of my ability.' Even Horace Walpole conceded that he 'would sooner pronounce Lord George a hero for provoking his trial, than a coward for shrinking from the French. He would have been in less danger by leading up the Cavalry at Minden than in every hour that he went down to Horseguards [where the court martial was held] as a criminal.'

At the trial in 1760, Lord George was found guilty of disobeying Prince Ferdinand, and pronounced 'unfit to serve his Majesty in any military capacity whatsoever'. He was stripped of his offices, and salaries and emoluments worth about £7,000 a year. But he was not sentenced to death, and this lenience – which infuriated George II, who described the disgrace as 'worse than death to a man who has any sense of honour' – cast some doubt on his culpability. It is a doubt shared by many historians today.

Lord George retired to Knole for a while, where a suite of rooms in the North Wing is named after him. He never really succeeded in shaking off the slur on his name cast by the Battle of Minden. In 1770 he challenged a Captain George Johnstone to a duel in Hyde Park for feigning surprise 'that the noble lord should interest himself so deeply in the honour of his country, when he had been hitherto so regardless of his own'. The protagonists exchanged two shots each at twenty paces, one of which struck Lord George's pistol, sending a splinter from it into his hand. Johnstone later declared that he had never known a man behave with more courage in a duel, and Horace Walpole reported that 'Lord George behaved with the utmost coolness and intrepidity . . . whatever Lord George Sackville was, Lord George Germain is a hero'. Lord George had recently changed his name as a condition of his inheriting Lady Betty Germain's house and estate at Drayton in Northamptonshire. The name change, argued Walpole, worked in favour of Lord George's sons who, by dropping the name of Sackville, 'might avoid great part of the disgrace that had fallen on their father'. It is something of an irony that the glorious name of Sackville, to which the family would cling so tenaciously in the nineteenth century, was seen then as such a liability.

Five years later, Lord George was made Secretary of State for the American colonies, although his rehabilitation was never complete. One scurrilous poem, called *Sodom and Onan*, dredged up once again the twin charges of cowardice and homosexuality:

> *Sackville, both Coward and Catamite, commands*
> *Department honourable, and kisses hands*
> *With lips that oft in blandishment obscene*
> *Have been employed . . .*

The man who, fifteen years before, had been found 'unfit to serve his Majesty in any military capacity whatsoever', was now the minister responsible for conducting a global war to subdue the colonies. In what was probably the most complicated war England had yet faced, Lord George had to supply an army 3,000 miles away, convoying food, reinforcements and equipment across the Atlantic, with Europe's top three maritime powers ranged against her.

Despite the loss of the colonies in 1782, Lord George emerged from the campaign with some credit – 'he had,' according to his friend Richard Cumberland, 'all the requisites of a great minister, unless popularity and good luck are to be numbered amongst them' – and he was awarded a peerage. He chose the title Viscount Sackville, thereby getting round the commitment to call himself Germain he had made on inheriting Lady Betty's estate. By clinging on to the name of his birth, this able, ambitious younger son was revealing, perhaps, his hopes of inheriting the other Sackville titles one day.

Lord George's disgrace at Minden had been a great disappointment to his father, who 'went into the country some time ago', according to the poet Thomas Gray, 'and (they say) can hardly bear the sight of anybody'. Sinking under his son's disgrace, the duke died at Knole in 1765, five years after his son's court martial (and the same year as his middle son, John), and was buried at Withyham.

During his father's last years, there had been some evidence of a thaw in family relations. Charles visited Knole in 1763 and, according to his brother George, 'he looks over the old place with a degree of curiosity and pleasure, but does not seem surprised at having been absent from it these twenty years'. His visit appeared to have done him some good, for at the end of ten days George wrote that Charles 'seemed really happy at being at liberty to please himself; and the air at Knole worked miracles in his favour, for he grew young and lively'.

When Charles became head of the family on his father's death, Lord George attempted some further reconciliation, although the use of the third person in his letter to his brother immediately conveys a certain distance: 'Lord George has nothing more at heart than to preserve that union in the family which he flatters himself now happily subsists, and he is sensible that any disagreement between Lord Middlesex and him will lessen the credit and consideration of them both. Lord George is resolved on his part to take every step that may prevent even the appearance of any misunderstanding, and trusts that he shall find the same friendly disposition in Lord Middlesex.'

They soon fell out, however, over the duke's will. Knole and the dukedom passed to the childless Charles as eldest son, but the duke had left much of the rest of his estate (other than that which had formed part of Charles's 1744 marriage settlement) to George for his life. George resisted any claims to the contrary from Charles. In any case, George had, at this stage, a clear interest in Knole either for himself or for one of his sons, should his twenty-year-old nephew, the future 3rd Duke, die without a male heir. Is that why George was so worried by the company Charles kept? His brother, he wrote in a letter to his friend General Irwin, was 'surrounded by . . . a set of bad people who are making him sign papers little to his credit and less to his advantage'. Lord George was doing all he could to prevent the mischief. He didn't want Charles marrying anyone unsuitable (Grace had died in 1763), and, in scenes reminiscent of the dying days of their grandfather Charles, the 6th Earl, sought legal opinion that the 2nd Duke was mentally incompetent to make a will.

Lord Shelburne reported that, towards the end of his life, Charles's appearance was that of 'a proud, disgusted, melancholy, solitary man', whose conduct was to 'savour strongly of madness, a disorder which there was too much reason to suppose, ran in the blood'. The history of the family – and their mental health – appeared to be following the course prescribed by the old verses: 'Folly and sense in Dorset's race,/Alternately do run.'

Charles died in 1769, aged fifty-seven, in a fit at his house in St James's Street, Piccadilly, 'having worn out,' according to Horace Walpole, 'his constitution and almost his estate. He has not left a tree standing in the venerable old park at Knole.' Lord George, who had raised some eyebrows by appearing at court before his brother had been buried, wrote, too late, to the steward at Knole, asking him to 'put an immediate stop to the cutting of any trees in the park'.

The diarist Lady Mary Coke was shocked by Charles's tree-cutting. 'The Duke of Dorset [Charles] is dead,' she wrote, 'and happy had it been if he had dyed three months ago, for since that time he has cut down all the wood in the Parke at Knowle, even the trees of his father's planting. How bad a use did he make of a very lively understanding – ruined himself, without doing any good to a single mortal!' Charles would have cut down the trees because it was a quick way to raise cash – and allowed by the trustees of his inheritance, in a way that selling land would not have been. But his actions must have seemed, at the time, a final act of patricide, a symbolic swipe at the trees planted by his father and at the whole aristocratic notion of hereditary responsibility for the land.

The bill for Charles's funeral survives: for 'two men dressing and laying out the corps (5 shillings)', for 'a strong elm coffin lined with fine quilt'd Persian (£4)', for 'the best velvet pall', for 'Eight Bearers to Move the Corps Early in the Morning', and so on, totalling £66 6s. As his cortège, a hearse, a mourning coach with a set of horses, led by six black-cloaked drivers, made its chilly way from London to Withyham, people must have wondered what would become of Knole: Charles had no legitimate male heir (just an illegitimate son, born a couple of years before his marriage), the estate was once again in debt, and Knole itself, that ancient pile, was once again little more than a curiosity adrift in a new age.

Chapter 7

A Grand Repository (1769–1799)

John Frederick Sackville, 3rd Duke of Dorset

Declining an invitation to Knole in 1791, the politician Edmund Burke wrote to John Frederick Sackville, 3rd Duke of Dorset:

> I who am something of a lover of all antiquities must be a very great admirer of Knowle. I think it the most interesting thing in England. It is pleasant to have preserved in one place the succession of the several tastes of ages; a pleasant habitation for the time, a grand repository of whatever has been pleasant at all times. This is not the sort of place which every banker, contractor or nabob can create at his pleasure. I am astonished to find so many of your rank of so bad a taste as to give up what distinguishes them, and to adopt what so many can do as well or better than they. I would not change Knowle if I were the D[uke] of Dorset for all the foppish structures of this enlightened age.

Knole is simply full of stuff. It is, indeed, a grand repository, and the ancestor as responsible as any other for this is John Frederick Sackville. John Frederick was only twenty-four, in August 1769, when he celebrated his succession to the dukedom with a feast for the county at Knole, 'at which sixty stones of beef, mutton and veal, a hogshead of strong beer, and five dozen of port at the servants' tables' were consumed. The 3rd Duke and his agents soon began to restore Knole and its estate, which his uncle had allowed to fall into disrepair. Parts of the roof were releaded, and new shelves and sash windows were added to the Library; sitting rooms along the south front, such as the Boudoir, were redecorated, giving them an airy eighteenth-century elegance which they still possess. In 1777 he built new hothouses for growing pineapples and other exotic plants, and he continued to replant the park, so that on a visit to Knole one beautiful late-September morning in 1794 Joseph Farington was marvelling in his diary at the fine order in which the park was kept, and in particular at its many magnificent beech trees – a complete contrast to the state of the place thirty years before.

But the 3rd Duke's greatest contribution to Knole was its art collection. In 1770, like his father, uncle and countless other young eighteenth-century aristocrats, he embarked on a Grand Tour of Italy, travelling to Rome, Naples, Florence and Venice. A notebook providing *An Account of the Number and Value of the Pictures, Busts etc.* records what he bought in Rome that year through the dealer, Thomas Jenkins, and his rival, James Byres, and in Venice in 1771 from Count Vitturi. His acquisitions included ancient marbles – for example, busts of Antinous and Pompey excavated by Gavin Hamilton at the Villa Adriana – and paintings by Garofalo, Teniers and Wouvermans that add spice to a collection which can appear overwhelmed by sombre, and slightly dingy, portraits.

The 3rd Duke was the only member of the Sackville family to create a collection of his own, rather than commissioning the odd portrait, or – as was the case with the 6th Earl – acquiring a collection through inheritance or the perks of public office. As well as the Old Master paintings from Italy, France and the Low Countries, the 3rd Duke was a prolific patron of contemporary painters, including John Opie, Ozias Humphry, George Romney, John Hoppner and Thomas Gainsborough. His particular favourite, though, was Sir Joshua Reynolds, who became a close friend and whose funeral he attended as a pall bearer in St Paul's Cathedral in 1792. By the time of the duke's death in 1799, there were twenty paintings by Reynolds at Knole, of which a dozen are still here. These include the fashionable 'fancy' pictures and the grand historical and mytho-logical paintings which, at the time, commanded prices far in excess of the portraits. When it was shown at the Royal Academy in 1773, Reynolds's most ambitious history painting, *Count Ugolino and his Children in the Dungeon*, excited more discussion than any other British picture. In it, Reynolds captures the gruesome moment when Ugolino realises that he will have to eat his own children who have died in prison beside him if he himself is not to starve to death as well. Two years after its first exhibition, the 3rd Duke paid 400 guineas for the painting.

This is more than he would have paid for the portraits he bought from Reynolds in the 1770s: the portrait of Wang-y-Tong, for example, a Chinese boy who had caught the duke's attention while in the service of an old schoolfriend on leave from the East India Company. The duke took Wang y Tong into his own household as a page and had him educated nearby at the grammar school in Sevenoaks. Sitting wistfully on a bamboo sofa, the square toes of his red shoes forming beautiful red highlights against the crimson and blue of his robes, Wang-y-Tong brings a touch of oriental exot-icism to Knole.

And it is more than the 150 guineas he paid for his own full-length portrait in peer's robes by Reynolds, which was painted in the year he inherited the title. Here is the devastatingly handsome man, whom the Duchess of Devonshire described in a letter to her mother, years before she herself had an affair with him, as 'the most dangerous of men . . . for with that beauty of his he is so unaffected, and has a simplicity and persuasion in his manner that makes one account very easily for the number of women he has had in love with him'.

Some of the smaller Old Master paintings acquired by the 3rd Duke now hang in Lady Betty Germain's suite of rooms, while many of the larger ones are in the private apartments. The 3rd Duke clearly enjoyed hanging pictures. It was a way of proclaiming to the world that he was a man of some refinement although, as Edmund Burke had noted, the duke always expressed his taste and that of his own generation within the context of an earlier house.

We know all this through the survival of an inventory of 1799, which catalogues the collection and its disposition within the 150 or so rooms then in use. The large portraits by Allan Ramsay of King George III and Queen Charlotte, which had been given to the 3rd Duke to represent their majesties in his embassy in Paris, took pride of place in the Great Hall, as did some of the larger Old Master paintings. In the more intimate setting of the Poets' Parlour, however, the duke self-consciously complemented the collections of his predecessors with portraits by Reynolds of his literary and theatrical contemporaries, Dr Johnson, Oliver Goldsmith, Samuel Foote and David Garrick. There is even a fine portrait of the duke himself by Gainsborough, dignified and sombre in style, and framed in an oval cartouche, that is reminiscent of a portrait painted 150 years earlier. It is an indication of the duke's respect for the age of his ancestors: a sentiment echoed in a 430-line poem addressed to the Duke of Dorset by a certain Revd Newburgh Burroughs in 1793:

> But when th' enamour'd eye excursive roves
> O'er Kent's rich plains and intermingled groves, . . .
> See with majestic pride, the work of years,
> Its rev'rend front the stately mansion rears,
> Within whose ample space the eye surveys
> The labor'd excellence of former days.

Particular works of art would have had a greater prominence then than they do now, for emotional as well as aesthetic reasons. The duke was as keen a collector of women as he was of art, and at least one of his conquests is represented in the collection. Accompanying him for a couple of years on his tour of France and Italy, which began in 1770, was the courtesan Nancy Parsons, otherwise known as Mrs Horton – 'the Duke of Grafton's Mrs Horton, the Duke of Dorset's Mrs Horton, everybody's Mrs Horton', as Horace Walpole described her (she had previously been the mistress of the Prime Minister, the Duke of Grafton). Walpole also elaborated how 'the charms of the young duke of Dorset had made impressions [on

Nancy] that seldom disturb the reason of professed courtesans. He was unusually handsome, was well made, and had an air of sentimental melancholy, which more than atoned with women for his want of sense. His silence had the air of amorous absence, and he looked so ready to sigh that it served him instead of sighing; it seeming charity to afford him that pity which he was formed to repay so delightfully.' The duke seemed equally taken with Nancy: there was even talk of their marrying. Lady Mary Coke disapproved, writing in her diary on Friday, 6 January 1769: 'I shou'd fear he must have the disorder of his Father [who had gone mad], to have done so shameful an action, for few people wou'd make a wife of a woman who had been the cast-off Mistress of so many other Men. For him, he deserves no pity, but for his Family I really grieve.' She could have spared herself, for the couple parted in 1773.

Next came Mrs Elizabeth Armistead – a well-known member of Mrs Goodby's upmarket establishment in Marlborough Street, and later the wife of the politician Charles James Fox – and Lady Elizabeth (Betty) Hamilton, both before and after her marriage to the Earl of Derby. Vita Sackville-West's mother Victoria claimed – improbably – that the 3rd Duke used to disguise himself as a gardener, working in the gardens at Knowsley Hall, the Derbys' country seat, by day, and climb through the windows of Lady Elizabeth's rooms at night. Elizabeth left her husband and children to go off with the duke. It was a public scandal, an offence 'against the laws of man and God', according to Lady Mary Coke – ever-ready with a note of censure – rather than a discreet, and therefore perfectly respectable, affair. 'It is imagined the Duke of Dorset will marry Lady Derby,' Lady Sarah Lennox wrote to her sister in February 1779. They never did, for although the Earl and Countess of Derby separated in 1779, the earl would not divorce his wife. She was ostracised, but not the Duke of Dorset, who continued to be friends with the earl and to be invited to Knowsley. There were even rumours, later, that the countess had borne the duke an illegitimate daughter.

But none of the 3rd Duke's lovers was as long-lasting as La Baccelli. Reclining voluptuously at the foot of the Great Staircase is a life-size plaster figure of a woman by John Baptist Locatelli. Light filters through the leaded windows of Thomas Sackville's open-well staircase, playing over her naked body. She props herself up, her elbows resting on tasselled pillows, and smiles with sleepy half-shut eyes. Her hair is piled high, but loose enough that a stray ringlet caresses the back of her neck. One breast, swelling slightly, sinks into the pillow; the modest folds of her stomach press into the rumpled sheets on the mattress on the floor, while the curve of her fleshy buttocks rises towards the Sackville leopard on the newel post. One leg is crossed over the other, the foot turned gracefully at the ankle.

She is a provocative presence in the midst of all those family portraits, a flash of fleeting sensuality in the midst of so much sobriety. Her nakedness is almost shocking as you stumble upon her, surrounded by all those well-dressed ladies and gentlemen in their fancy frocks and powdered wigs, ceremonial robes and wands of office. 'A good friend of the family' is how, as children, we heard her described by the National Trust guides at Knole.

Her full name, in fact, was Giovanna Francesca Antonia Guiseppe Zanerini, but she was better known by her stage name of La Baccelli (and as Jannette by the 3rd Duke himself). Born in Venice around 1753, she trained in France, where ballet masters such as Jean-Georges Noverre and Gaetan Vestris were transforming ballet into an art form independent of opera. La Baccelli made her English debut as the Rose in *Le Ballet des Fleurs* at the King's Theatre, Haymarket on 19 November 1774, and it was here that she caught the duke's eye. By 1779 she was his mistress and living for long periods at Knole. Baccelli bore the 3rd Duke a son, also called John Frederick Sackville, who was born around 1779 and brought up at Knole, the son of a gentleman. Scenes from their domestic life are revealed in the household accounts from this period: in the laundry bills for silk stockings, shifts, petticoats and drawers for Madame Baccelli, the bills for cat food, the payments for her son's wet-nurse and, later, for 'toys for Master Sackville': a drum, gingerbread, 'a pair of Spatterdashes', gloves, repairs to his watch, pocket money (from the age of eight) and, most significantly, 'butts and stumps – £0. 8s. 6d.' for playing cricket.

In 1783 an itinerant painter called Mr Almond painted portraits of the Knole staff, including La Baccelli's personal servants Daniel Taylor and Elinor Low, Philip Louvaux, Mrs Mary Edwards and Andrea Coronin, bringing, quite literally, a touch of domesticity to Knole. On a visit to the house in October that year Madame D'Arblay (Fanny Burney) complained in her diary that, although the Duke of Dorset was not at home, 'we were prevented seeing the Library, and two or three other modernised rooms because Madlle. Baccelli was not to be disturbed'. It is in this sunny suite of rooms on the south front – the Library, Music Room and Boudoir – that Baccelli's spell still lingers, her stay at Knole still remembered in the name of Shelley's Tower (a corruption of Baccelli) that rises beside these rooms.

La Baccelli was charming, beautiful and, by all accounts, sweet natured and 'generally respected for her benevolence'. The duke had her painted by Gainsborough in 1782, and the following year by Reynolds, but the portraits are very different. Gainsborough's full-length of Baccelli, described when exhibited at the Royal Academy of Arts in 1782 as like 'the Original, light airy and elegant', is the portrait of an artist. It captures the dancer mid-movement, her pointed right toe poised in a pool of light in the foreground while, in a moment of perfect equilibrium, she stretches her left arm to hold the hem of a skirt cascading down her figure. The Reynolds, on the other hand, is the portrait of a courtesan. Her hair wreathed in vine leaves, she is depicted as a Bacchante, a follower of the ancient god of wine. But the oval face, olive eyes and long nose are unmistakably those of La Baccelli, as she glances at you sideways over her bare shoulder, that stray lock of hair, curling down her back, and, with a carnival mask in her right hand, invites you on to the revels.

In rooms such as the Boudoir, there is a sensuality that simmers beneath the surface of a generally strait-laced Knole. The 3rd Duke was an admirer of Reynolds's so-called 'fancy' pictures, with their sexual innuendo, and – among several others – he acquired one, which was then known as Lesbia, after the lover of Catullus, the Roman poet. Catullus had devoted twenty-five poems to Lesbia, including one on the death of her pet sparrow, and there in the painting, perched on the shoulder of a minxy-looking girl, is a sparrow – a symbol at the time of lechery and promiscuity. While her right hand feeds the sparrow, her left hand rests on a gilded birdcage – an allusion, commonly understood at the time, to captive love.

In 1783 the 3rd Duke was appointed British Ambassador to the Court of Louis XVI in Paris. That year the *Whitehall Evening Post* observed that, 'In the estimation of many people, the Duke of Dorset is the most extraordinary accomplished nobleman we have – at cricket, tennis and billiards his Grace has hardly any equal.' Each summer the duke returned to England for several months, possibly for the cricket – giving rise to the caricature in *The Prophecies of Delphos* (1791) as 'a most admirable cricket-player – more cannot be said of him as he is not in possession of any brains'.

The duke even tried to introduce cricket to France, *The Times* reporting in 1787 that 'horse-racing is already on the wane in France, as it is in England. Cricket, on the recommendation of the Duke of Dorset, is taking its place, and making a far better use of the turf.' The newspaper also claimed that the duke had presented the Queen with a cricket bat which she 'kept in her closet'. Who knows, had he succeeded – and had the social historian G. M. Trevelyan's claim that 'If the French *noblesse* had been capable of playing cricket with their peasants [as the English aristocracy and their tenants and labourers did], their chateaux would never have been burnt' proved right – the French Revolution might never have happened?

Until the final days of the ancien régime, when his accounts of the French Revolution assume a personal drama, the duke's dispatches are full of gossip – Montgolfier's hot-air balloon, the affair of the Queen's stolen necklace – or they describe the fulfilment of commissions to supply Marie Antoinette with English gloves (which he continued to do after his recall from Paris). Ministers in London were so exasperated by the stream of trivia that the Foreign Secretary Lord Carmarthen was forced in 1784 to write to Dorset's second-in-command in Paris, Daniel Hailes, begging him, 'For Heaven's sake', to 'have pity upon the Department, and either prevail upon our friend the duke to write something worth our Master's [King George III's] perusal, or else suppose your principal absent, and let your own zeal and abilities have fair play. Consider for a moment the importance of the present moment.' For Horace Walpole, 'our Ambassador at Paris' was a 'proverb of insufficience'.

In fact, there is a world-weariness to many of his letters. On 8 March 1787 he complained to the Duchess of Devonshire:

All the French are *aimable si vous voulez*, but they are capricious and inconstant, especially the women – in short I have really no friend here but Mrs B. [short for Mrs Bourbon, the French Queen, Marie Antoinette] and then I see her so seldom that I forget half what I want to say to her. The Frenchmen are all jealous and treacherous for they tell everything to one another so that between the capriciousness of the fair sex and the want I have of confidence in the other *je me sens vraiment malheureux* – I assure you my dear Duchess this is a true picture of my feelings, *mon ambassade m'ennuie* I feel there is very little pleasure in serving an ungrateful minister . . . I suppose you will hear talk of my ball it has made a great noise at Paris . . . I am spending at the rate of near £11,000 a year . . . for to do honour to those who have never shown me the smallest mark of attention or civility.

The ease and insouciance, the self-deprecation that people had found so charming in his youth, masked a deep-seated vanity in the 3rd Duke that became ever-pricklier with age. This was particularly clear in his anxious attempts to be made a Knight of the Garter. In a letter to the Prime Minister, William Pitt, dated 20 October 1786, he presented his credentials: 'my fortune tho' not great (considering my rank) is quite sufficient to keep up the dignity of my title; my parliamentary interest is independent, it being my own property, and my interest in both the Counties of Kent and Sussex are sufficiently considerable, in the former to turn the scale in favour of a friend, and in the latter I could carry a great number of votes owing to my being possessed of one of the most considerable estates in that county.' He then referred to a conversation with the Prime Minister the previous year, when Pitt had told him that he 'saw no person who had a better right than myself to the Garter'. Imagine, then, how 'amazed and hurt' he had been when others had been created in his place: 'But I will not, indeed I cannot dwell upon it; it is too humiliating for me to think any man, let his property be what it may, ought to stand in competition with me, when I consider the zeal and earnestness with which I have *invariably in every instance* given you my support . . . in the eyes of the world I can have no competitor . . . I know the King has some regard for me, and I am almost certain were you to mention me to him in a real friendly way, but what he would comply with my request.'

Dorset was eventually made a Knight of the Garter in 1787. The following year La Baccelli shocked Horace Walpole by dancing at the Paris Opéra with 'a blue bandeau on her forehead, inscribed *Honi soit qui mal y pense*' – the Order of the Garter that the 3rd Duke had recently received.

The duke's dispatches also recorded the extravagance of the French court, and the growing opposition to the royal family and its attempts to raise taxes. In his letters to Georgiana, Duchess of Devonshire, he detailed the concerns of Mr and Mrs Brown [or Bourbon, the King and Queen of France], reporting that, as popular uprisings gathered pace, Mrs Brown was 'amazingly out of spirits'.

The round of balls, receptions and lavish entertainment came to an abrupt end with the French Revolution in 1789, although as late as 9 July, five days before the fall of the Bastille, the duke was asking William Pitt: 'If I find my presence not absolutely necessary here, I shall avail myself of my congé about the latter end of this month if you have no objection to my coming away about that time.'

Events overtook him. On 14 July the duke wrote to Lord Carmarthen, now Duke of Leeds, announcing that 'the greatest revolution that we know anything of has been effected with, comparatively speaking – if the magnitude of the event is considered – the loss of very few lives. From this moment we may consider France as a free country, the king a very limited monarch, and the nobility as reduced to a level with the rest of the nation.' The mood, however, became increasingly Anglophobic – partly as a reaction to Marie Antoinette's love of all things English – and the duke had on one occasion to sword-fight his way through a mob besieging the British embassy. In early August, he scuttled back to England.

The whole experience shocked him deeply, and confirmed in him a deep-seated horror of the French – particularly after the execution of Marie Antoinette. 'I hope you will not return by that vile country [France],' he wrote in a letter to Georgiana, Duchess of Devonshire, in 1792. 'I begin to hate the name of the country as I lose having *any* opinion of *any* of the inhabitants. They are almost all intriguing, low, artful and treacherous people . . . We must *take care* or else democracy will gain ground.'

La Baccelli had made her debut as a guest ballerina at the Paris Opéra in 1782, and had accompanied the duke to France for some of his posting the following year. He and his embassy were later described as 'arrogant and haughty, ignorant and illiterate . . . Under his roof fiddlers and buffoons, w--res and parasites, sharpers and knaves were always welcome . . . Billiards and hazard engrossed almost the whole time of our A-b------r – unless when he relaxed from the fatigues of gaming in the arms of beauty.'

By 1785, La Baccelli was a star, and her comings and goings were reported in the gossip columns with much the same interest as a celebrity today. The *Morning Herald and Daily Advertiser* noted on 9 February that 'Madame Baccelli lives in great splendour in Paris, and no lady more truly deserves good fortune than herself. Her house is the resort of all the fashionable English in that gay metropolis and it is the chief pleasure and study of her life to shew her gratitude to our nation for the protection with which she was honoured by our nobility.'

But the duke generally had several women on the go at any one time. That same year he had begun a short affair, in Paris, with Lady Elizabeth Foster, the mistress of the Duke of Devonshire, with whose child she was pregnant. After a brief interlude the following year, 1786, with Mademoiselle Gervais, another dancer at the Paris Opéra, the 3rd Duke, not content with Devonshire's mistress, moved in on his friend's wife, Georgiana. He wrote her several letters a week from Paris, flirting with her and flattering her with his inside accounts of events in France and, on one occasion, even asking her to promote La Baccelli: 'I must tell you the Baccelli will soon be in London. I don't wish you to do anything for her openly, but I hope *que quand il s'agit de ses talens* you will recommend her. I assure you she is *une bonne fille very clever and un excellent Coeur*, her dancing is really wonderful.'

The 3rd Duke's letters to the duchess were heavily censored by her descendants in the nineteenth century – with any endearments obliterated. In letters to her family and friends, Georgiana referred to Dorset as the 'Pride', an allusion to his vanity, and broke off the affair in the summer of 1788, writing to Lady Melbourne: 'When the Duke of Dorset returned, he express'd great misery at the idea of my having, without any cause of his side, spoken to him in an angry and harsh manner, especially as he was ready to give up every wish to mine, to be contented with seeing me and being on a friendly footing with me – he was particularly shocked at the idea of my forbidding him Chatsworth, at the time when he gave up to me what he said was the greatest sacrifice a man could make me.'

The following year, she wrote to her mother, Lady Spencer, who had always been worried by Georgiana's attachment to such a serial seducer: 'You have no need to fear the Duke of Dorset. The complexion of the times is such that we can scarcely see him at all.' In any case, Dorset had already told Georgiana that he intended to marry the first heiress who would have him. There were also reports in the newspapers of 1789 that he was to marry Miss Coutts, the daughter of the wealthy banker, and that the 'lady's father will make the Grace an opulent man'.

From 1787, La Baccelli had been having an affair with Henry Herbert, the 10th Earl of Pembroke, although she was still on good terms with the duke. In 1789, Baccelli left Knole for good, one newspaper reporting in December that 'the Duke of Dorset and the Baccelli have just separated, and she is said to have behaved very well'.

In the great tradition of his forebears – indeed of many aristocratic families – the duke decided to settle down to a respectable marriage with an heiress. The series of Sackville brides – Clifford, Curzon, Compton, Colyear – continued with Cope, Arabella, one of two

HIRLEY TEMPLE'S

BIRTHDAY
BOOK

ERYTHING
COLOR !

Paper Dolls and Dresses · Toys · Puzzles
Cut-Outs · and over 40 Pictures of Shi

1.25

In 1604, the first year of his ownership of Knole, Thomas Sackville attended a conference at Somerset House in London to discuss peace with the Spanish. He is seated (*top right*), facing the Spanish and Flemish delegates. On Thomas's side of the table, the English delegates include Robert Cecil (*near right*), his successor as Lord Treasurer and the builder of Hatfield House, a palace as splendid as Knole.

The richness of Knole's interior decoration was designed to celebrate the wealth, taste and learning of Thomas Sackville. A carved wooden frieze of mermaids and mermen runs along the top of the walls in the Great Chamber (*top*); the marble chimneypieces designed by Cornelius Cure, such as the one in the Reynolds Room (*above right*), are masterpieces of Renaissance sculpture; and the painted surfaces of the Great Staircase (*above left*) depict the four ages of man, the five senses, and the triumph of virtue over vice. As important as any of these allegories, however, were the symbols that announced to the world that the Sackville family had finally arrived: the heraldic Sackville leopards on the newel posts; and the initials TD (for Thomas Sackville, Earl of Dorset) stamped, with an earl's coronet, on lead drainpipes all over the house.

Lady Anne Clifford (*above*, by William Larkin) spent ten, mostly miserable, years at Knole in the early seventeenth century, married to the feckless, fashion-conscious Richard Sackville, 3rd Earl of Dorset (*top right, also by Larkin*). As her diary of life at Knole records, Richard used the threat of separation and custody of their beloved daughter Margaret (*right*, by Paul van Somer) in his attempts to get his wife to sign her fortune over to him. Vita Sackville-West saw in the tightening of Anne's mouth and the watchfulness of her gaze the strengths that enabled her to resist her husband's demands.

With his gleaming breastplate, scarlet doublet and the key of office as Lord Chamberlain to King Charles I hanging on a ribbon from his waist, Edward Sackville, 4th Earl of Dorset (studio of Van Dyck) was, according to Vita Sackville-West, the 'embodiment of Cavalier romance'.

Loyalty to the King resulted in the sequestration of Edward's estates, the occupation of Knole by parliamentary troops, and – most grievous of all – the gratuitous murder by a Cromwellian soldier of his younger son Edward (the boy, with the fair curls, on the right of this double portrait by Cornelius de Neve).

Edward's older son and heir, Richard Sackville (the boy on the left of the double portrait, *facing page*) gradually restored the family fortunes – partly through a strategic marriage to the heiress Frances Cranfield (*left*, by Anthony Van Dyck). Their union was fertile, if occasionally fractious, producing thirteen children of whom six reached maturity.

On either side of the marble tomb in the family chapel at Withyham in Sussex, the final resting place of at least a dozen generations of Sackvilles, the two kneeling parents, Richard, the 5th Earl, and Frances mourn the death, aged twelve, of their favourite youngest child, Thomas, who lies on top of the tomb clutching a skull.

Restoration rake, patron of poets and playwrights, 'the Maecenas of his age', Charles Sackville, 6th Earl of Dorset (*left*, by Sir Godfrey Kneller), acquired for Knole the unique collection of Stuart furniture that has come to define the house today.

One of the perquisites of his office as Lord Chamberlain to King William III, from 1689 to 1697, was the disposal of unwanted furniture from the roy palaces, such as the X-framed chair of state (*left*). The royal provenance of some of the chair was confirmed by the discovery, on the webbing beneath the seat of inventory stamps, such as 'H(1661' (*above*) for 'Hampton Cou

Other 'perks' included the richly carved and gilded royal state bed in the King's Room. When this bed was restored in the 1970s and 1980s, each of its six curtains involved around 9,000 hours of conservation work.

Knole was at its most magnificent in the eighteenth century, as the Sackville family continued its steady rise – in terms of wealth, office and title. Lionel Sackville (*right*, by Kneller) was promoted from Earl to Duke of Dorset. Money was spent, conspicuously, on the mansion and its grounds. In a topographical engraving (*below*, by Jan Kip), avenues of trees radiate proudly from the house, the centre of power, out across the park.

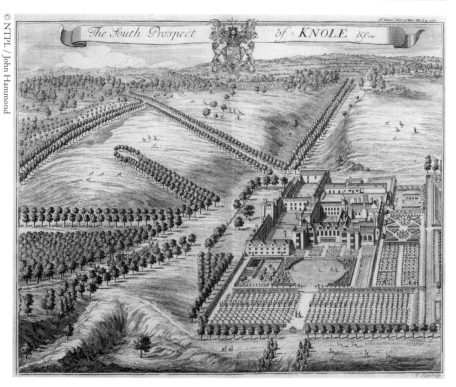

The South Prospect of KNOLE &c.

Inside, the house was transformed into a place for entertainment, its state rooms adapted to suit the social requirements of the eighteenth-century assembly. The Colonnade (*above*), one of the most beautiful rooms in the whole of Knole, was glazed, and its walls decorated with trompe l'oeil arches and niches containing giant urns. The Great Chamber became the Ballroom, and was candle-lit from gilt sconces (*above right*), bearing the Duke's coronet and Garter, to a design by William Kent.

By the 1760s, the 1st Duke's party-loving eldest son, Charles (*left*, by Rosalba Carriera) – note the carnival masque in his cocked hat – had, according to Horace Walpole, 'worn out his condition and almost his estate. He has not left a tree standing in the venerable old park at Knole.'

John Frederick Sackville, 3rd Duke of Dorset, was the first serious Sackville art collector. As well as Old Masters acquired on a Grand Tour of Italy, he was a prolific patron of contemporary painters. In 1769, the year he inherited the dukedom, he commissioned a full-length portrait of himself in peer's robes by Sir Joshua Reynolds (*left*). Here is the devastatingly handsome man, described by the Duchess of Devonshire as 'the most dangerous of men'. He also commissioned from Reynolds a portrait of Wang-y-Tong, his Chinese page-boy, bringing a touch of oriental exoticism to Knole (*below*).

From Thomas Gainsborough he commissioned a full-length portrait of his mistress, the Italian dancer Giovanna Baccelli (*left*), who lived with him at Knole for several years in the 1780s and bore him a son. Like 'the Original, light airy and elegant', is how the portrait was described when exhibited at the Royal Academy of Arts in 1782.

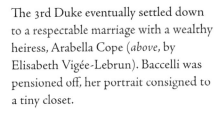

The 3rd Duke eventually settled down to a respectable marriage with a wealthy heiress, Arabella Cope (*above*, by Elisabeth Vigée-Lebrun). Baccelli was pensioned off, her portrait consigned to a tiny closet.

Their son and heir, George, the 4th Duke (by George Sandars) was killed in a hunting accident soon after his twenty-first birthday, at which point 'the very name of Sackville' appeared 'to be near extinction'.

When Mortimer, 1st Lord Sackville, attempted to close the park at Knole to visitors, a crowd of more than 1,000 people from Sevenoaks broke down the posts he had placed across the entrance and, singing 'Rule Britannia', marched on the house. The 'tumultuous' proceedings were reported in the *Penny Pictorial News* on 28 June 1884.

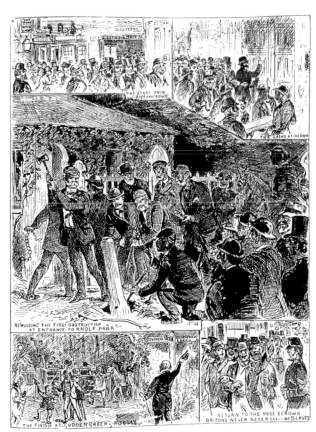

In the 1860s, my great-great uncle Lionel (*above*) raised a secret family in France with his mistress, a Spanish dancer known as Pepita (*above right*). When Lionel, who had never married, unexpectedly inherited in 1888, he brought two of his three illegitimate daughters to Knole.

The eldest daughter Victoria (*left* and *above*) had, by the end of her first year in England, met and married her first cousin, the heir to Knole, another Lionel Sackville-West (*left*). By doing so, she effectively legitimised her name and became mistress of Knole. Victoria owed her Mediterranean looks and her lustrous, hip-length hair to her mother.

By the turn of the nineteenth century, Knole was a magnificent place to enjoy a lavish weekend house party. From the living rooms on the south front, guests could flow through French windows out into the garden. In this photograph of a visit made by the Prince and Princess of Wales to Knole in July 1898, the six-year-old Vita Sackville-West holds Princess Alexandra's hand. Her mother, Victoria (*seated, second on the left, next to the Prince of Wales*) leans forward slightly, looking on anxiously.

Despite Victoria's many home improvements – she claimed that she had 'made Knole the most comfortable large house in England, uniting the beauties of Windsor Castle with the comforts of the Ritz' – Knole still had a fussy Victorian feel at the end of the nineteenth century, with knick-knacks cluttering every surface of the Boudoir (*above left*). Some of the exteriors – the Pheasant Court, for example (*above right*) – had a similarly overgrown, forlorn look.

On 16 February 1910, Lionel and Victoria, with their daughter Vita, returned to Knole in style after winning the High Court action over the disputed Sackville succession. They rode through Sevenoaks in a horse-drawn victoria. At the top of the drive, a triumphal arch welcomed them home, the horses were led away, and the victoria was then pulled by members of the local fire brigade through the park.

Later that year, aged eighteen, Vita was painted at Knole by Philip de Laszlo.

Vita's lover, Virginia Woolf, first visited Knole in 1924. Here she is with Vita's sons, Nigel and Ben. One of Nigel's many memories of Virginia is captured perfectly by this photograph: 'I think of her at Knole, leaning S-curved against a doorway, finger to her chin, contemplative, amused. She instinctively assumed attitudes expressive of her moods.'

As a caricature of 1936 (*above left*) reveals, my golf-playing great-uncle Charlie and his son, the music critic, writer and all-round aesthete Eddy, were very different in character. Their relationship was further complicated by the fact that Eddy disliked his stepmother, Anne (*above right*, with Charlie). Eddy never cared that much for Knole either, describing it as 'that big place in Kent' and eventually settling in Ireland. The portrait of Eddy (*left*) by Graham Sutherland was described by his cousin, the art historian Benedict Nicolson as a 'magnificent image of controlled distress'.

Knole residents and members of the estate staff assemble in front of the house to clear up after the storm of 1987: my father Hugh is on the far left; my uncle Lionel in a cloth cap and carrying a walking stick in the centre.

The Retainers' Gallery is now in better shape than it was at the time this photograph was taken in the 1980s. There is always a delicate balance between preserving the magic of a place where you can still make discoveries and not allowing it to fall into decay. On the right of this photograph, you can just see one of the discoveries, a Boulle cabinet, its pieces of tortoiseshell and brass marquetry slowly flaking onto the floor. It was very nearly consigned to a skip during a periodic clear-out of the attics, but was rescued instead, and went on to sell for over £1 million at Christie's, paying for the restoration of the park after the devastating storm of 1987.

daughters of Sir Charles Cope, who had died in 1781 leaving estates in Staffordshire and Oxfordshire in trust. In January 1790, the duke married Arabella, who came into her estates, worth £140,000, at the age of twenty-one later that year. The statue of La Baccelli was banished to 'the Top of the Stairs, next the Wardrobe', according to an inventory of 1799. Here, described starkly as 'A Naked Venus, whole length, plaister', she spent the following century gathering dust in an attic. A similar fate befell Gainsborough's full-length portrait of Baccelli, which is recorded in an inventory of 1864 as hanging in the King's Closet, a room far too small to allow the picture to be viewed properly: it was sold in 1890, a hundred years after Baccelli had left Knole, by the 3rd Duke's grandson, Lionel. At some point, even the fancy picture of the minxy-looking girl by Reynolds, known as Lesbia, was retitled 'Robinetta' [little robin], thereby removing all the saucy significance of the sparrow.

The duke had in 1785 settled an annuity of £400 a year on Baccelli for life, charged to property in Withyham and Hartfield. In preparation, perhaps, for his marriage plans, the charge was transferred in 1789 to property in Warwickshire and Gloucestershire, a more discreet distance from the Sackville estates and final resting place in Sussex. This little piece of tidying-up, of financial housekeeping, had a similar sanitising effect as the removals and redesignations around the house. The reordering of history continues to this day. One of the pleasures of living at Knole, as it was for the 3rd Duke, is the opportunity to hang and rehang pictures, to unmake the more censorious moves of previous generations. You can begin to reintroduce characters who would not necessarily have felt at ease beside each other at the time, placing the portrait of a wife next to a mistress, a first husband next to a second: a reunion in retrospect of a mildly dysfunctional family.

Arabella bore the duke three children: Mary, a legitimate male heir, George, and Elizabeth. But contemporary accounts of the duke's ill temper during the 1790s make rather dismal reading. He had suffered a small stroke in 1785. 'You hardly ever saw any Person more alter'd than he is, – he has a catching in his right Eye, as if he had had a paralytic stroke, and in order to conceal it he constantly carries a Handkerchief to his Face', wrote William Humphry to his father, Ozias. He was also beginning to suffer from the depression that had dogged his father to his dying day in Switzerland. The disappointment with life had begun to turn to disgust. Like his ancestors and like at least two of his grandsons, he was sinking into a slow, reclusive despair at Knole, the victim of a rogue gene that eventually robbed him of his mind.

The man who had claimed to spend around £11,000 a year while in Paris (well in excess of his official salary, and much of it on the opera) and who had gambled up to 1,000 guineas on the result of a single cricket match, was now worried about money. He fretted massively when the painter John Hoppner, who was staying at Knole to paint the couple's three children, won 15 shillings off him at a game of cassino. Pride in his family and in their place were losing all sense of proportion. 'He cannot bear to hear other places described as beautiful,' Joseph Farington reported in his diary; 'Knowle, he considers as possessing everything . . . The Duchess is a woman of most excellent temper, and is unmoved by the duke's peevishness; never seeming to be discomposed.' Farington also reported that another painter, Nathaniel Dance, had found the duke 'Humoursome & uncomfortable' on a visit to Knole, 'not suffering the dinner to be all placed on the table – the Duchess feels the inconvenience of it but prudently submits'. The duchess was in her late twenties at the time, married to a decaying roué more than twenty years her senior. Shortly before his death, 'his faculties were so entirely gone, & he was so much debilitated, that He was fed like a child, & did not even know the Duchess'. He did, however, have occasional flashes of recall. In 1798, Joseph Farington recorded how the duke passed the funeral procession of his former lover Lady D[erby] at Bromley and, on being told whose it was, 'turned pale and fainted'.

The 3rd Duke died on 19 July 1799, aged fifty-four, after a long period, according to Nathaniel Wraxall, 'of intellectual decay or mental alienation', during which for 'nearly twenty months, the duchess, his wife, discharged towards him, in a most exemplary manner, every conjugal duty and office'.

La Baccelli, who had settled in Sackville Street, London, with a Mr James Carey after the death of Henry Herbert in 1794, died two years after the duke, in May 1801. She had suffered 'a most lingering and painful illness', according to the *Morning Chronicle*, 'which she bore with the most exemplary resignation and with that sweetness of temper which rendered her so attractive in the days of her youth and beauty'. She left an estate of around £6,000 and died surrounded by her treasured possessions: paintings and prints of herself and her two noble lovers; a bird cage which she left with the birds inside to the care of her faithful servant and friend Mrs Edwards; and some 'cups of the late Queen of France', a memento of her years in Paris with the duke.

And what of the other loose ends? After La Baccelli had left Knole in 1789, her son John Frederick stayed on in the big house and went to school in Sevenoaks. He joined the 69th (South Lincolnshire) Regiment of Foot as a lieutenant; and died of a 'deadly fever' – probably yellow fever – in Port-au-Prince, Santo Domingo, on Christmas Eve, 1796. Before leaving for the West Indies, however, he too had had an illegitimate son – by Amy Skoulding, the daughter of a pastry cook in Bury St Edmunds. The young boy, who was to be called Sackville Sackville, was disowned by his aristocratic family, but remembered by his grandmother, Baccelli, in her will. After Baccelli's death, he was sent to school in Lowestoft where he proved a poor student, his manners apparently 'quite neglected', his accent provincial. It was a trajectory so different from that of the 3rd Duke's other grandsons, including my own great-grandfather. Sackville Sackville joined the army of the East India Company and died of a 'remittent fever' in Ceylon in 1815. Despite the double declaration of his ancestry in his name, Sackville Sackville died thousands of miles from the ducal home, a doubly illegitimate, inconvenient and disinherited son.

Edmund Burke was absolutely right, Knole really is a grand repository of stuff: of statues and paintings, of scraps of paper, bills, letters, accounts, 'the succession of the several tastes of ages'. But the significance of these objects lies not just in the objects themselves, but also in the buried memories they recall, the fleeting moments, the fugitive figures. A payment record in an accounts book for a cricket bat and stumps brings back a summer's afternoon in the 1780s, when a beautiful Italian ballerina – in a snapshot of surprising domestic intimacy – plays cricket in the gardens at Knole with her illegitimate son John. An inventory of 1799, listing a statue recently consigned to the attics, recalls the fate of a mistress pensioned off and, for the time being at least, removed from the record. And a series of letters tells the short life story of an illegitimate Sackville dying from disease in the East Indies, joining the ranks of those family members who were let go.

Chapter 8

'The very name of Sackville . . . near extinction' (1799–1888)

The Dowager Duchess and Her Descendants

On 15 November 1814 the young duke's coming of age was celebrated with parties at Knole and Buckhurst. Church bells rang from Sevenoaks to Seal, from four in the afternoon till late at night, bonfires blazed in the park, and a band played during and after dinner. As Thomas Neill, the steward at Knole, reported to the Dowager Duchess, Arabella, who was in Ireland at the time, 'Beef and Bread were distributed to 3,673 persons and it gave me great pleasure to observe the uniform feeling and gratitude that pervaded the whole of the poor people for their benefactor.'

All in all, the celebrations at Knole were a great success, 'notwithstanding that there were upwards of forty persons at one time laid upon straw in the Bishop's Stable, who were unable to move further without a little repose, they were chiefly composed of the working people at Knole, and as we expected they would make pretty free with the ale, we arranged matters so that those who could not walk home with safety, should be taken to the stable until they recovered the use of their legs'.

The object of these celebrations had been painted shortly before his birthday by the portraitist, George Sandars. The 4th Duke of Dorset was a handsome young man, with a pink-and-white complexion, and fair, curly hair. He had recently become engaged to Elizabeth Thynne, daughter of the Marquis of Bath, and hopes for this dynastic union ran high.

Within three months, however, the young duke was dead. He had accompanied his parents to Ireland where his stepfather, Lord Whitworth, was viceroy, and had gone to stay with a former schoolfriend Lord Powerscourt, near Dublin. On 14 February 1815 he went out hunting on a lively Irish mare. Just as they were about to return home after several uneventful hours in the field, a hare sprang up and they gave chase. The duke jumped a wall, but on the far side the ground sloped and the mare's front feet slipped on the large stones. The horse fell headlong, turned over and landed on her rider, crushing his spine.

The duke's body was brought back from Ireland to Knole, and laid to rest at Withyham. A ducal coronet, like the one beside which he had posed so proudly, hand on hip, in the Sandars portrait a few months before, now rested on his coffin. 'His premature death was by two Nations, Deplored as a publick calamity', according to the inscription in the Sackville Chapel. At Knole, the long-necked rocking horse that has traditionally been assumed to be his, and which was passed down through generations of children including Vita, serves as a poignant reminder of his life and as an eerie premonition of his death.

The poet Lord Byron described in a letter to his friend Tom Moore how 'very much shocked – or, rather, ought to be' he was by the death of the Duke of Dorset. 'We were at school together, and then I was passionately attached to him ... there was a time in my life when this event would have broken my heart; and all I can say for it now is that – it is not worth breaking.' The young duke had been Byron's fag at Harrow School, and had accompanied the poet on 'rambles through the neighbouring country'. He had even had a poem dedicated to him about the dangers of wealth: 'Thee, on whose head a few short years will shower/The gift of riches, and the pride of power' should not be seduced by the flattery of 'passive tutors' or 'youthful parasites' – but should look to his ancestors and uphold their glory and fame.

Such a glorious future was not to be. With the death of the 4th

Duke, the connection between Knole and the Dorset title, which stretched back over two centuries to Thomas Sackville, came to an end. The dukedom of Dorset (but not the property) passed back up the family tree and then down again to Lord George's eldest son, Charles Sackville-Germain, who became 5th Duke of Dorset. Charles had inherited Drayton, Lady Betty Germain's 5,000-acre estate in Northamptonshire, from his father, and Dorchester House, a magnificent house in Park Lane, from his aunt.

Even the connection between Knole and the name of Sackville became increasingly tenuous. Vita herself devoted no more than a couple of pages in her book *Knole and the Sackvilles*, first published in 1922, to the years after 1815. It is something of an irony that, in an inheritance determined, in theory, by male primogeniture, Knole was, between 1815 and 1870, owned and run – very capably – by women, and more particularly by women whose married name was not Sackville.

The 4th Duke's mother, Arabella, had in fact been running the Sackville estates since the death of her first husband, the 3rd Duke, in 1799. The 3rd Duke had left Knole and his estates to his widow for life, and then to his son – or failing that, to his two daughters. When the 4th Duke was killed, Charles Sackville-Germain searched for legal loopholes in the 3rd Duke's will, in the hope that he could inherit the lands as well as the Dorset title. But these attempts came to nothing, and Arabella – partly through this inheritance and partly on her own account – became a wealthy woman, with extensive estates in Kent, Sussex, Essex, Oxfordshire, Gloucestershire, Warwickshire, Derbyshire and Staffordshire. In the last years of the 3rd Duke's life, there had been some consolidation around Knole, with the acquisition of properties that remained at the core of the Knole estate into the twentieth century: Stake Farm in Godden Green, Blackhall Farm which became the Home Farm supplying goods to Knole House, Bow Petts, and land in Fawke Common, Stone Street and Bitchett. In 1795 the 3rd Duke had also acquired the Sussex estates around Buckhurst of his uncle, Lord George Sackville.

These estates had been yielding more and more. Over the second half of the eighteenth century, there had been a general increase in rental incomes. This accelerated during the Napoleonic Wars, when rents doubled, tracking (through the rack-rent system, which allowed landlords to take full and immediate advantage of rising prices) the inflationary rise in grain prices.

Arabella was a good businesswoman. According to the memoirist Nathaniel Wraxall: 'Her person, though not feminine, might then be denominated handsome, and if her mind was not highly cultivated or refined, she could boast of intellectual endowments that fitted her for the active business of life. Under the dominion of no passion except the love of money, her taste for power and pleasure was always subordinate to her economy ... So great an accumulation of wealth and of parliamentary influence had rarely ever vested among us in a female and a widow.'

Wraxall had his own reasons for such faint praise of Arabella. His parliamentary career having come to an end in 1794, when he lost his seat as MP for Hindon in Wiltshire, he was forced to cast around for other means of support. Lord George Sackville introduced him to his nephew, the 3rd Duke, and Wraxall, spotting an opportunity, perhaps, to find permanent employment as the duke's librarian, proposed a plan for arranging and publishing the more important papers at Knole. In 1797, he set to work among the papers which had for years lain in a great tumbled mess 'in a chamber at the top of the house [Bourchier's Tower]' – papers which, now catalogued and meticulously cared for at the Centre for Kentish Studies in Maidstone, have provided so much of the material for this book.

What Wraxall particularly hoped to find was literary correspondence and anecdotes from the time of Charles Sackville, 6th Earl of Dorset: the twitter of Restoration poets and playwrights so popular at the time 'for gratifying and elegant entertainment'. Wraxall's search proved fruitless, and in the process he contributed considerably to the disorder of the manuscripts in the Muniments Room. When he dragged a document, almost at random, from the pile and it didn't suit his purpose, he penned a cross and – horrifying archivists today with his amateurishness – wrote 'Of no use', 'Business matters' or simply 'Curious' on it, before tossing it aside. On those that he found more interesting, he expounded at length on the back, providing rather banal historical commentary.

Nevertheless, according to Wraxall, the duchess encouraged him to continue his researches after the duke's death; and to this end, he carried off a number of the papers from Knole to his house in Frant, near Tunbridge Wells. A year after the duke's death, the duchess demanded the return of the papers, but Wraxall refused, claiming payment for work which he said he had been commissioned by the duke to do upon them. At arbitration in 1801, it was agreed that Wraxall should bring the papers back to Knole in return for a ransom of £700, which he did on 22 February 1802.

The disagreement between Wraxall and Arabella partly explains his persistent bitchiness towards members of the Sackville family in his *Memoirs*, which were published after his death and brought him a degree of distinction, albeit posthumous, that far exceeded his reputation as a politician or an archivist. But there are accounts by others, too, of Arabella's squabbles over money: with the painter Ozias Humphry, for example, for non-payment for copies of some family portraits at Knole, which the painter claimed the duchess had commissioned, but which she denied.

There is even a slightly chilly account by the French painter Elisabeth Vigée-Lebrun of a visit to Knole, when the duchess was sitting for her portrait:

> The first time we met for dinner, the duchess said to me: 'I'm afraid this will be terribly boring for you: you see we never talk at dinner.' I reassured her on this point, saying that I was used to this since I had eaten alone for many years. She must have been very entrenched in this habit for during dessert, her son [the 4th Duke], then aged about eleven or twelve, came over to her, and spoke very briefly to her; eventually she dismissed him without the slightest mark of affection. I could not help recalling what I had been told about the English – they care little for their children once grown, and only love little babies.

In April 1801, two years after her husband's death, the thirty-one-year-old Dowager Duchess of Dorset married Charles Whitworth, then aged forty-eight. Whitworth's early career was 'more distinguished ... by success in gallantries than by any professional merits', according to Wraxall, who goes on to describe how he was forced by the financially embarrassed circumstances in which his father had left him to leave the army for a career in the corps diplomatique. There may, indeed, have been something of the adventurer about Whitworth. Wraxall repeats a rumour, referred to in many sources, of how Whitworth's salary as Minister Plenipotentiary in St Petersburg was inadequate to 'sustain the dignity of his official position' and that he therefore 'did not hesitate to avail himself of female aid'. The female aid included a Countess Gerbetzov, a married woman of considerable fortune, who 'provided, clothed, and defrayed his household from her own purse', in the hope that Whitworth would marry her as soon as she could obtain a divorce. By this time, however, Whitworth had returned to London, and met and married the widowed Duchess of Dorset, the memory of the Russian countess 'an eternal subject of remorse' to him.

From then on, Whitworth's diplomatic career mimicked aspects of the family into which he had married: in September 1802 he was appointed Ambassador to the French Republic (his wife's first husband, the 3rd Duke, had been the last Ambassador to the Court of King Louis XVI); and in 1813 he was appointed Viceroy of Ireland (a position held by the 1st Duke half a century before). The salary of £30,000 a year was considerably more than the 1st Duke had earned in the job, and Charles and Arabella were a very wealthy couple. During his time as ambassador in Paris, he shopped extravagantly, purchasing in 1802 a Boulle cabinet (the sale of which paid for the restoration of the park at Knole after the devastating storm of 1987). Charles himself had a number of plantations in the park laid out in 1811, and at Buckhurst too. Just as the 1st Duke had, a hundred years before, brought touches of the eighteenth century to Knole, Charles and Arabella brought touches of the early nineteenth century to the house. In 1823 they converted a range on the southern side of the Green Court into an orangery, with large Gothic sash windows facing the garden, and filled it with classical sculptures; and they built an arched window beneath the clock and belfry, giving a Gothic character to Bourchier's Tower.

They were, by all accounts, a devoted couple, and Arabella was inconsolable when Charles died in May 1825, leaving an estate worth £70,000 to his wife. She died three months later, at Knole, on 1 August. But whereas Charles was buried at St Nicholas's church, Sevenoaks, opposite the entrance of the drive to his adopted home, such was the pull and exclusivity of the family vault, that Arabella joined her first husband and their son at Withyham.

Wraxall lamented the approaching end of an association between a place and the people who lived there: 'Even the dukedom itself seems to be deprived of its greatest ornament, and to be half extinguished by the loss of Knole,' he wrote. 'That venerable pile, where the Earls and Dukes of Dorset have resided in uninterrupted succession for more than two centuries . . . it is highly probable it will be transferred to the Earls of Delawar, in consequence of a will which, whatever legal validity it may possess, militates against every feeling of justice and propriety.' He concluded: 'The very name of Sackville appears to be near extinction.'

The will to which Wraxall was referring was the settlement made on Arabella's death. In 1825 the Sackville estates were divided between Arabella's two daughters, Mary and Elizabeth. Mary, who had married the Earl of Plymouth in 1811, received Knole and the Kent estates, while Elizabeth, who had married George West, the 5th Earl De La Warr, at Knole in 1813, inherited Buckhurst and the Sussex estates. Mary, however, had no children, and it looked increasingly likely that on her death, her younger sister, the Countess De La Warr, would inherit.

After her mother's death, Mary lived for much of the time at Knole with her husband, the fabulously wealthy Earl of Plymouth (after whom the lodge at the north-west corner of the park is named) until his death. I have a particular affection for the beautiful Mary, whose portrait, larger-than-life, hung throughout childhood above my bed in Bourchier's Tower. The Earl of Plymouth died in

1833, and six years later, Mary remarried and brought her second husband, William Pitt, Earl Amherst, to Knole. Almost twenty years older than Mary, Amherst had been a diplomat and a former Governor General of Bengal. Early in his career, Amherst had been sent as British envoy to China and had returned with a rare breed of golden pheasant, *Phaisanus Amherstiae*, which he introduced to England. Several of these birds were housed in one of the seven courtyards at Knole, which is still known as the Pheasant Court, while others lived in an aviary in the park, beside the Gothic Revival building called the Bird House.

Mary and Amherst also remodelled the bedrooms in the North Wing, and it was here that Knole's only documented ghost was heard. When Mary's niece, Elizabeth, spent her wedding night at Knole in January 1844 with her husband Hastings Russell, the future 9th Duke of Bedford, they were kept awake all night by a thumping noise from the floor above. They had arrived from their marriage service and reception at Buckhurst at about five o'clock in the evening and, as Hastings Russell described in a letter to his brother, he was at once struck by the 'deep silence and the solitude' of the place. 'The servants live, heaven knows where, & when you ring they come, but otherwise you never meet, or hear, or see them – at dinner they brought in the dishes & disappeared. Breakfast and luncheon we always found ready to the minute but no sign of how it got there.' Bride and groom went to bed at about 11.30 p.m. and at about midnight heard:

something fall with a heavy thud on the floor above us, in some room over our own – after this, the noise continued till near 4 o'clock in the morning. This sort of *Boglerie* [ghostly activity] was a bore, but even if I had known my way up to the Black Boy's Passage (over us) & to the Devil's room, where someone once was murdered – even if I had known my way there, which being the first night in the house I did not, I should not have felt much inclined to run up in my nightshirt & in the dark to stop the thumping – so I laid still, when all on a sudden & without any previous warning, the handle of the door was sharply turned & a push made to open it – I had bolted it – without which I do not know what we would have seen – nor cared to see it.

Paradoxically, at a period when it seemed as if the association between Knole and the Sackvilles was becoming increasingly tenuous – at least, in name – the identity of the place was being firmly established in the popular imagination. This was partly through the publication of guidebooks to the house. The first of these, *An Historical and Topographical Sketch of Knole in Kent; with a Brief Genealogy of the Sackville Family* (1817), was written by John Bridgman, the 3rd Duke's former steward, and dedicated to his widow, 'Her Grace, the Most Noble Arabella Diana . . . with sentiments of profound respects, by her Grace's obedient and ever-devoted Servant'.

One of Bridgman's claims, which looked increasingly hollow in the light of later events, was the story of an unbroken succession of Sackvilles: 'It is not less singular than extraordinary, that during so many centuries as have elapsed since the [Norman] Conquest, filled with wars, rebellions and insurrections, in which the Nobility and Barons, chief instigators of those events have been engaged, while so many have become extinct and are forgotten; that it should have descended regularly from father and son during so long a period . . . There are many more ancient creations, but no other instance can be produced of a family inheriting in so direct a line.' This unbroken succession was just one of the many myths that first surfaced in guidebooks to the house. Bridgman also claimed that there were certainly 'above eighty staircases' at Knole and possibly as many as 500 rooms – predating a later myth about Knole as a calendar house with 365 rooms.

The *Visitor's Guide to Knole*, written by J. H. Brady and published in 1839, added to the mix, and offered an insight into the style of early-nineteenth-century country-house visiting. Mary, Dowager Countess of Plymouth, it explained, 'now constantly resides here, notwithstanding which, every facility is afforded by her to gratify the curiosity of all respectable applicants to view the state rooms of the mansion and their treasures of art – an indulgence to the public kindly continued by her ladyship, in imitation of the liberality of her noble ancestors'. It also noted that 'Knole was built for a mode of life utterly at variance with modern habits.' Brady's guidebook was the first to tell the story of how Charles Sackville, 6th Earl of Dorset, won the poetry competition judged by John Dryden – with the particularly poetic entry: 'I promise to pay Mr. John Dryden, or order, five hundred pounds, on demand' – a story that has been repeated and embellished in all later guides to the house.

Knole has always been celebrated because it is so venerable, so obviously old. This was as true in the nineteenth century as it is today. When the novelist Maria Edgeworth visited the house in 1831, she wrote in a letter to her mother the following day: 'And then King James's *Silver Room* as it is called. How it was gilt by the genius of Romance! ... In the Silver Room a bed as the show woman trumpeted forth of gold tissue which cost 8 thousand guineas new now in tarnished tatters not worth Christies best puffing 8 thousand pence this day.' The King's Bed, which she was describing, was one of many pieces of sumptuous furniture acquired from the royal palaces by the 6th Earl, as a perk of his office as Lord Chamberlain. Displayed in the same rooms then as now, the 6th Earl's collection of the 1690s and early 1700s had come to define the house by the nineteenth century, giving it that special feel, that fading magnificence, that lustre.

Overlaying that, in the nineteenth century, Knole was attributed further personality traits that have persisted to this day. The house caught the Victorian imagination as a perfectly preserved relic of 'the Olden Times', a period somewhere between the Tudors and the Stuarts, between the Middle Ages and modern times. It was an era popularised in the novels of Sir Walter Scott, whose portrait was – appropriately enough – acquired in 1822 and hung in the Poets' Parlour at Knole, complementing the collection of Restoration poets and playwrights.

Much was made of any connection between Knole, a Sackville, and a Tudor or Stuart monarch. This, for example, is when stories originated of Good Queen Bess giving Knole to her trusted cousin and courtier, Thomas Sackville; and of Mary, Queen of Scots presenting Thomas with the wooden Calvary in the Chapel for the tact with which he broke the news of her death sentence. Literary associations and anecdotes also caught the popular imagination, sometimes cropping up in nineteenth-century guidebooks to the house: Knole's association with the Restoration poets and play-wrights, for example, or the setting in the King's Room at Knole of Sir John Millais's wonderful painting *The Eve of St Agnes*, which was inspired by John Keats's poem.

In 1839, the year in which Brady's guidebook celebrated Knole's 'numerous relics of ancient magnificence, which afford a pleas-ing illustration of the domestic decorations, manners and customs of our ancestors', an architectural painter and lithographer called Joseph Nash published the first of four volumes of drawings of *Mansions of England in the Olden Times*. Over the next thirty years or so, these drawings were copied so many times that they gradually came to represent everything that the Victorians found romantic about these historic houses, to define visually the spirit of 'the Olden Times'. In Nash's series of around a hundred plates, there are seven interiors of Knole – more than of any other house.

In his *Descriptions of the Plates*, Joseph Nash set out what he was hoping to achieve:

> In producing a set of views of the picturesque architecture of the mansions of England, the artist's object has been to present them in a new and attractive light ... glowing with the genial warmth of their firesides, and enlivened with the presence of their inmates and guests, enjoying the recreations and pastimes, or celebrating the festivals, of our ancestors ... in attempting this the artist has endeav-oured to place himself in the position of a visitor to these ancient edifices, whose fancy peoples the deserted halls, stripped of all movable ornaments and looking damp and cheerless, with the family and household of the 'old English gentleman' surrounded by their everyday comforts, sharing the more rare and courteous hospitali-ties offered to the guests, or partaking of the boisterous merriment of Christmas gambols.

The Knole pictures conform to this vision, and the composition of each is similar. In the foreground, people go about their everyday lives: a group is escorted through the Great Hall, children play skittles in the Retainers' Gallery, a mother reads to her child in the Brown Gallery, a woman does her toilette at a looking glass in the Spangle Bedroom, a lady strums her lute in the Pheasant Court Room, there's a conversation in front of the fireplace in the Cartoon Gallery, and so on. In the background is a riot of ornamental detail, ceilings and elaborate friezes. All the architectural detail is authentic – and accurate enough to be used by historians locating and tracking the movement of features such as chimneypieces around the house. The costumes – the brocaded dresses, the doublets and the breeches – look properly researched, too. But the combination of these activities in those rooms is not authentic. Nash had missed the point about Knole. In his attempt to domesticate the house, he had filled and furnished the show rooms with all the life that had left them almost as soon as they were built. Nevertheless, Nash's flawed Victorian vision of daily life in a Stuart home has proved particularly enduring, and is still echoed in descriptions of the house today.

Also in 1839, the *Penny Magazine* launched a series on 'Olden Time mansions'. It raved about Knole, not just for 'its antiquity and the air of primitive grandeur that reigns throughout the domain', but also for 'the memories of the distinguished men who have found a home beneath its roof'. When, claimed the author of the Knole article, we step into the 'lofty and extensive Gothic hall, with its characteristic-looking table fitted for playing the old English game of shuttle-board' (this was pure fabrication), it makes 'us centuries older: we not only think of, but feel with, the past. The loneliness seems suddenly to be broken, the bustle of countless attendants going in and out begins, the tables groan with the profusion of the feast, bright jewels and still brighter eyes begin to sparkle, gorgeous vestments and sacerdotal robes mingle together, the solemn strains of music peal forth.'

What all these publications celebrated was a notion that stretched back to the country-house poem of the early seventeenth century, to a mythical Merry England, where all strata of society were joined together in a great bustle of jollity by the hospitality of the landowner. What actually was happening at Knole was rather different.

The near-extinction of the Sackville name, which Wraxall had lamented, should have become total on the death in 1843 of the 5th Duke of Dorset. For the death of this 'little, smart-looking man ... a favourite with the ladies', according to Thomas Raikes's *Journal*, marked the passing of the last male heir to a name and a title that reached back almost 250 years to Thomas Sackville. One of the preoccupations of the English aristocracy has always been to preserve the country seat as a symbol of family status and continuity; and keeping hold of the family name has been crucial to this. The reluctance to see a surname disappear resulted, particularly in the nineteenth century, in multiple surnames as much of a mouthful as Pleydell-Bouverie-Campbell-Wyndham. The Sackvilles were no different in the contortions to which they would go to compensate for sheer biological bad luck.

On 30 October 1843, a royal licence was issued, allowing Elizabeth's husband George West to take the name of Sackville before that of West, and allowing his children, too, to call themselves Sackville-West. This typically Victorian fudge, then, is the origin of my name, and the reason that this book is not called Knole and the Wests (Vita had chosen, perhaps correctly, to end her *Knole and the Sackvilles* in 1815).

Elizabeth and George brought up their six sons and three daughters, first at Bourn in Cambridgeshire and then at Buckhurst. They cultivated their royal connections – George was Lord Chamberlain of the Royal Household from 1841 to 1846 (at the time of the name change), and then again in 1858–59 – and Queen Victoria was a regular visitor to Buckhurst in the 1830s and 1840s. It is from this era that date the forlorn royal mementoes at Knole, now in a cardboard box in a corner of the Estate Office: a tracing of the young Queen Victoria's foot, and a desiccated wreath of hops that she gave to Elizabeth's sixth son, my great-grandfather, William Edward.

The extensive correspondence between Elizabeth and her children, and between the siblings themselves – with its breezy retailing of family gossip – charts the careers of the boys, and the marriages and confinements of the girls. Together, the five surviving sons (the eldest, George, had died in 1850) had a full range of the very few careers considered suitable for Victorian gentlemen. Charles joined the army, serving in India, and in the Crimea, at the battles of Alma, Balaclava, Inkerman and at the siege of Sebastopol; he eventually rose to the rank of major-general. Reginald chose the Church, becoming rector of Withyham from 1841 to 1865, and from 1846 to 1865 a chaplain to Queen Victoria. Mortimer, the next one down, held a series of arcane court appointments, first as Gentleman Usher – Quarterly Waiter – and then from 1852 as a Groom in Waiting. Lionel joined the diplomatic service, starting his career as an assistant précis writer for the Secretary of State for Foreign Affairs, the Earl of Aberdeen. And the youngest, William Edward, became a land agent (this last was still a career option for younger sons in the 1960s, when my father, William Edward's grandson, became agent at Knole for his elder brother, Lionel).

Two of these careers at least – the court, where roles such as equerry and private secretary were more ceremonial than dynamic, and the Foreign Office, which resembled a gentleman's club – remained bastions of the aristocratic closed shop, with recruitment by connection rather than by competition. It was no coincidence that two future Lord Sackvilles, Mortimer and Lionel, neither of whom, dare I say it, was that able or dynamic himself, had chosen to make their way in two of the least demanding of the careers available.

The correspondence also begins to capture the character of each of the sons: William Edward, the sweet-natured baby of the family; Lionel, the slightly feckless gad-about, for ever getting 'into scrapes with other swells' (his words); Mortimer, the courtier, desperately trying to wangle his next appointment; Reginald, whose idea of a fun night out was a round of glee singing with his siblings; and Charles, the introspective, tortured soul, who would eventually commit suicide.

The hole in the correspondence, and in the life of the family itself, was that left by the adored eldest son George, Viscount Cantelupe, who died in his thirties in June 1850. The death had momentous consequences for the family, and particularly for the troubled Charles, who was terrified of being 'thrust forward to fill the gap which has been created in the family'.

'I am tormented with the anticipation of future unhappiness,' he wrote to his mother on mourning paper in October 1850, 'arising from the incompatibility of my temper and disposition with the duties I shall have to perform and the life I shall have to lead. Sometimes I think it would be better if I could abdicate altogether, renounce all interest in the property, and let Reginald, Mortic or Lionel live as eldest son, I keeping the title which I suppose cannot be renounced, and continue in the army, never of course to marry . . . I do all I can to drive away the morbid melancholy which haunts me – but I cannot succeed.'

He was making himself ill with worry, so unworthy did he feel of 'treading in the shoes of one who was deservedly beloved in every Society, and that I with my reserved and unsociable Temper, must ever provoke a most fanciful Contrast'. A letter from one of his family advised him to lay off the opium: 'It must be sometime before the mind recovers its usual tone after so many weeks of sleeplessness, but you must also recollect that opium produces excitement at the time that it is being taken but that the effects are injurious afterwards now that you are enabled to get natural sleep, you will soon feel the benefit of leaving off the habit!'

The jostling for position amongst the siblings, that drives any large family, was given added momentum by a series of wills – and a sequence of events that none of these wills anticipated. In 1860 their aunt Mary – now in her late sixties, and without children from either of her two marriages – made a will that left Knole and the estates in Kent to her sister Elizabeth for life, and after to Elizabeth's eldest surviving son, Charles. In the event of his death without children, Knole would pass to Elizabeth's third surviving son Mortimer, completely bypassing the second son Reginald.

This plan was changed in 1864. Ever since 1843, Elizabeth had been hoping that some special consideration would be given to the loss of so many family titles (including that of Buckhurst) on the death of the 5th Duke of Dorset. But despite her appeals, all that she and her husband had received was the consolation of a hyphenated surname. On 27 April 1864, Elizabeth's loyalty to the monarch was rewarded when she was created Baroness Buckhurst of Buckhurst for life, with the title to pass to her second surviving son, Reginald (her eldest surviving son, Charles, would be expected to inherit his father's title, as Earl De La Warr). The patent creating this title had an unusual proviso, however, to the effect that if any Baron Buckhurst subsequently succeeded to the Earldom of De La Warr, then the Buckhurst barony should pass to the next male heir in line – the so-called shifting clause – and so on. What this meant was that if Reginald should succeed to the earldom De La Warr, then the third surviving son Mortimer would become Baron Buckhurst.

On 3 May, less than a week after the letters patent creating this new title, Mary made a codicil which effectively revoked her will. She now intended to settle her estates in a way that mirrored the provisions of the letters patent. The family arrangements were overturned. By the will of 1860, her nephew Charles had stood to gain the most, her nephew Reginald had been completely omitted, and Mortimer was in with a chance of inheriting Knole if the unmarried, forty-five-year-old Charles died without children. By the codicil, Charles was stripped of any prospects of Knole and the Kent estates, Reginald was reinstated and stood to gain Knole, and Mortimer's prospects (and those of his younger brothers) were diminished.

Mary died in July 1864, before a legal settlement, based on the will and its codicil, had actually been made. There was no question that her younger sister Elizabeth should inherit for her lifetime, thereby reuniting – temporarily at least – Knole and Buckhurst, the Kent and the Sussex estates. But the further implications of the will and codicil, and Mary's change of mind, reverberated through the family for the next decade. The first challenge came from Charles over the proving of the will. In 1865, in the Court of Probate, Lord

West (as Charles styled himself) contested the will on the grounds that, at the time of adding the codicil, his aunt Mary 'was not of sound mind memory and understanding' and that the codicil had been 'obtained by undue influence'. Her servants were called to testify to her sound state of mind, and the will was proved.

Legal cases over the inheritance of Knole continued throughout the 1860s, reflecting the shifting alliances and rivalries between the siblings. In 1864, when Mary added the codicil, none of Elizabeth's five surviving sons, who were all in their thirties and forties, had any legitimate children. The three daughters, on the other hand, were considerably more fertile and poked fun, in particular, at Reginald's attempts – which were ultimately successful, in his fifties – to produce an heir. The unpredictable order of births, as well as deaths, would alter the course of the inheritance, and determine which siblings found common or separate cause as family circumstances changed. These legal actions culminated in a case before the Court of Appeal in February 1870, just a month after Elizabeth's death.

What had prompted Mary to change her mind? One of the law lords argued convincingly that it was the grant of the Buckhurst peerage alone which had caused Mary to change her 'testamentary disposition'. 'It was in order to furnish a provision for the dignity created by this grant that she was willing to place in abeyance her own personal predilections, excluding a son of her sister whom she had included and placed first in her will, and, on the other hand, including and placing first one which she had in her will altogether excluded.'

The Court of Appeal adopted this argument, and decided that it had been Mary's intention to endow a newly created peerage, separate and distinct from the De La Warr peerage. Knole and the Kent estates should therefore follow the course of succession prescribed by the letters patent, even though there was some doubt as to the validity of the shifting clause. 'I cannot but express my astonishment at finding such a proviso in letters patent of nobility,' argued another of the law lords. 'It is, I believe, quite unprecedented. Whether it is valid in law, and capable of being made legally effective, are questions on which it is not for this House now to pronounce an opinion.' The law lords had decided, therefore, on the succession to the property, even if the succession to the title was unresolved, and would become a matter for the House of Lords in 1876.

Whatever Mary's intentions had been precisely, they were tested by a series of three family deaths in the space of four years. The first two were not unexpected: George, the 5th Earl De La Warr, died in 1869, and was succeeded as 6th Earl and owner of Buckhurst by his oldest surviving son, Charles. George's widow Elizabeth died the following year, and was succeeded as Baron Buckhurst and owner of Knole by the second son, Reginald, as the letters patent and the codicil had provided. During what proved to be a very brief tenure of Knole, Reginald had his surname changed by royal licence in 1871 to Sackville (rather than Sackville-West, or indeed West as he had been born). At last, and for the first time in almost a hundred years, there was in Reginald Sackville, Baron Buckhurst, an owner of Knole whose name and title mimicked the name of the first family member to live at Knole, Thomas Sackville.

But the third of the deaths was totally unexpected, and pointed to the impossibility of providing, in wills, for every eventuality. In April 1873, Charles travelled to Cambridge, purportedly on business, and put up at the Bull Inn. As his brother-in-law Edward Stanley, Earl of Derby, reported in his diary on 24 April, Charles went out 'leaving letters behind him from which it is inferred that he intended to destroy himself'. His body was then found in the river, but 'the motive is a mystery. He was well in health, habitually cheerful, temperate in his habits, fond of society in a quiet way, though detesting the bustle of London life: his affairs were not embarrassed, and by economy and good management he was rapidly putting the family estates into order. Few men seemed to enjoy life more.'

He may have had some 'little oddities', as Lord Derby noted in his diary, and he may have been rather highly strung. Derby's wife Mary, Charles's sister, had told him how 'when excited by family troubles, of which in earlier years there were many, [Charles] would discuss them calmly and quietly in the evening, go to bed, pass a sleepless night, and come down in the morning excited by want of rest and his own thoughts, so that his language & manner then would be in complete contrast with what they were a few hours before'. These oddities were not, it was thought, of a serious kind, however, and 'nothing in the nature of insanity was ever suspected'.

It emerged, at the inquest, that Charles had been devastated by the recent death of a lady friend, Miss Nethercote, 'to whom he had been attached' and beside whose grave he had lately been seen in great distress. According to Lord Derby, it became clear that 'her death was caused by drink ... poor [Charles] felt it deeply: and probably his idea of being responsible for her death arose from a notion that he had either not exerted himself enough, or exerted himself injudiciously, to check her propensity'. Charles had committed suicide by drowning, the coroner decided, in a moment of 'temporary insanity'.

All in all, 1873 had been a bad year, as Derby recorded in his diary for 1 January 1874: 'The last year has been the least happy of my married life, though solely from external causes: ... the death of poor Delawarr [Charles] by his own hand, the embarrassed circumstances of one brother [the feckless Lionel] and the almost public quarrels of two others.' Family troubles had taken their toll too on his wife, Mary, who was beginning to suffer from chronic depression.

'There is something not quite consistent with sanity in the continual and ceaseless quarrels which arise in the family,' Derby wrote in his diary. These family dynamics underlay the litigiousness that was to be such a feature of the Sackvilles over the next forty years. The first of the quarrels arose immediately after Charles's death, when, in line with the Court of Appeal ruling of 1870, Reginald had to move from Knole to Buckhurst and Mortimer took possession of Knole.

During his three-year tenure of Knole, Reginald had removed a number of family heirlooms and sold others. An inventory was taken of 'heirlooms missing at Knole' on 10 October 1873. Many of the items were of little value, except retrospectively in identifying the names of Knole's rooms in the nineteenth century: a crib mattress from the Nursery, a mahogany toilet table and a tumbler from Lady Amherst's dressing room, glass scent bottles and pomade pots from the Chintz Room, a violin bow from the Music Room, a poker from the Library, a stuffed hare from the Guard Room, eleven billiard balls from the Billiard Room, an old bedstead from the Dairymaids' Room, a copper stock pot, a fish kettle and a stag's head and antlers from the Servants' Hall, three milk pails and two skimmers from the Dairy, and any number of pieces of 'broken' china or squares of worn-out oil cloth. But there were several items of value, and Mortimer successfully sued Reginald for these: a Spanish mahogany escritoire, a pair of ormolu candelabras, and a pair of 'rosewood cabinets and ebony winged cabinets, inlaid with Buhl and tortoiseshell, mounted on ormolu from Ball Room'. At court in 1874, Mortimer was awarded £2,180, plus costs.

The next quarrel concerned the Buckhurst title. When Reginald succeeded his brother Charles as 7th Earl De La Warr, he clung obstinately to the title of Baron Buckhurst, despite Mortimer's claims. In 1876 Reginald took his case to the House of Lords, contending that the shifting clause in the letters patent 'has never been recognised as valid by your lordships' House, and ought, in fact, to be treated as of no force or validity'. The insertion of the shifting clause, his lawyers argued, was 'wholly without precedent': it was simply not right to take away the honour of a peerage from someone who had sat in the House of Lords and voted under that name.

In July, the House of Lords' Committee of Privileges confirmed that, despite the letters patent and provisions to the contrary, Reginald should continue to retain the barony even after succeeding to the earldom. Later that year, as consolation – and as a reward for his appointments in the Royal Household – Mortimer was created Baron Sackville of Knole. The current title – the one that I hold as 7th Baron Sackville – is, therefore, like the name Sackville-West, a relatively recent creation. However timeless the phrase Knole and the Sackvilles may seem, its sense of continuity is a fiction based on name changes and new titles.

Derby had questioned whether Elizabeth had been wise in obtaining, through her personal friendship with the Queen, a title for her second son in 1864, leaving 'two peerages scantily endowed, instead of one, which would have been abundantly wealthy'. This division of the family estates, and its inevitable consequence – the creation of an inheritance that was too costly to run – was everything that the principles of primogeniture and strict settlement, whereby estates, houses, heirlooms and titles, descended together to the oldest son, had been designed to prevent. As a result, Knole, that great treasure house of Britain, mansion of the Olden Times, ancient and venerable pile, passed to a series of younger sons; while the elder son was left with Buckhurst, a house which until recently had been used as a grand hunting lodge or a home for a younger son. Thomas Sackville had chosen Knole as his principal house, and when it had passed to Mary, the elder of the 3rd Duke's two daughters, in 1825, it had certainly been considered the senior inheritance. However, by the second half of the nineteenth century, through a strange sequence of wills, titles and family circumstances, Knole had mutated into the junior inheritance, passing in 1873 to Mortimer, a fourth son.

At the time, and as the legal battles indicate, the elder sons may have thought they had got a rather poor deal. I am not sure that they would today. Buckhurst Park has many of the hallmarks of a prosperous private estate: a raked gravel drive between crisp grass verges, a picture-postcard cricket pitch and pavilion, a handsome house and well-kept terraced gardens overlooking Ashdown Forest. The view can have changed little in the past 400 years, since these fields (rather than Knole Park) formed the heart of Thomas Sackville's estate. But the crucial difference between the two parts of the divided inheritance is that Buckhurst is still privately owned by the De La Warr family, whereas Knole was to prove too big, too meagrely endowed, and was to pass less than a century later into the hands of the National Trust.

The fourth and last edition of John Bateman's great statistical survey of landowners in Great Britain and Ireland makes the reasons for this very clear. In 1883 Mortimer's Sackville estates, based on Knole, consisted of a total of 8,551 acres, yielding £11,250 a year, while the De La Warr estates, based at Buckhurst Park, consisted of 23,366 acres, yielding £21,606 a year. The De La Warrs were therefore twice as wealthy as the Sackvilles, and had a much smaller house to maintain. To put these figures further into perspective, two of Mortimer's sisters had married extremely well, into the small group of super-rich landed families, with incomes of over £75,000 a year. Elizabeth had married the Duke of Bedford from Woburn (with 86,335 acres, yielding £141,793 a year); and Mary had married first the Marquis of Salisbury from Hatfield, and secondly the Earl of Derby from Knowsley (with 68,942 acres, yielding £163,273 a year).

With an estate of less than 10,000 acres, the Sackvilles were no more than middle-ranking landowners – within the top thousand landowners in the country, rather than within the top ten they had been in Thomas Sackville's day. The divided inheritance accounted for some of this slippage, but what had happened to the profits of public office, on which the fortunes of Mortimer's ancestors had been built? Mortimer was a career courtier – just as many of his ancestors had been. He had spent decades in Queen Victoria's service, just as his ancestors had done at the courts of previous monarchs. But, by the second half of the nineteenth century, being a courtier, and the search for sinecures, was not the gravy train it had once been. Mortimer's reward was a peerage, not the opportunity to fill his pockets.

Like all landowners, he was also hard hit by the agricultural depression of the 1870s and 1880s, as cheap grain from the Americas and Australia flooded the European market. Prices, land rents and values fell by around 50 per cent, ensuring that the Sackville estates were too small to support aristocratic life on a scale demanded by Knole – particularly when this lifestyle entailed a certain amount of noblesse oblige.

By 1874 some 10,000 people were visiting Knole House every year, making it one of the most popular show houses in England. This was a very different phenomenon from the country-house visiting of the eighteenth century, when a handful of connoisseurs – or simply curious gentlefolk – were shown around a house by the housekeeper, and admired the place as a repository of ancient treasures and fashionable taste. Many owners felt increasingly beleaguered by the number of new tourists and by the seemingly inevitable rise in petty vandalism. Some tried to limit them by instituting fixed visiting hours and admission charges, while others, like Mortimer, simply shut their doors. 'People strayed from their parties,' Mortimer later claimed in an interview with the *Evening News*, 'broke into our rooms, tore the fringe off the chairs and couches, and did all manner of things, whereupon I felt obliged to shut up the place; and then the "row" began. Thirty Royal Academicians came down the other day and I was delighted to see them; but I don't like people to come here and destroy my property.'

Knole House was effectively closed to the general public from the autumn of 1874 until after Mortimer's death in 1888. *The World*, a nineteenth-century journal, was sympathetic, reporting that 'Knole is now too near to London to be shown to every 'Arry who comes, and Lord Sackville is perfectly justified in stopping what must have long been a prodigious nuisance.'

Nevertheless, the number of visitors to the house was small compared with visitors to the park. Although the park was – and is – privately owned, the paths across it had come to be seen as rights of way, and the park itself as a public amenity. Sevenoaks was only an hour by train from London, and by the 1880s there were thirty trains every weekday tunnelling through the North Downs from London, and fifteen on Sundays. As well as improvements in the rail network, people had more free time – what with Saturday half-holidays and the new Bank Holidays – and, as a result, Knole became a popular destination for a day trip to the countryside from the crowded capital.

The park was also treasured by the inhabitants of Sevenoaks themselves. The population of this market town had doubled over the previous twenty years, rising to 8,000 in 1881. Local residents liked to stroll in the park; mothers wheeled their children in prams along the paths; people from nearby villages, particularly those on the eastern side of the park, rode on horseback or in carts across the park to do their shopping in town; and everyone, particularly shop and hotel owners, benefited from the passing weekend trade that the park attracted.

Mortimer had had enough. He complained that people abused the privilege, 'galloping all over the park, frightening the deer, and defying the keepers'. In 1883 he had wooden posts placed across the main gate on the west side of the park, and closed the Fawke Gate on the east side, thereby blocking the bridleway that ran across the park. This prevented horses, and even prams, from entering the park. It was claimed that the new pedestrian entrance was so narrow that not even a butcher's boy with a basket nor an old man in a bathchair could get through. On Bonfire Night that November, a giant sketch was carried through the town, showing a bridleway through the park, and a pig – Mortimer – perched on top of Knole House.

The Sevenoaks Local Board protested, on behalf of the ratepayers, about the blocking of the bridleway. The Commons Preservation Society, an organisation established in 1865 to protect open spaces from enclosure and property development, argued that historic usage of the path conferred a legal right of access. But the dispute rumbled on for months. In June 1884, Mortimer had the wooden posts at the main gate reinforced with wrought iron and secured by a chain. There was a public outcry.

On the evening of 18 June, which was overcast and very cool for the time of year, a protest meeting was called in the grounds of the Rose and Crown hotel in Sevenoaks. It was chaired by Major James German, a local JP and Liberal politician, who declared, quite reasonably, that: 'In the old days, the feudal barons claimed to have the right to do as they pleased with their own, not only as regarded property, but the people on it; but now civilisation had so advanced that it was generally conceded by all right-thinking men that if property had its rights it also had its duties.' Mortimer, on the other hand, was informed by two men he had at the meeting that 'the language used there was worse than you would hear in the slums of London'.

When the meeting closed at 9.30 p.m., the crowd, now swollen to over a thousand citizens of Sevenoaks, decided to take the law into their own hands. They broke down the posts across the entrance and, singing 'Rule Britannia', marched on the house. Mortimer was at dinner at the time and 'heard a terrific noise – a tremendous yelling and shouting – and the next minute my butler ran into the room and said that hundreds were coming up to the gate. You may imagine the state of alarm, into which Lady Sackville, and the household generally, were thrown.' He ordered the gates to be shut, whereupon the mob deposited the posts and chains at the main door and, according to Mortimer, 'hammered continuously at the knocker', yelling and shouting "Bring him out and let's hang him!"'

The next evening they entered the park again, surrounded the house, smashed a few windows, and hissed abuse at Mortimer, before proceeding to the Fawke Gate, at the far end of the park. There they forced the gate open and the crowd, led on horseback by William Stepney, a forty-year-old solicitor's clerk, passed ceremonially back and forth through the entrance. Men dressed as women wheeled prams symbolically through the park, contributing – in a bizarrely British way – to the midsummer carnival spirit.

Mortimer had been so alarmed by the events that he asked the chief constable to increase the number of policemen stationed at Sevenoaks; by the second evening, there were sixty-two of them; and by the third, which passed off peacefully, there were 114 (a third of the entire Kent Constabulary).

Even after the situation had calmed, Mortimer felt threatened and left Knole temporarily to live in the Grand Hotel, Scarborough. There, during his self-imposed exile, he had privately published a justificatory 'Account of the Disturbances at Knole, with Letters and Press Opinions on the Subject'. Many of these opinions were drawn from the sympathetic, politically conservative *Evening News*, which described the 'invasion' while it lasted as 'a veritable reign of terror'.

The Bonfire Night celebrations for November 1884 featured a coffin, paraded through the streets of Sevenoaks, inscribed: 'In memory of the Knole Park Obstructions removed June 18th 1884, taken to Knole and there left to be for ever with the Lorde.' Nevertheless, Mortimer continued to press for a legal injunction that there was no public right of way across the park and for the prosecution of the 'prime movers in these disturbances', including Major German. In a letter to the Lord Chancellor, Mortimer restated his case that 'a County Magistrate [German] advised an enormous crowd of people to do, after dark, in a violent and tumultuous manner, that which could have been done quietly in the light of day, and to invade my privacy at night for no legal purpose whatever, but for mere vengeance and intimidation, if not for actual destruction'. When no public prosecution was forthcoming, he brought a civil action against the ringleaders for trespass. This Mortimer won in the High Court in 1885, and was awarded the nominal sum of £5 in damages. A compromise had, however, at last been reached. In return for the defendants abandoning their claim to a public bridleway through the park, Mortimer allowed pedestrians to use the footpaths.

Mortimer died childless in 1888, and was succeeded as 2nd Lord Sackville and owner of Knole by his younger brother Lionel. By the time of his death, Mortimer had broken off all relations with his family and, it is said, had sacked some of his servants whom he thought were trying to poison him. Lionel was unable to take possession of Knole immediately because – once again – there were complications over a Sackville will. Mortimer had thrown one posthumous spanner into the works by leaving much of his personal estate (he was only a life-tenant of Knole itself) to Queen Victoria's four Maids of Honour. Whether this provision was an extraordinary act of spite towards his relatives or whether, as Vita suggested, 'he had private reasons for wishing to benefit one of them, and hit on this method of doing it without singling her out into scandalous publicity', it was contested by Lionel – and settled out of court. A pair of gloomy portraits of Mortimer and his wife were soon consigned to a dilapidated passage in the house, where his whiskery, dark-hearted presence still casts a pall. In 1890 the guidebook to Knole stated that 'The Park is always open to the public.'

Lionel, a grandson of the 3rd Duke who had inherited in 1769, would live at Knole until his death in 1908. Over just three generations, then, spanning almost 140 years, the Sackvilles were to maintain their hold on Knole. It was a surprising continuity, in view of the strange contingencies of the succession, and in the face of a more general erosion of economic and political power. But it was a survival, with all its name changes and new titles, that demonstrated the Victorian genius for reinvention.

Chapter 9

An Inheritance in Crisis (1888–1908)

Lionel Sackville-West, 2nd Baron Sackville and His Daughter, Victoria

On 3 July 1889, a young woman with striking Mediterranean looks and a distinctly French accent visited Knole for the first time, in the company of her father, the new Lord Sackville – a portly, grey-bearded man in his early sixties. In her diary that evening, she wrote in French, her first language, how struck she was by the orderliness and scale of the house – so big that you could easily get lost in it. Many years later, her daughter, Vita, found these first impressions of her mother, Victoria, a little underwhelming, expecting her to have been more struck, on that midsummer's day, by the 'sheer loveliness of the grey Elizabethan pile rising above the brilliant turf', rather than by its order and its size.

We know something of how the house looked and was furnished around this time from a copy of the photograph album that Mortimer, the previous Lord Sackville, had given Queen Victoria, when staying at Balmoral in November 1881. Knick-knacks clutter every surface; what-nots and display cabinets are packed with plates, ornamental fans, cups and saucers; antimacassars cover the backs of chairs and sofas; and tassels dangle from curtains and upholstery – no wonder there are so many of them today, stuffed into cupboards all over Knole. Screens designed to stop draughts occlude every perspective and line of sight; ferns protrude from pots to obscure the Jacobean decoration and the eighteenth-century trompe l'oeil; and cast-iron fires and grates fill and diminish the magnificent early-seventeenth-century marble fireplaces. Pride of place, and a whole page, in the album is given to a close-up of a sentimental statuette in the Boudoir of 'The Queen's Piper'. (Queen Victoria had fallen in love with bagpipe music on a visit to the Highlands in 1842, and the following year had made a permanent appointment of a personal piper to play for her.) As Knole disappears beneath a veneer of fussy Victoriana, oh, how one longs, in the words of Lytton Strachey, for the spaciousness of the eighteenth century.

Outside, the photographs show a similar picture. Massive glasshouses protrude from the wall of the house into the garden, providing hothouse grapes, peaches, nectarines and melons for the family, but obscuring the south and east fronts (you'd never get Listed Building Consent for that today). Ivy clings to and corrodes the walls of the house, making parts of it resemble a ruinous, overgrown medieval abbey. A fashionable monkey puzzle tree occupies a prominent position on the lawn. And striped awnings shade the length of the Colonnade, giving it a jaunty seaside, rather than a stately seventeenth-century, air.

In some ways, these photographs of Knole, and its inhabitants, make the past more immediate and less impenetrable than the paintings and portraits of previous generations. And yet, spotted and mottled with age, these sepia photographs bring their own mellow romantic glow to the place, masking the decay in its dank and derelict courtyards. With the age of photography, we are also entering the era of recent memory. My grandfather was born in 1872 and, although not playing a prominent part himself in the domestic dramas that were to unfold, he was closely related to all the characters involved – his father, uncles and aunts, cousins, brothers, and nephews and nieces. To the documentary record, therefore, is added the record of family anecdote, of stories and half-secrets handed down from generation to generation.

On her first visit to Knole, the twenty-six-year-old Victoria was nervous and uncertain about her future. She had every reason to be. For the woman who was to become Lady Sackville, the future mistress of Knole who would drag the house into the twentieth century, and – quite literally – electrify it, had, what she would describe as a 'stain' on her name. She had first learned of her illegitimacy nine years previously. She was to find this 'a terrible strain and stumbling block' for the rest of her life.

As a young diplomat, Victoria's father Lionel had, in 1852 in Paris, met and fallen in love with Josefa Duran, a dancer known as Pepita. Pepita had been born in the slums of Malaga, in southern Spain, the daughter of a barber and a door-to-door half-gypsy pedlar of secondhand clothes. When she met Lionel, she was twenty-two, already celebrated as 'The Star of Andalusia', and recently estranged from her husband, Juan Antonio de Oliva. So began a romance that echoed the relationship seventy years before of Lionel's grandfather, the 3rd Duke, with the Italian dancer, La Baccelli.

Pepita gave birth to her first child, Maximiliano Leon Jose Manuel Enrique Bernardino ('Max'), in 1858 in a town called Albolote, near Granada, and over the course of a nineteen-year relationship that lasted until her death in childbirth in 1871, the couple had more children: Victoria, Flora, Amalia and Henry. Victoria was born in a furnished apartment that Lionel had taken for his mistress at No. 4, Avenue de l'Impératrice, Paris, on 23 September 1862 and baptised a Roman Catholic, Victoire Josephine Dolores Catherine. In the register of the parish of St Honoré d'Eylau, she was described as the daughter of Josefa Duran and of an unknown father (*fille de père inconnu*). It was to her mother, then, that Victoria owed her Mediterranean looks, her dancer's figure and tiny waist, the lustrous black hair that hung to her hips, her long dark eyelashes, and skin so fine that she would never in her life wear make-up.

At first, their affair was conducted around the diplomatic capitals of Europe – Stuttgart, Berlin, Turin, Madrid, Paris. Then, in 1865 Lionel installed his growing family in the Villa Pepe – a house he bought for Pepita – in Arcachon, a small seaside resort in south-west France, where he would visit them four or five times a year from postings in Madrid and Paris. Always something of a fantasist, Pepita styled herself Countess West, and both the gates to the house, and her visiting cards, displayed a coronet. However, everyday life among the holiday homes of the prosperous Bordeaux merchants in the pine-scented Ville d'Eté was marked by petty humiliations. These were to have a profound effect on Victoria. Pepita could never be introduced to any of Lionel's diplomatic colleagues; nor, because she was living 'in sin', could she take Holy Communion. Victoria was shunned by Minna and Bella Johnston, the children of their next-door neighbours; and years later, when Lionel was appointed to a post in Paris in 1868, Victoria was forced to turn back ten minutes before they got to the British Embassy when she accompanied her father on his walk to work.

Victoria's world was shattered when her mother died a couple of days after giving birth to a short-lived son, Frederic, in March 1871. Gradually, the full story of Lionel's expensive secret life was revealed to his grand aristocratic siblings, from whom he was reduced to borrowing money. His brother-in-law, the Earl of Derby, was uncertain about the extent of Lionel's financial embarrassment, but he was sure that 'the beginning of the mischief was a connection of many years standing with a Spanish woman, I believe, originally a dancer, by whom he has a family left on his hands to maintain. She died last year. It is an awkward business altogether.' Lionel, as Vita Sackville-West later noted of her grandfather, was not the sort of 'man ever to enjoy dealing with a difficult situation', and he escaped to Buenos Aires in 1873 as British Minister to Argentina.

The children, meanwhile, were consigned to the care of a French family, the de Béons, first in Arcachon and then in Paris. Victoria was sent to the Convent of St Joseph in the Rue Monceau in Paris, where she was to spend seven very unhappy years – relieved only by gloomy holidays with the nuns in Berck-sur-Mer, a windblown resort in northern France for sufferers from tuberculosis. At the end of these seven years, Victoria's only qualification was a certificate enabling her to work as a governess, a role for which, later, her daughter Vita could scarcely imagine anyone less suited – 'to think how she would have turned any employer's household upside-down within a week'. In 1880, a Mrs Mulhall, whom Lionel had known in Buenos Aires and had chosen because she was 'the only

Catholic of [his] acquaintance', escorted Victoria from her convent in Paris to England. And it was she who broke the news of her illegitimacy to Victoria on the Channel crossing. With the exception of Max, who had been dispatched to South Africa, Victoria's siblings followed her to England the following year. And it was Victoria who, in turn, told Henry the truth about his parents, just before he was sent to the Roman Catholic boys' boarding school, Stonyhurst, in October 1881.

One of the great surprises that greeted this little band of bastards on their arrival in England was the social grandeur of their relations. Victoria was taken to visit her uncle Reginald, the Earl De La Warr, at Buckhurst in Sussex, and discovered that she had another uncle, Lord Sackville, who lived in even greater splendour, at Knole. Her aunts included the Duchess of Bedford (Aunt Bessie), who disapproved of her illegitimate nephews and nieces, and the Countess of Derby (Aunt Mary), who was to assume the role of fairy godmother. Nevertheless, the children were not allowed to meet other guests when they visited Aunt Mary at Derby House, and she advised them to drop the Sackville from their surname and call themselves plain West.

Aunt Mary used her influence to get the nineteen-year-old Victoria sent to Washington as her father's hostess and mistress of his house, after his appointment as British Minister to the United States in 1881. She had obviously noticed that the young woman, however insecure and ill-educated, and speaking English that was little better than broken, had something special about her; and persuaded the Foreign Secretary, Lord Granville, that this would be a good idea. Queen Victoria agreed, so long as Washington society acquiesced; and, to this end, a committee, consisting of Mrs Garfield, the wife of the American President, the wives of the Secretary of State and the Under Secretary of State, and Mrs Cameron, the wife of a leading Republican senator from Pennsylvania, was formed – and gave its approval, too.

Victoria was an instant – and spectacular – social success, and spent the next seven years in Washington, until her father's recall in disgrace. Lionel had been tricked into expressing an opinion as to which of the candidates in the forthcoming presidential election of 1888 would best represent Britain's interests. Contravening all protocol, Lionel wrote a letter suggesting the Democrat candidate; the Republicans (who had devised the trick question in the first place) then published Lionel's response. Compounding his error, he then gave unauthorised interviews in the press, justifying his behaviour. There was an outcry. 'It was ironical,' someone later remarked to Vita, 'that your grandfather, the most taciturn of men, should have been sacked for expressing himself too freely.'

There was, however, some consolation. Unexpectedly for a fifth son, Lionel had recently inherited Knole. His older brother, Mortimer, the 1st Lord Sackville, had died in great distress at the house in October, his last mad months made miserable by the paranoid delusion that he had committed treason and that his servants planned to poison him. By the time Victoria made her first appearance at Knole on 3 July 1889, she had already long established herself as the companion and confidante of her father. The following month, in the pouring rain on 24 August, the pair arrived at Knole again, but this time to take up permanent residence. Victoria's sister, Amalia, the third of Lionel's illegitimate daughters, was soon to join them.

Victoria slept in the room that had once been occupied by Archbishop Cranmer, and immediately threw herself into the running of the great house with the same energy and style that she had brought to the British legation in Washington. '*Cela me semble drôle* to keep house,' she wrote, but it did at least provide her with some distraction from thoughts about the future which preyed on her mind. 'I keep house!' she repeated in English in her diary, or '*Ai kip haoose*,' as her daughter Vita later reproduced her accent.

She visited the kitchen garden, discussed menus with the chef, and talked business with Captain Glasier, the Sackvilles' agent. Should they raise money by selling some of the Gainsboroughs and the Reynolds at Knole? Or could they get by, as her father preferred, by selling pheasants at 6 shillings a brace and camellias at 5 shillings a dozen? These first weeks were for Victoria an intense immersion course in Sackville history. She visited Buckhurst again, and the Sackville almshouses at East Grinstead, and she swathed herself in the fabric of Knole itself. She rummaged through wardrobes and chests of drawers stuffed with old lace, tried on the family jewels (loving the tiara but finding the diamond necklace a bit 'maigre'), poked around in china closets and in the plate room with its wonderful silver, and flicked through the books in the Library. In the show rooms she posed for a series of professional photographs.

In her first week at Knole, Victoria had read Lady Anne Clifford's diary, an account of daily life and domestic drama in the house 270 years before. Victoria's own diary was to prove even richer and more revealing about life at Knole than Lady Anne's. But it was, eventually, to echo many of the same feelings of bitterness and betrayal, of disappointment and disinheritance.

Victoria loved the grandeur of the place and the deference with which she was treated. Never secure of her place in the world, she was always reassured by the approval or love of others. She noted the magical effect which the very name of Lord Sackville had on people, and the 'bowing and scraping of the servants' as they saw her all dressed up to go out to dinner. She soon realised that she would find it very hard to get used again to an 'existence pauvre', and she loved it when visitors described her as the 'jolie châtelaine', for it confirmed in her a sense that her position at Knole was in every way an excellent one. 'Quel roman est ma vie!' she wrote in her diary.

Towards the end of July, while staying with friends of her father on the south coast, Victoria met for the first time her cousin, also confusingly called Lionel, a good-looking young man almost five years younger than her. If her father – to whom I will refer from now on as Old Lionel, as the family did then – failed to produce any legitimate sons, this young Lionel Sackville-West was heir to Knole. In 1922, in The Book of Happy Reminiscences for My Old Age, Victoria recalled – rather selectively, for her actual diary records a less dramatic encounter – how: 'We fell in love with each other the very day we met . . . I remember feeling I was looking my best that night . . . I was wearing a tight-fitting bodice and skirt of a pale yellow striped satin dress . . . Lionel never took his eyes off me during that dinner. I felt much disturbed, as he attracted me immensely.'

Over the coming summer weeks, the couple saw a lot of each other, and Lionel, at least, fell in love with Victoria, enchanted by her French accent, her beauty and her vivacity, which was such a contrast to the bleak Sackville reserve. They played draughts together in the Library at Knole after dinner, and on 6 September Lionel 'literally dragged' her into the King's Room, and by the glow of its tapestries and smouldering silver furniture, spoke his heart. 'God help me, V., I love you so,' she recorded.

Victoria was already beginning to appreciate that Lionel's love might provide a solution to the problem of her future. He had already told her that he would give up Knole if it would make a difference, that – in his words – 'Vicky's house [as he described Knole] could always be her house.' But there was also another way. And on 29 September, when someone told her what a pity it was that she couldn't stay at Knole for ever, she exclaimed, 'Ah! . . . if only they knew how easy that would be.'

First, there was some disentanglement to be done. During her years in Washington, Victoria had always had several suitors on the go, including two diplomats on her father's staff, Charles Hardinge, later head of the Foreign Office and Viceroy of India, and Cecil Spring-Rice, later British Ambassador to the United States. Poor Spring-Rice came to Knole on 24 September to declare his passion for Victoria. Before he left, however, he had to concede that nothing would make her happier than to stay at Knole and marry Lionel (he had no idea how realistic a proposition this was). 'If only he knew that Lionel asks for nothing better than to marry me,' Victoria confided in her diary.

The love letter, in which Spring-Rice bade Victoria a final farewell – 'Goodbye my tormenter. I forgive you but can't forget just yet!' – captures something of her character and attraction. Accusing her of being a flirt, a charge which she always denied, he described that when 'people, men & women, are once attracted, once in your power, you are very careful that they shan't get you in theirs – At first you seem defenceless, humble, longing for sympathy – And when the trap has once fallen on the victim everything changes . . . some people deal in sport, others in books, or society and make friends over that. Your speciality is love – You are an accomplished mistress of that art: only it's not art, it's nature – You play with it and use it and manage it, like a seagull the winds; on which he floats but which never carry him away.'

The Marquis de Löys Chandieu, whom Victoria had met in the South of France in the spring of 1889, posed a greater dilemma. Victoria told Lionel about their courtship and, in Lionel's letters to her, he acknowledged the fact that she was 'half-engaged' to the marquis. As ever, she was scrupulous, at least in her diary, to be straight – '*toujours loyale*' – to both her suitors, echoing one of the ancient Sackville family mottoes.

At first, what had prevented Victoria marrying the fabulously wealthy 'L.C.' was her religion – the marquis's mother was fervently anti-Catholic. But it was not long before other considerations became apparent. There is no doubt that Victoria was in love with the marquis. On 1 October he came to stay at Knole for four nights, at the end of which Victoria agonised over her future. 'Here I am between Lionel and Löys . . . *Je serais ou marquise ou pairesse; je sais bien celui que je préfère.*' ['I'd be either a marchioness or a peeress; I know which one I like better.']

Löys begged Victoria not to abandon him, although he did realise that this was the only way she could keep hold of her 'fine castle'. It was only three months since Victoria had first set eyes on Knole, and already she was weighing up a choice between love of a place and a person.

For several weeks that autumn, Lionel was sent abroad to study German for his Foreign Office exams, writing to Victoria up to twice a day. In his letters, which became increasingly desperate in tone whenever he feared that the marquis was gaining the upper hand, he acknowledged that, although in many ways the marquis – or 'Abroad', as he referred to him – was a better match, he didn't, of course, have Knole. Lionel feared that he may have behaved badly towards the marquis, but nevertheless hoped that Victoria would 'try and arrange everything loyalement with Abroad', that is, ditch

him with dignity. There is a touching faith in his belief in her goodness. 'Physically you are perfectly lovely,' Lionel wrote to Victoria,
'and morally you are the most noble, pure-minded person I could
ever have imagined possibly could exist.'

When Lionel returned from Germany, he came to Knole to
declare his love. On 11 December, less than six months after her
first visit to Knole, Lionel and Victoria went up to the King's Room
after dinner, and in the moonlight he asked her again to marry him.
This time she accepted. 'I will be so happy with him,' she wrote in
her diary that night.

Lionel left Knole the next morning, and Löys arrived the day
after that. When Victoria told him about Lionel, he simply wouldn't
accept the news at first, sobbing that she was his. Gradually, and
'heroically', he began to understand what Victoria was telling him:
how marrying Lionel was a way for her to secure the future of her
brothers and to legitimise her name. From her diary, it is clear that
at this stage Victoria didn't know whether she was marrying for love
or not, although she did think that Lionel would make her a faithful and devoted husband, and she was tired and fed up with battling
'contre l'existence'. 'Pauvre L.C.' left for Paris on 18 December 'dans
un état de prostration complète'. He didn't, however, lose much time
in securing his own future, announcing his engagement to a French
aristocrat Agnès de Pourtalès three months later, and marrying her in
June 1890 (a week before Victoria and Lionel's wedding).

Over Christmas, at Knowsley, the Derby seat, Victoria gave
her Aunt Mary another reason why she could never have married
L.C.: it would have meant leaving not just Knole but her father too.
If Victoria had her motives for accepting Lionel, there were also
practical advantages in the marriage for him. By basing his life at
Knole, he would not have to concentrate quite so hard on getting
a job, for he was constitutionally quite lazy. There was talk later
on of him becoming an MP, and of a directorship in a company
that manufactured bicycles, but his only real job application, to the
Foreign Office, failed.

Just as it appears from the diaries that she has finally made up
her mind to accept Lionel, she entered another agony of indecision.

She began 1890 *'avec angoisse, ne sachant a quel . . . me vouer; que je me marie avec L.C. ou avec L* [in agony, not knowing which one to pledge herself to].' She went for long walks in the Wilderness, seeking solace like Lady Anne Clifford, and many Sackvilles before and since, among the dripping trees, and beside the tiny streams, mooching and mulling over her future. Her father told her that he hoped she would marry Lionel, as did her sisters who argued that this way she would be able to stay with Papa at Knole, and look out for Max and Henry (and presumably them too).

The following month, however, her mood changed. There were fewer references in her diary to her duty towards her siblings or her father, and more a sense of acceptance, and even pleasure, in her final decision. On 1 February, Lionel asked for, and received, Victoria's father's consent. She was further reassured by the fact that, on learning the news, Lionel's family generally approved the decision. In early March, Lionel's father, William Edward, wrote to say that he was surprised by the news and worried by considerations of their age (Lionel was only twenty-two), by the difference in their respective religions, and by the fact that they were first cousins, but that if they loved each other, and were prepared to bring up their children in the Church of England, he would be happy to give his consent. Lionel's sister Cecilie was also pleased (although there are some hints that Lionel's sisters were suspicious of Victoria), and a visit to her prospective father-in-law, my great-grandfather, William Edward, near Bangor in North Wales in April was a great success. There are photographs of Victoria looking foreign and glamorous in the company of her dowdier, future sisters-in-law on windswept family picnics beside the Irish Sea, or amidst the clutter of tennis rackets and dogs. Aunt Mary saw 'a hundred thousand advantages to set against the objections'; and a neighbour, Miss Boscawen, on one of many visits to Knole, told Victoria that it was a great blessing for Knole always to have her now as mistress of the house. Even the Prince of Wales, whom she had met the previous year in the South of France, wrote to congratulate her.

Along with acceptance by family and friends came a growing pleasure in Lionel's company. 'Mon L. est vraiment such a darling,' she wrote on 15 March; '*je me sens si heureuse, excepting quand je pense au pauvre L.C.* [I feel so happy except when I think of poor L.C.].' There were 'conversations interminables', and coy references in her diary to a growing number of physical intimacies and liberties. Victoria allowed Lionel to help her with her hair, permitted him a peek at her bare foot, and showed him the petticoats she had bought as part of her wedding trousseau. Every evening, in their bedrooms at Knole, they kissed each other good night.

Lionel and Victoria were married in the chapel at Knole on 17 June 1890. '*Jour de ma Vie*,' she headed the page in her diary, repeating the rather strange family motto adopted by Mortimer in 1876: '*J'ai dit:* Obey!' Through this marriage Victoria made her position as mistress of Knole more than a temporary one, for in the likely event of her father failing to produce any legitimate heirs, her husband was heir to Knole. The wedding presents included cheques from Aunt Bessie and Aunt Mary; a Gladstone bag for Lionel from his middle brother Charlie, and a fan for Victoria from his youngest brother Bertie (my grandfather); a gold quill pen for Victoria from Amalia and Flora, a silver tea-caddy from poor Cecil Spring-Rice, a Brussels lace fan from Mr and Mrs Joseph Chamberlain, and a silver blotting-book and envelope case from the Knole household and its employees.

So began a marriage of great physical passion, of which Victoria's diaries tell you as much as you could possibly want to know. Although thinly disguised in code, with love-making referred to as 'e.g.', 'n.f.' or 'commotion', they provide a sexual tour of the house, of where and how often the young couple made love: on the lawn in front of the house, under the big tree in the Wilderness, on the sofa in Victoria's upstairs sitting room, in the Library, in bed, in the bath, on a 'black rug', in the 'fire brigade suite', four times on 18 September. 'Stallion', she applauded in her diary.

In a note addressed to his brother Charlie, but found in Victoria's papers, Lionel wrote:

I thought it might interest you to know how we get on together. First I must tell you that V. is simply a dream of beauty in bed – She has the most lovely drawers and night-gowns and to see her undress and display all her charms is enough to make me mad. She is most beautifully made – has the most lovely olive skin and superb hair. Her breasts are too delicious for words – round firm and soft with two darling little buttons which I adore kissing. She has the most magnificent hips & legs with the most ravishing little lock of hair between them which is as silky and soft as possible. Farther I must tell you she is the very incarnation of passionate love ... We go to bed awfully early and I often undress her – I unbutton her dress at the same time caressing her under her stays – I lift up her skirt over her head taking good care to feel her on the way.

Nevertheless, life at Knole with her husband, father and younger sister must, at times, have been tedious and tense. Her father had withdrawn completely into himself, and was morose and occasionally ill-tempered. When her husband told her that she talked a lot, Victoria replied that she was simply doing her best to keep conversation going, especially at meals. Apart from the occasion when a Mr French came to stay, 'who could talk to death a swarm of bees, one at a time', Victoria complained that there was so little 'small talk' in England – echoing a remark made by Mme Vigée-Lebrun about dining at Knole with the Dowager Duchess of Dorset.

Victoria's relations with her siblings – particularly Amalia – were strained by her marriage. The tone of their correspondence in the 1870s and 1880s had been relatively affectionate, as the five children, with a dead mother and an extremely distant father, supported each other in their unhappiness and displacement to different parts of the world. As Victoria increasingly took charge not just of household matters at Knole, but also of family affairs in general, they became jealous. In April 1890, a couple of months before her marriage, she had had a 'stormy interview' in Paris with Flora and her husband Gabriel Salanson (whom Flora had met in Washington). Flora and Gabriel didn't want to look after Amalia – she was too extravagant – but wanted her to live, instead, with Papa and Victoria at Knole. The problem was that Amalia got so bored there, irritating everyone with her bad moods, her frequent requests for money, and her constant bad-mouthing of Victoria. Victoria tried to stop her from bitching to mutual friends who visited the house, but Amalia countered by threatening to tell their friends that Victoria had forbidden her from speaking to them at all. After yet another of these unpleasant conversations with Amalia, Victoria broke down in tears in the Library, 'so discouraged by trying to be so kind to her to live in peace with her', and to be treated, in return, with such ingratitude.

Amalia, for her part, felt like a prisoner at Knole. Her father and older sister were obliged to keep an eye on her, for the sake of economy and propriety (although given Old Lionel's own secret history, and the muddle that keeping up appearances was to get him into, this stress on propriety seems a little ironic in retrospect). When, in June 1895, Amalia asked to stay in Victoria and Lionel's London house in Berkeley Square while they were at Knole, Victoria refused, recording in her diary that Amalia would simply not behave well enough.

There was an obvious solution, as the wife of the adjutant of the West Kent Yeomanry said to Victoria: 'Amalia was so trying to all her friends, that anything ought to be done to get her married.' Amalia did have a number of suitors, but, unfortunately, most of them came to nothing. In January 1894 a Mr Jackson suddenly appeared less suitable when it was revealed that he had one older brother, five sisters, and very little money; in any case, his family opposed the match on the grounds of religion. Amalia reacted by sulking in her bedroom for days. In 1895 there was a Mr Tobin, but his family telegraphed him that they would only give him any money if he married an American and, as a result, he told Amalia that he couldn't marry her. 'Quel disappointment,' noted Victoria. Amalia's engagement to a Mr Louis Dease in 1899 was also broken off.

The staple sibling rivalries over money, the use of the car and a fair share of parental affection poisoned the atmosphere at Knole for most of the 1890s. In October 1896, Amalia was still asking Victoria for her own sitting room at Knole – Cranmer's Dressing Room – so that when the sisters were at Knole together, they could at least have a little space: 'I am not asking anything I have not got a right to . . . Believe me, this is the only possible way of living in peace under the same roof.' The alternative was to beg her father for money to live on her own. 'You know how utterly impossible it is for Victoria and I to get on together more so now than ever. The six years I have spent at Knole have been simply miserable on account of the endless rows and quarrels,' Amalia wrote on 2 December 1896. 'I am twenty-nine, quite old enough to take care of myself.'

From the distance of Paris, Flora kept making trouble, claiming for example that she didn't consider Lionel and Victoria properly married: they had been married in the chapel at Knole, rather than in a Roman Catholic church, and Victoria had not yet received the papal dispensation she was eventually to get from Pope Leo XIII. Flora always tended to encourage Amalia to 'hold her own' against the Sackville-Wests and 'fight to the end'.

Victoria kept herself distracted in those first years at Knole by reading, by taking walks in the park, to the kitchen garden to eat gooseberries, or to the Bird House to take tea, or to visit the farm at Blackhall that her husband had taken in hand. There were a hundred and one little household projects, such as embroidering footstools or decorating a screen with postage stamps – she was later to wallpaper an entire room with stamps she had collected.

On her first wedding anniversary, 17 June 1891, Victoria recorded an '*année parfaitement heureuse avec mon amour de mari si aimé* [a year of perfect happiness with my beloved husband]'. In the evening, at a party for the staff, Lionel – or 'Tio', as Victoria called him – made a speech which went down very well, in which he said that the last year had been the happiest of his life. The following month Victoria realised that she was pregnant.

In her diary, Victoria referred during pregnancy to the squirming unborn child, who gave her such trouble sleeping, as 'Vita'. She had anticipated a difficult birth, rewriting her will and penning a letter of goodbye to her husband, but when it came, it was '100 times worse than she was expecting'. She writhed in the arms of her husband and the nurse Mrs Paterson, asking them to kill her and begging for chloroform. When 'mon pauvre Tio' couldn't open the bottle, '*J'étais affolée* [out of my mind]'. The experience would put her off the idea of having any more children, although in December 1895 she had still not ruled out the possibility, given that her husband was so keen on 'baby No. 2' and, she claimed, she 'would do anything to make him happy, even if it meant undergoing the horrors of childbirth'.

Vita was born at 4.15 a.m. on 9 March 1892. 'I shall never forget the intense happiness I felt when Lionel brought me Vita on a pillow at five in the morning after my terrible confinement,' Victoria wrote many years later in her *Book of Happy Reminiscences*. 'One's own little baby is such a miracle; such an incredible marvel. Nothing else can be so wonderful! I had the deepest gratitude to Lionel, who I was madly in love with, for giving me such a gift as that darling baby . . . Vita's babyhood is one of my happiest recollections. Lionel was perfect to me in those days. He gave me ten perfect years of the most complete happiness and passionate love which I reciprocated heartily. I adored him, and he adored me.'

Victoria also adored her daughter, particularly as a young child, recording all her little doings with pride: the first time she said 'Dada' (3 September 1892) or 'Mama', her first teeth, her first tottering steps. She often called Vita 'the Child' in her diary, copying the way Lady Anne Clifford had referred to her daughter, Margaret, in her diary.

Vita had many wonderful memories of Knole at the turn of the century, with her grandfather, father and mother. One of her most affecting descriptions was of her grandfather, whose heavy-lidded eyes always reminded her of Thomas Sackville, the 1st Earl of Dorset. 'Old Lionel,' she wrote, 'never did say anything; he had his own occupations, which included . . . whittling paper knives from the lids of cigar boxes. He liked the garden, where two cranes (called Romeo and Juliet) and a French partridge with pink legs followed him sedately about.' From early childhood, Vita was thrown into the company of O'Mann, as she called him – short for Old Man – and grew to know him 'as intimately as a child of that age could ever know a very reserved old man of nearly eighty'. She observed that, 'Of all human beings he was surely the most inscrutable. I lived with him for sixteen years, and had I lived with him for yet another sixteen I have no doubt that he would have remained just as much of an enigma.'

One particular vignette from Vita's childhood shows just how deep some of those still, secret, Sackville waters, ran. Once, when Vita followed Victoria into Old Lionel's sitting room, holding on to the end of her mother's long hair, her grandfather jumped up and said: 'Never let me see that child doing that again Victoria.' The sudden memory of how Victoria had played with her own mother's hair momentarily broke through Old Lionel's reserve, and exposed his feelings for Pepita.

Vita Sackville-West grew up at Knole, the house that was to inhabit her soul in a way that no human being ever would. She learned at an early age to take parties of visitors round the house, or simply wandered around on her own, playing imaginary games. She particularly loved the attics, which opened through unexpected skylights on to the roofs, and were crammed, as they are today, with the flotsam and jetsam thrown up by previous tides of Sackvilles. Here she would poke around in trunks and rifle through chests of drawers, just as our children do today, each successive generation making its own discoveries.

Vita was in many ways a lonely and secretive little girl, and when other children were invited over to Knole, she tended to be rather fierce with them, as she recalled years later in 'Shameful Reminiscences', a piece she contributed to a collection of childhood memories. When the Battiscombe children – whom Vita renamed the Thistlethwaites – came to tea, they all reenacted battles from the Boer War in the garden, digging trenches among the rhododendrons. Vita was Sir Redvers Buller and the Battiscombe boy Lord Roberts, and they ganged up on the four Battiscombe girls, tying them up to trees, stuffing their nostrils with putty, and thrashing their legs with nettles. Vita claimed, perhaps wishfully in this memoir, that 'the girls enjoyed it masochistically, as much as the boy and I [did], sadistically'.

Occasionally her cousins visited Knole: little Lionel Salanson, Flora's son, came for the summer of 1894 and, several years later, her uncle Charlie's son Eddy. He, like Vita, remembered the house very well in the early 1900s: the ticking of the grandfather clocks, the wood-smoke smell, and the long, dark-panelled dining room which, when the wind blew, 'seemed to contract and expand irregularly like the heart of a dying man'. His great-uncle made a particularly vivid impression as an 'old, sad, disgusted man', with a great white beard and hooded eyes, who suffered from 'the temperamental melancholy which dogs all Sackvilles and has driven many of them to end their lives in blackest solitude'.

From time to time, Lord Sackville would emerge from a study, which contained nothing more than a leather armchair and a glass case with a wasp's nest inside: 'In this cold and cheerless cell,' wrote Eddy, 'the possessor of some of the finest furniture and silver in England would immerse himself for hours at a time, perusing either Gibbon's *Decline and Fall* or the works of Josephus. These books he read through regularly every year, and as he closed the last volume of either he would remark: "Good book, that." He was never known to vary this comment, nor to enlarge upon it.' Eddy also recalled the 'fantastic personality – so charming yet so unsafe' of his Aunt Victoria.

Eddy used to play with his cousin Vita, who was nine years older than him, a friendship he described as 'one of the most intimate and enduring' of his life. The terrible irony, as it transpired, and the cause of an underlying tension in their relationship, was that Eddy was the eventual heir, by virtue of his sex, to Knole. And yet he didn't particularly like the house, and would probably have been just as happy as a girl, whereas the tom-boyish Vita was excluded by her gender from the inheritance of a place about which she cared passionately. Nevertheless, they shared a liking for very black toast, and Vita would work the bellows as the musically gifted Eddy strummed on the 'sturdy little Jacobean organ' in the chapel: 'the gently stirring air of the twilit chapel, the great gothic tapestry representing the crucifixion, which filled the whole of one wall with its livid fanfare of primary colours, the plaintive ciphering of the organ when a certain stop was pulled out, and the mysterious affection of kinship spun between myself on one side of the organ and my cousin on the other'.

As well as the attics, Vita also liked the little wooden summer-house in the garden, overlooking what is now the swimming pool, then known as Looking-glass Pond. Here she wrote – at a phenomenal rate. Between 1906 and 1910, from the age of fourteen to eighteen, Vita wrote eight full-length novels and five plays, almost all of them inspired by Knole and her ancestors. Her favourites were Herbrand de Salkaville, who crossed from Normandy with William the Conqueror; Thomas Sackville who looked exactly like her grandfather, and, best of all, Edward Sackville, 4th Earl of Dorset, 'the embodiment,' Vita wrote 'of Cavalier romance'. She penned a story of 65,000 words called *The Tale of the Cavalier* about him.

Though the Sackvilles were, as Nigel Nicolson describes in *Portrait of a Marriage*, on the whole 'a modest family given to lengthy bouts of melancholia', they were transformed in Vita's childhood romances into veritable troubadours, playing 'the most romantic roles at the most dramatic moments of English history', and behaving 'in every situation with the utmost gallantry'. It is precisely this romantic vision of her family that informs Vita's book about her ancestors, *Knole and the Sackvilles*, published in 1922.

Whereas Vita had a romantic vision of Knole, Victoria had a more materialistic one, as if, her daughter sometimes complained, she had actually made the place. Vita's mother, Victoria, was a woman of massive energy: 'a powerful dynamo,' observed one male friend 'generating nothing. There was no driving belt attached to her whirling wheels.' As mistress of Knole, she had some twenty-four servants working in the house. At the top of the hierarchy were the butler, Mr Hicks, and the housekeeper, Mrs Knox; at the bottom were the footmen, laundrymaids and the housemaids, who got up before six every morning to polish the grates and to carry brass cans of hot water up to the bedrooms. There were twenty people working for Mr Stubbs, the head gardener, in the pleasure gardens and in the walled kitchen garden; four blacksmiths in the forge; a gamekeeper, Mr Findlay, with five or six men working for him; a carpenter,

Mr Jeffery, with three men and an apprentice under him; six or seven foresters; and a staff of ten on Home Farm, which supplied milk, eggs, butter and cream to the big house. Every Christmas, there was a party around a tree in the Great Hall for the children of all the staff, and Victoria would give each of them an orange, a toy and an article of clothing.

Victoria also set about making Knole more comfortable. A telephone was installed in her father's bedroom in 1891; bathrooms with hot running water gradually replaced the brass cans; central heating was introduced; and the house was fully electrified by 1902, with magnificently ornate brass light fittings. Her father was completely terrified by the electric lights, and continued to go about with a candle. Comfortable guest rooms were done up and decorated in the North Wing, each with a little brass frame on the imitation-Jacobean oak doors, into which was slotted the name of the guest who was to occupy the room. Victoria later boasted: 'Everyone says that I made Knole the most comfortable large house in England, uniting the beauties of Windsor Castle with the comforts of the Ritz and I never spoilt the old character of Knole.'

By the turn of the century, Knole was a magnificent place to enjoy a lavish weekend house party. From the living rooms on the south front, guests could flow out into the garden through the French windows. There's a photograph of just such a scene on a visit made by the Prince and Princess of Wales to Knole on 10 July 1898 – by all accounts a great success. 'We were delighted to revisit your beautiful home – after an interval of thirty-four years!' wrote the Prince. 'It is so beautifully kept & I am sure owing to the tender care *"de la charmante Châtelaine!"*' In the foreground, a six-year-old Vita, the future chronicler of Knole, holds Princess Alexandra's hand; while in the background are the ivy-covered walls of the house, dappled in the afternoon sunlight. This was the house, and the period, immortalised as Chevron in Vita's novel, *The Edwardians*: 'a medieval village,' she wrote, rather than a house, 'with its square turrets and grey walls, its hundred chimneys sending blue threads up into the air . . . The house was really as self-contained as a little town; the carpenter's shop, the painter's shop, the forge, the sawmill, the hot-house.'

The invitations and visitors' books, now in the Library at Knole, are a roll call of the rich and famous. There were shooting parties in the autumn, and 'dine and sleep visits' (the equivalent of a sleep-over) throughout the year. The guest list for 3 July 1899, for example, included W. W. Astor and Mr John Singer Sargent, the Keppels (Mrs Keppel was to become the mistress of the Prince of Wales), the Iveaghs, the Dufferins, the Sassoons, the J. P. Morgans, the Bentincks, and recorded the rooms in which they slept, many of which go by the same names to this day – Cranmer's Room, the Gateway Room, the French Library, George III's Bedroom, the Stamp Room.

The apparent elegance and ease of aristocratic life at the turn of the twentieth century was captured perfectly by Vita in *Pepita*, the double biography of her mother and grandmother:

> Life must have been extremely pleasant ... for those who were blessed with money and possessions, and whose ears were not turned to catch any sound of ominous cracking going on around them. One spent the winter months in London (Mayfair, of course), then a few weeks in Paris with the chestnut trees coming out and the spring sunshine sparkling on the river, then the deep summer beauty of Knole, with weekend parties and the adulation of stray ingratiating people who wanted to 'see the house', then the freedom of Scotland and plenty of time to read – a nice book of memoirs, or the latest novel by Mr E. F. Benson, who was so amusing, or Mr Robert Hichens, who understood so well the workings of a woman's heart – not the horrid H.G. Wells, who was a Socialist and wrote about things which were much better left unsaid. It was all extremely agreeable. One had an enormous motor ... plenty of servants, a lady's-maid and a valet who always went ahead by train and had everything laid out ready for one's arrival; one had a chef, and as much pâté de foie gras and plovers eggs as one wanted.

Victoria, too, was ecstatic about the arrival of a magnificent new 25 horsepower motor, costing £921, in November 1903, although it tended to break down quite frequently, unnerving and infuriating her father as much as the electric light.

Over the years Victoria's diary tended to become less intense and introspective, and more a record of her social life, the people she met at dinners and what she wore at Henley, Ascot and other events of the season: '*Robe bleue Worth, gros diamants; robe satin bleue et mauve, perles; robe mauve et ruban orange, turquoises & diamants*', and so on. Her year followed a pattern: February and March with Lionel in Paris and the South of France; the London season in a rented flat or house in the capital; July at Knole; grouse-shooting, fishing and stalking in Scotland in August and September (often stopping off at the in-laws in Bangor en route); visits to other grand houses, such as Cliveden, in the autumn, where Victoria was often shocked by the fast talk and behaviour of her fashionable fellow guests; and Christmas at Knole.

There was still a tendency to list, but now it was more likely to be the number of animals Lionel had shot on a shooting weekend than the number of times she and her husband made love. The young woman whose diary eight years before had been so anxious, so insecure, so impressionable had become more obviously materialistic and mercenary, obsessed with her losses and gains on the stock market or at the Casino in Monte Carlo, where she experimented compulsively with systems for beating the bank. This aspect of her personality was to become increasingly pronounced.

But the opulence of life at Knole was little more than a façade. The agricultural depression of the 1880s had continued to eat away at the fortunes of many aristocratic families, and the estate that Vita's grandfather, Old Lionel, had inherited in 1888 yielded only £11,250 a year – a relatively modest income with which to maintain such a house. In 1897 *Cornhill* magazine published a survey of the relative sizes and expenses of establishments needed to service different country houses. Knole, it seemed, got by on the level of staff considered a minimum for a house of the 'third magnitude' – and Knole was considerably larger and grander than that. There were wages of around £3,500 a year to be paid, the costs of external repairs to the roofs, chimneys and stonework, bills for internal decoration and home improvements, and the expense of Victoria's housekeeping and entertainment (which came to about £3,000 a year). On top of all that, were Lord Sackville's continued attempts to support his and Pepita's other children, including setting Max and then Henry up as farmers in Natal, and giving money to Flora and Amalia.

The Sackvilles reacted to the changed economics by selling paintings, part of a general trend in which works of art collected by aristocratic families over the previous two centuries were now widely dispersed over a couple of decades. In July 1890, *The Fortune Teller* by Reynolds and a portrait of the actress Mrs Abington by the same artist, together with the Gainsborough portrait of Signora Baccelli that had languished in the King's closet for almost a hundred years, were sold for £50,000 to the dealers Messrs. S. Wertheimer & Sons of New Bond Street, London. Flora's husband, Gabriel, who emerges from the diaries a shady and manipulative figure, encouraged the sisters to think that Victoria had pocketed the money herself – a suggestion for which she was never to forgive him. These three paintings were just the first of several sales from Knole. Nevertheless, when Victoria heard of other families, such as the De La Warrs, selling family heirlooms, she was always the first to claim how she couldn't 'bear to think of family pictures going out of the family'.

There was also the prospect of a new tax, death duties, which was introduced in 1894, with a top rate of 8 per cent. Victoria used all her considerable powers of charm and persuasion on the Chancellor of the Exchequer, Sir Michael Hicks-Beach, whom she had met at a house party, to modify the scheme. Her efforts were rewarded. In her diary on 17 April 1896, Victoria wrote: 'Last night Sir Michael Hicks-Beach proposed in his budget to abolish death duties on pictures and heirlooms. This will save Knole. He has written to me telling that it was I who made him understand the injustice of the law.' The principle of exemption from death duties of works of art, defined in the 1896 budget as of 'such national or historic interest that they would be purchased or accepted as a bequest by one of the national collections', has survived, with revisions and more demanding conditions, to this day. It has enabled the collection at Knole to survive relatively intact. And, for her part in establishing this principle, Knole has a lot to thank Victoria (however many other works of art she may have sold and dispersed).

Potentially more damaging than any other threat were the lawsuits, the prospect of a court case casting a permanent shadow over the house. The Knole inheritance had been the subject of lawsuits since the 1860s, and these were to continue until 1910 – a span of almost half a century. Back in 1890, Henry had written to Victoria that 'when you come to think of it, a father could not have done more for his children than Father has done for us; how kind he has always been to us. Remember we are his illegitimate children . . . He is a grand old man, that is what I think of him.' By 1893, however, Henry's tone had become more self-pitying. He was asking Victoria for money: 'It has been a hard lot for us boys, especially for me who has felt and still feels my presence would not be at all appreciated in England among my own relations. It is a cruel blow to my pride, however I will endure it for your sake until the bitter end.' By the time Victoria met him in Paris in the spring of 1896, he had become very 'disagreeable and aggressive'.

But no one had anticipated the bombshell. In October 1896, Lionel and Victoria were staying with Lord and Lady Iveagh at Elveden for a shooting party, when they heard that Henry had written to his father with papers supposedly proving his legitimacy and laying claim to the title and to Knole. Henry also bombarded his noble uncles and aunts – the Earl De La Warr, the Duchess of Bedford and the Countess of Derby – with letters commending his cause and threatening that unless his legitimacy was proved, he would 'make declarations which will drag the honour of an ancient family into the dust'.

The fault lines in the family opened further. In a letter to Victoria in January 1897, Max complained that his farm had suffered from rinderpest and locusts, in fact 'every scourge you can think of'. He asked her for money, noting that 'you find it a difficulty to bring up one child & to provide for the future with your thousands a year, while I have three with only £150 . . . leading at best a hand to mouth existence'. Victoria found 'the tone of his letter most unpleasant & the letter full of jealousy', and concluded: 'What is the use for me to have been so kind to them all; I am rewarded only with bitterness and jealousy?' Two years later, a letter from Max to his 'dear father', accompanied by an 'In Memoriam' card, announced the death of his eldest son Lionel Philip Sackville, Vita's first cousin.

Flora took Henry's side (there were even rumours, reported by Victoria in her diary, that Henry had the 'very worst designs' on his sister). Relations between Flora and Victoria had been strained anyway by Victoria's casting doubt on the paternity of Flora's daughter, Elie. Flora's marriage was breaking down (the divorce was settled in 1899 on the grounds of her adultery), and she needed money. Victoria heard from Flora's friend, a Miss Evans, that Flora was threatening to 'go to the bad', and in early 1899, according to Miss Evans, she was living the life of a 'common prost[itute]' in a fine apartment in Paris. The following year, Flora threatened, in a letter to Victoria, to start a bonnet shop in London 'with her name and Sackville-West on the door'. By 1901, however, 'the poor wretched thing' was living in 'miserable lodgings' at the top of a house in Gower Street, and asking the Sackvilles for money, to be found, she suggested, by selling more pictures from Knole and replacing them with copies. Finally, she threatened to go on to the music-hall stage and perform '*Poses Plastiques*' – in which the entertainers titillated the audience by dressing up in skin-tight, flesh-coloured costumes to look like naked, living statues. 'That will never do,' Victoria wrote in her diary, 'as she would have to be in tights etc. It must be stopped at all costs.' By 1904 it was being reported to Victoria that Flora was leading a very disreputable life in Paris, her demi-monde a complete contrast to the beau monde Victoria inhabited on her frequent trips to France.

Amalia sided with Henry, too, which made her position at Knole increasingly untenable. Victoria recorded in her diary how Amalia would arrive at Knole in a fly (a horse-drawn carriage), enter by the backdoor, go up to her room for five minutes, and then leave as furtively as she had come, without seeing or asking for Papa. She would then dash off to scheme with Henry in London and to spread rumours: that Victoria was angling to get Vita made heiress of Knole, that Victoria and Lionel had tried to make Amalia enter a convent or go on the stage, and that Lionel, at dinner, had dissected Amalia's character in front of the servants. Amalia's most pernicious trouble-making was to tell Mai Cornwallis-West that she had, in her possession, several compromising letters written by Mai's husband to Victoria (of which Victoria, in her diary, denied all knowledge).

Like Flora, Amalia threatened to bring the Sackville name into disrepute by earning her own living, by loose living – Victoria learnt from Amalia's maid in January 1897 that Amalia was 'tout à fait perdue' and that 'her behaviour with men [was] perfectly awful' – and by running up large debts. In March 1897, for example, Amalia was writing to her father from Cannes, asking him for an advance on her allowance 'as I have not got a penny left and the washing woman must be paid'. She also put pressure on her father by using the threat of Henry's lawsuit to blackmail the Sackvilles into settling out of court. As a result, relations at home became very unpleasant, and in December 1897, Amalia left Knole to live in Eaton Place on an allowance, provided by her father, of £360 a year. Amalia nursed her bitterness towards Victoria to the end, writing to *The Times* on her sister's death in 1936, to claim that Victoria had never been Lord Sackville's daughter.

Henry's claim to be the legitimate heir to Knole rested on two propositions: that Pepita had never been married to Oliva; and that she had, in fact, married his father, Old Lionel. Whereas Max had been registered as the son of Pepita and Oliva (which everyone knew to be untrue), and Victoria as '*fille de père inconnu*', Henry and his other sisters had been registered as the legitimate children of 'Lionel Sackville-West and his wife Josefa (Pepita) Duran'. Henry was therefore, he contended, the legitimate son and heir.

As Henry's threats continued – alternating with demands for money – the Sackvilles began to prepare their case. A private investigator, Mr Littlechild, was sent by the family solicitors, Meynell and Pemberton, to Spain to investigate the falsification of the register in the church of San Millan in Madrid, where Pepita had married Juan Antonio de Oliva in 1851. And Victoria's father was encouraged in 1897 to record his life with Pepita and the circumstances surrounding the registering of his children's births. Old Lionel's statement was to form part of an 'action for the perpetuation of testimony' – testimony to be used in a court case that could be brought only after his death. His statement began with the words: 'I am a bachelor', and went on to admit that previous false declarations about the legitimacy of some of his children and his marriage to Pepita had been done 'simply and solely to save the reputation of Pepita, and at her earnest request'. He had done it out of indolence and pity, to indulge the woman he loved, but the muddle that he made, the tissue of secrets and lies that he created, and the wandering, evasive manner with which he gave his evidence, were to cost the family dearly.

In July 1897, Victoria had to juggle visits to Meynell and Pemberton with rehearsals for a magnificent fancy-dress ball to be held at Devonshire House. Victoria had been invited to join Lady Warwick's exclusive quadrille, and went dressed as the late-eighteenth-century Duchess of Dorset. The guests were welcomed by the Duchess of Devonshire, 'gloriously apparelled' as Zenobia, Queen of Palmyra, and the duke as the Emperor Charles V. But Victoria was preoccupied throughout by rehearsals for the action for the perpetuation of testimony. 'Papa makes a great mess of his answers & contradicts himself every minute,' she wrote on 6 July. 'It is hopeless and Pemberton thinks he will be a very bad witness.' When the examinations began in the Law Courts at the end of the month, Victoria, by her own account, made a 'splendid witness', and Papa turned out to be 'not quite as bad . . . as we expected although he does not listen to the questions'. Papa and Henry occasionally stared at each other threateningly across the room.

The following year, Henry turned up at Knole at five in the afternoon of 5 October. Victoria saw him forcing his way across the Green Court, and hurried Vita away to protect her from any unpleasantness. Lord Sackville rang for a footman to help Lipscombe the porter throw his son out, but Henry kept shouting that he was the rightful heir to Knole before bursting into hysterical tears and trying to break into the house. It was then that Lord Sackville gave the order to fetch the police. Henry stayed for about two hours talking to the servants and threatening to kill himself (which he would do, sixteen years later), and then left just before the police arrived. He returned to Knole the next day, telling the policeman on permanent guard at the front door that he would go to 'extremities' on Saturday, but in fact he didn't return to Knole, and his father settled an allowance on him the following week – to buy time and peace. Over the next few years, Henry continued to make trouble from Paris, claiming that he couldn't live in London because Lionel and Victoria had tried to 'poison' him there, and forming a syndicate to invest in the his lawsuit.

Victoria's dissolving relations with her siblings began to poison her marriage. 'I had quite an unpleasantness last night with Lionel about my charming brothers and sisters,' she wrote on 26 November 1898; 'I am afraid they will be the cause of a good deal of unhappiness in my married life & my relations with L. That is the worst of it.' The couple spent more and more time apart from about 1899, Lionel with the West Kent Yeomanry or following his sporting interests. Victoria still pined for her husband when he was away, and enjoyed his amorous attentions on his return, amused, for example, when he took a series of décolleté photos of her in her room and in the garden in 1899. On 24 March 1900, she described how she loved staying in for a tête-à-tête dinner with her husband. 'I do love him more & more & do appreciate his tactful way with me; I don't think he can know how much I love him and what he is to me, for ever!!!' But was there something slightly defensive about her protestations of love?

By this time, Lionel was having an affair with Lady Camden – a fact played down by Victoria in her diary: 'Lionel is apparently having a mild flirtation with Joan Camden! Dear boy! I have such implicit confidence in my darling husband; how I love and worship him.' As she was to do on subsequent occasions, Victoria befriended her husband's mistress, feeling 'so sorry for poor little Joan' being married to a man as cantankerous as Lord Camden. 'How different my darling husband is to me,' she wrote; 'I love him all the more when I see such a striking contrast.' When Lionel did confess his affair in December 1902, Victoria was very upset and spent a wretched day at Bayham, the Camden home fourteen miles from Knole, where they were staying.

Early in 1903 Lionel went off sailing in the West Indies, which Victoria hoped would 'do him good, morally and physically'. She continued to think fondly of him – 'My darling husband is all the world to me' – but she started referring to him in her diaries as a friend as much as a lover. When Victoria consulted Dr Ferrier for her neuralgia in 1904, he found her circulation 'extremely slow' and her 'nervous system out of order'. He prescribed iron and valerian pills and a stop to marital sex. It 'won't please my darling husband', she wrote in her diary, 'but my nervous system *must* be left in peace'.

Since the late 1890s, Victoria had been spending a lot of time – in London, Paris and Scotland – with Sir John Murray Scott, an immensely wealthy and overweight (25-stone) bachelor. 'I never could get a five foot measuring tape to meet around the place where his waist should have been,' wrote Vita. 'Seery', as he was nicknamed by the Sackvilles after the way his French servants pronounced the title 'Sir', was perfect platonic company for the lonely Victoria. Several of her old suitors reappeared, too, bolstering her confidence somewhat. Baron Bildt, a Swedish diplomat whom Victoria had met in Washington, told her that he would never get over his feelings for her, although Victoria wrote in her diary that she was 'much too fond of her husband to flirt with anybody'. Charles Hardinge, also from her Washington days, came over rather 'spoony' as he took her into dinner at a party one day. 'He does not seem to get over it' either, she added. And in Paris, in 1904, she re-met the Marquis de Löys Chandieu, who told Victoria that he still held a flame for her. Victoria, however, was 'determined not to see him. I am not a flirt!' she wrote in her diary (for the umpteenth time).

Lionel's affair with Lady Camden continued until around 1905, and there are several photographs of her in the family albums, wasp-waisted, and wearing a smart pin-stripe and jaunty yachting cap, on board the Camdens' boat. Victoria chose to turn a blind eye to her husband's infidelities, at the very most urging him to exercise greater discretion, to stop him getting 'into a scrape'. But occasionally the brave face crumpled, and eventually the strain of maintaining it caused her to break.

In August 1905, Lady Constance Hatch, who was replacing Lady Camden in Lionel's affections, came to stay at Knole, and Victoria noted how she had 'struck a great friendship with L. She is a very nice-minded woman & she admires how independent Lionel and I are, of everybody; she is in the transition stage yet and has an awful bedint [Sackville slang for lower-class] of a husband. Poor Connie.' As with Joan Camden, Victoria befriended her husband's mistress, patronising her with pity, and counselling her as a means of staying in control. The exercise of discretion still lay at the heart of the accommodation Victoria had reached with herself and her husband. Connie accompanied Lionel, Victoria and Seery to Paris in the spring of 1906. In the daytime the four of them formed a perfect *'partie carrée* [foursome]', as Victoria described in her diary, with Lionel and Connie going off to play golf, and Victoria 'loafing' with Seery in galleries and antique shops. In the evening, however, Victoria was keen to drag Lionel to as many parties as they were invited to, solely 'for propriety's sake', so that they should be seen in society together.

As her marriage soured, Victoria felt increasingly alone. The house that had once given her such inspiration and strength began to exhaust her, just as it had oppressed Lady Anne Clifford three hundred years before. Like Lady Anne, she began to resent the injustice of the succession, complaining on 26 January 1906 that she had to 'spend a lot of my own money for Knole – and Eddy [her husband's eventual heir]'.

You would not be able to tell this, however, from the portrait that the French artist Carolus Duran painted of her at Knole in July 1906. A handsome woman, sitting in 'a big red velvet & gilt armchair from the ball-room', stares confidently at the viewer. Wearing 'a gauze dress trimmed with pale blue ribbons, and a light blue velvet cloak falling from her shoulders', she exudes an air of scented opulence, with a big emerald pinned to her bosom, and others around her neck and on a finger and earrings. This is Victoria at the age of forty-three, revealing nothing of the weariness and disappointment inside, of the hurts that she would confide to her diary. According to her, Carolus Duran thought it 'one of the best portraits he has ever painted', but she preferred it when people said that the portrait was 'not half good enough', and in particular when they found her expression not 'soft enough'.

Victoria entranced and exasperated those around her, and a hundred years later she remains a puzzle. I have spent many days in her company, immersed in the detailed personal diaries she kept during her life at Knole between 1889 and 1919. Reading these is a confusing, and occasionally exhausting, experience as Victoria comes over as a chaos of contradictions: one moment, extravagantly generous; the next mean and penny-pinching; sometimes shocking and sometimes shockable; passionate and yet prudish. One of the few consistent aspects of her behaviour is that she tended to be extremely nice to people who adored her, and allowed her to get her own way. She needed to be the centre of attention, and the object of everyone's appreciation and gratitude. This is the way she was with her daughter, Vita, with her friends, and with her family – dispensing advice on 'matrimonial affairs' to her sister-in-law Cecilie (who at the age of thirty-five was just about to marry a sixty-one-year-old) or to one of her husband's mistresses.

Money was to become the main means by which Victoria exercised control over her nearest and dearest, although, as the illegitimate daughter of an impecunious peer, and the wife of an unemployed aristocrat, goodness knows where it came from. When 'poor little Tio's' speculations went wrong, she was there to bail him out – and to chide him. 'That was a bad speculation on his part!' she wrote on 10 September 1903; 'I have never complained about it, but it has been very tiresome to me, having to find all the money for those shares which he bought against my consent.' It was the same with her father. On 17 November 1906, she came down to Knole to find: 'Papa very much taken up with the Knole accounts of which he does not understand a word. We must retrench! He has not told us for several years that he was living beyond his income and now the crisis has come. We must try and live away from Knole a great deal, and come back only for the summer. The waste in the garden, especially in Vegetables, has been awful.' And it was later to be the same with her daughter, for holding the purse strings was one of the few ways Victoria had of controlling Vita.

Victoria had always complained about the ingratitude of her own siblings, but she was now irritated by that of her husband's family, too. When her father-in-law, William Edward, died in 1905, she noted that he had not left her the smallest remembrance in his will, despite her generosity to him over the years. 'There seems so much ingratitude in this world! I am always doing things to help other people and yet, I very seldom find that the smallest grati-tude is shown.' Her brother-in-law Charlie and his wife Maud were so 'eaten up' by jealousy, she believed, that all they could do at Christmas was club together to give her a book costing 2 shillings and sixpence, when Maud thought nothing of spending over £4 on hats for herself. On New Year's Day, 1906, Victoria resolved as a result to 'turn over a new leaf & not wear myself out doing things for other people, especially the family, as I have done it till now. I shall use a great deal of "judicious neglect". I am sick of the ingrati-tude I see on all sides.'

Lionel and Victoria were leading increasingly separate lives; when they were together Lionel was often moody and preoccu-pied. On 17 June 1908, Victoria sent a telegram to 'my little Tio' on their eighteenth wedding anniversary, 'but he never took any notice of it! He has been as cold & indifferent lately & gets easily irritated if I propose anything or invite anybody here who is not entirely in his little set. *Cette aridité de coeur me fait tellement souf-frir* . . . [this cold-heartedness makes me suffer so much].' Victoria was surrounded by reserved Sackvilles, who could never give her as much as she gave them. This was not just a problem with her father and her husband, but with her daughter too. When Victoria had finished reading *The King's Secret*, Vita's 75,000-word, childhood novel about Charles II and the 6th Earl of Dorset, she questioned whether the character of the young Cranfield was an accurate self-portrait of Vita, as Vita had intended him to be. Cranfield was 'a dear loveable child', but Vita 'does not appear, on the surface, to be quite like little Cranfield. I should like her to be more open, less reserved.

She seems indifferent, too much so & is inclined to be rather self-ish . . . If only she could change and become warmer hearted! It has been rather hard to live all my life with Papa & Lionel who are both so cold on the surface, and now I find the same disposition in my child. I like my old Seery because he is so sympathetique and I want that so much, with my Spanish nature.'

Living with Papa (which she did more than with her husband) had become a terrible strain for Victoria. Old Lionel was now the last survivor of his eight brothers and sisters, and hated being left alone. On the other hand, he made himself very disagreeable in any sort of company. He was 'more silent than ever', and on his return to Lionel and Victoria's house at 34 Hill Street, Mayfair, after an operation for prostate cancer, became cross and 'contrary in every way', the victim of a deep despair. 'Papa gets on my nerves terribly,' Victoria wrote in August 1908, '& rubs me the wrong way all the time. He can't help it, poor man, as there is not an atom of sympathy in his nature: that is why I have taken to Seery as a Father.'

Towards the end of the month it was clear that Old Lionel was dying. The family gathered at Knole, with Victoria in constant attendance. She described, in detail, his final hours, as his mind wandered and his breath slowed, and how, 'in his last look, he seemed to beg my pardon for all the harshness and unfairness he had often shown me. I forgave him from my heart.'

Chapter 10

A Family at War (1908–1928)

Lionel Sackville-West, 3rd Baron Sackville

Vita's grandfather, Old Lionel, died on 3 September 1908. Over the previous twenty years, this most inscrutable of men had become increasingly withdrawn and depressed. But he had always inspired devotion in Vita, who was staying with Seery – Sir John Murray Scott – in Scotland when she heard the news. 'One of Seery's sisters,' she wrote, 'the big one, whom her family called the duchess – came to my room before breakfast with the telegram; she had on a pink flanelette dressing gown, and no false hair, and I remember noticing how odd she looked. She kissed me in a conscientious sort of way, but I wasn't very much moved over Grandfather's death just then; it only sank in afterwards.'

Seery's reaction, on the other hand, was more immediate and more emotional. In *Pepita*, Vita described how 'still moving in this world of unreality, I made my way down to Seery's room. I found him sitting in front of his dressing table, clad only in a suit of Jaeger combinations. He was sobbing uncontrolledly, and his sobs shook his loose enormous frame like a jelly. He was quite oblivious of his appearance. He was just overcome by the fact that "the old man" was no more.'

There is a photograph of Old Lionel's modest funeral procession, making its way down the drive at Knole. Sixteen members of the estate staff carry the coffin, several of them from families that were to be associated with Knole to the end of the twentieth century: Potter, Hodder, Tye, Doggett. The scene is timeless and decorous enough, but the trouble that had threatened since 1896, when Henry returned to England from Natal and failed to get himself acknowledged by his father as a legitimate son, was now precipitated by Lionel's death.

The Sackville family solicitor, Mr Pemberton, asked Henry's solicitor, Mr Fellowes, to use his influence to prevent Henry from attempting to enter Knole or attending the funeral. In reply, Fellowes gave 'his assurance that Henry West would not go to Knole though he would go to the funeral but would merely attend as an ordinary individual and go straight away after it was over'. Henry was to bring his case in 1909, producing evidence that he was his father's legitimate son and the rightful heir not just to the title but to Knole as well. At first, though, there was the immediate problem of settling the expectations of the other siblings.

The oldest of them, Max, initially sided with his younger brother, Henry. Letters from Max in South Africa to his cousin, 'young' Lionel, in the summer of 1909 indicated a shift in his loyalties and an acceptance that the inheritance was due to Lionel. 'I repeat that far from bearing you any grudge I will stand loyally by you. The assistance, such as it was, I may have given Henry at the very beginning . . . is a vastly different thing from assisting him, against my better judgment, in a fraud.' They are the letters of a sad and broken man, who had never been reconciled to a father whom he had loved, and who grieved on behalf of his mother – 'Poor mother! I think she was more the victim of circumstances than the author of the cross her children have to bear. She threw away the substance for the shadow, and she exchanged sterling gold for the glitter of brass.' He was disappointed by his sisters taking Henry's part, and on top of it all, his throat had been troubling him – 'I have had a wolf or a tiger at my throat for the last five years and I am only a shadow of my former self.' Although aged fifty, 'I look sixty & more, and what is more, I feel it.'

In 1910, Max visited England but, out of deference to his powerful younger sister, promised Victoria that he would not reveal any connection with the Sackville family. 'While I am in England my name is plain Mr West, which means nothing . . . I shall nowhere claim relationship with the family, on the contrary deny it.'

Flora was not so accommodating, actively helping Henry with his legal costs. In one letter, for example, she offered him 100,000 francs, with more to come. 'I would be too happy to help you crush them [the Sackvilles], wipe them out, which I haven't the least doubt will be done. Don't forget to find me a very elegant motor car in London, to take me backwards and forwards from the court. P.S. Don't forget to send me postcards of Knole.'

In a letter dated 11 June 1909, Lionel wrote to Vita that he had heard that 'Flora had sunk very low indeed & went with pretty near any body – she was now living with a rich young man whom she would probably drop as soon as she had squeezed all the money out of him.' After that, references to her are patchy, although there is a photograph, dated 1912, of a semi-clothed, bosomy Flora, her dress parted provocatively at the top of the thigh, that suggests she did succeed in carrying out her threat to go on the stage.

Amalia, the youngest girl, was appeased by offers of money. Like her siblings, she had been left £1,300 by her father, which Victoria raised to £2,500 by forfeiting her share; on top of this, Lionel and Victoria were to give her an annual allowance of £100. As the case drew near, it was Amalia who attempted to engineer a face-saving settlement between the Sackvilles and Henry: 'ridiculous propositions,' according to Lionel after a meeting in January 1910, 'about H. being allowed to be acknowledged legit and give up all his right.' Lionel was now set against all compromise, and relieved that Sir Edward Clarke, the lawyer engaged by Henry, was said by Pemberton to be 'not much good now'.

Knole, meanwhile, was shut up, its revenues from estates in Kent, Warwickshire, Gloucestershire and Sussex frozen in the hands of trustees pending the outcome of the succession case. Not for the first time its contents were shrouded by dust sheets, in the care of a reduced staff. For the next two years the new Lord and Lady Sackville lived on and off in a small hotel, the St Petersburg, in North Audley Street, near Grosvenor Square.

*   *   *

On 1 February 1910 the case opened in the High Court in London
before the Rt Hon. Sir John Bigham. An application the previous
year by Henry – Ernest Henri Jean Baptiste West – to have the
case heard by a jury had been turned down on the basis that the
body of evidence, some 2,000 folios collected over thirteen years,
with all the consequent questions of admissibility, was too large
and unmanageable for a jury. At stake was a house – Knole – which,
as Vita described in *Pepita*, had assumed a monstrous importance
and 'meant as much as any human being' (although to Vita it probably meant more). The case was described as 'the Romance of the
Sackville Peerage' and it attracted massive press coverage on both
sides of the Atlantic, with its heady mixture of ancient manners and
modern wealth, high life and low life. The greatest irony of the case
was that Victoria, Lady Sackville, was in the invidious position of
needing her illegitimacy (always a very sensitive subject with her)
to be proved in order for her husband to inherit.

On the third day of the case, Vita attended the court for a few
minutes after lessons at Miss Woolff's school. Her father had not
wanted her there, but Victoria got her way, and Vita came. 'Look at
your relations,' Victoria said dismissively to her daughter. To Vita,
they seemed 'very drab and black-suited and bowler-hatted, – not
romantic at all. My Spanish relations! They looked like plumbers
in their Sunday best.' The same day, Henry's counsel, Sir Edward
Clarke, withdrew abruptly from the case, following a disagreement
with his client. The judge suspended the sitting to allow Henry to
consider the situation and, when the court reconvened, the peti-
tioner said he wished to plead his own case, adding: 'I know that I
shall lose, but I will have a good try.' Henry's petition was dismissed
within six days, although the case was to cost the Sackvilles around
£40,000. Henry would commit suicide four years later.

On 16 February, Lionel and Victoria, with their daughter Vita,
returned to Knole in style. The couple rode through Sevenoaks
in a horse-drawn victoria. At the top of the hill, a triumphal arch
welcomed them home, the horses were led away, and the victoria was
then pulled by members of the local fire brigade through the park.
'An abominable nuisance,' is how Lionel described the celebrations.

Vita, however, enjoyed herself immensely. The staff lined up to welcome them, and Vita was given a box of chocolates. 'Never, before or since, have I felt so much like royalty . . . Then there were more speeches, with everyone in the most amiable humour, and as the doors shut behind us and we laid down our heavy bouquets in the familiar library we felt with relief that we had really come home. Now we could go and have dinner quietly and comfortably in the dining-room, with the oil lamp in the middle of the table as it always had been.'

The family had reclaimed their inheritance. Vita was given her grandfather's old room, overlooking the Pheasants' Court, while her maid, Emily, had a room in the Little Duke's Tower above. Vita wanted her room to be 'stern and austere, not the bedroom of a young girl', and certainly not the pink that her mother had had it done up in. She would repaint it in a mock-Italian style, blue and gold.

Vita was immersing herself in Knole, as her mother had done just over twenty years before – not just in the fabric of the place but in the whole notion of her possession of it. As she wrote on 27 February 1912: 'Mother has gone to Paris, and I am all alone here for the moment, and all this big house is mine to shut up if I choose, and shut out all the rest of the world by swinging the iron bars across all the gates. But instead of doing that I have locked all the doors of my own tower, and nobody will come near me till tomorrow morning, or even know whether I am still alive.' She claimed, disingenuously, that although she used to be jealous of her cousin Eddy, who would one day inherit Knole, she now realised she didn't want it and was happy to accept that he would be an excellent person for it. What Vita described as her atavistic passion for Knole often clouded her feelings for people: Eddy, certainly, but her future husband too.

Vita had first met her husband-to-be, the twenty-four-year-old diplomat, Harold Nicolson, at a dinner party in London in June 1910, days after she had 'come out' as a debutante. He was invited to Knole and sat in the pouring rain in the park to watch Vita's performance as Portia in an open-air Shakespearean masque.

Between 1910 and 1913, or between the ages of eighteen and twenty-one, Vita lived what was superficially at least a life of great privilege. Although she recalled that 'we were very poor then', her life was a whirl of social activity and journeys abroad: to France, Italy, Switzerland and Russia, often in the company of Rosamund Grosvenor. 'I really worshipped Rosamund then,' she later reminisced about her first love, with whom she had shared lessons at Knole as a girl and whom she often referred to as 'the Rubens lady'. Vita went to dances, including a '100-years-ago ball' in June 1912 where she dressed (as her mother had done for the Devonshire House Ball of 1897) as Arabella, Duchess of Dorset, with 'three nodding white plumes, and ring-miniatures of John Frederick the Duke on my fingers'. Many of these balls were held at houses – Hatfield, Burghley and so on – that had been built four centuries before when Vita's ancestor, Thomas Sackville, was Lord Treasurer and the ancestors of her hosts were his colleagues and rivals. As Vita later wrote of those times, 'genealogies and family connections, tables of precedence and a familiarity with country seats formed almost part of a moral code'.

She also began to see a lot more of Violet Keppel. The two had met in 1904 at a tea party at Lady Kilmorey's, when Violet remembered Vita as a shy, gawky girl of twelve. Over the next years they met from time to time – even holidaying together. Vita particularly enjoyed the tea-time visits to the Keppel home in Portman Square where Violet's mother entertained her lover, King Edward VII. Vita would occasionally see a horsedrawn carriage waiting outside 'and the butler would slip into a dark corner of the hall with a murmured "One minute, miss, a gentleman is coming downstairs".' In December 1908, she recorded in her diary: 'Went to tea with Violet, and stayed to dinner. The King was there.'

But it was not until 1912, after a couple of years of not seeing each other, that Violet became completely enthralled by Vita: 'I expected a "representative Englishwoman", perpendicular, gauche, all knobs and knuckles. No one told me that Vita had turned into a beauty. The knobs and knuckles had disappeared. She was tall and graceful. The profound, hereditary Sackville eyes were as pools from which the morning mist had lifted.' In her memoirs *Don't Look Round*, Violet observed with great perspicacity about Vita and the Sackvilles: 'One thing was common to them all, a detachment, part morgue, part melancholy, which in the end drove them to see in Nature the stable compensations that they failed to find in their fellow creatures.'

Vita enjoyed watching her girlfriends vie for attention. Over New Year 1913, she was performing in *An Eastern Fantasy* in the Great Hall at Knole. Vita had written the prologue herself, and took the principal part of the Caliph loved – appropriately enough (because they were both in love with her) – by Zuleika, a dancing girl played by Rosamund, and a slave girl played by Violet, dressed in yashmaks and veils. A couple of months later, Vita was describing another event in a letter to Harold. 'Violet Keppel and I gave a party,' she wrote from Knole on 24 February 1913. 'It was the success of the year. The Rubens lady, who is jealous of VK, was furious. Especially when Violet and I acted afterwards, and ended up in each other's arms.'

Rosamund had another reason to be miserable. In July, after much prevarication, Vita became officially engaged to Harold, and Rosamund, according to Vita, 'used to cry all night and every night, as I very well knew, because her bedroom was next door to mine at Knole, but as I had ceased to care for her and thought only of Harold, I was only exasperated by her tears'.

The emotional intensity of life at Knole was complicated further by the unhappiness of Vita's parents. The cracks in Lionel and Victoria's marriage, on which they had embarked with such minutely documented passion, were by now apparent. In her various reminiscences, Vita made much of the differences in character and background between her two parents. For her it partly explained the duality in her own nature – her mixture of unconventionality and conventionality; the Spanish and the English, the gypsy and the grandee.

Her father, she saw, as 'the best type of English country gentleman; just, courteous, and conscientious, he was truly loved and respected by all. Five days a week he devoted to the service of his

county; Saturday he would give to his duties as owner of Knole.'
She went on to describe, perhaps a shade too romantically, a man
who would know about every tile that came off one of the estate
cottages, who hand-copied every important letter, and who might
just manage to squeeze in a round of golf or a game of tennis on
Sunday.

However, the impression Lionel gives in his letters is of a man
slightly bored by his 'duties' – 'my agricultural dinner at Dartford'
or a county council meeting. He was actually quite lazy, his philosophy of life summarised in one of his pet sayings: 'Never do today
what you can possibly put off until tomorrow.' Some advice he gave
Vita in September 1913 as she prepared for her wedding revealed a
lot about his own attitudes to marriage: 'the difference is really a
very big one to a man [thinking of Harold]. He gives up a lot of
liberty and takes on a lot of responsibility in having to think for
two.'

That this feckless and weak man was very fond of his daughter is
clear from the letters he wrote to Vita, often teasing her for her love
of literature and intellectual people. 'Of course,' he wrote to her
about some acquaintance, 'he is not a friend of Botticelli's, but does
that matter? Cimabue himself would be a little out of place in the
Paddock.' To his wife Victoria, he confided about Vita: 'I can't help
being sorry she doesn't like more normal and ordinary things . . . I
am very much afraid she will end up marrying a "soul" [by which
he meant, an intellectual or anyone with the slightest interest in the
arts or ideas].' Lionel was resolutely unintellectual, almost revelling
in his philistinism. When Vita attended 'a very arty party' with John
Singer Sargent, Henry James and Percy Grainger, she wrote that
her 'Dada', who much preferred the pleasures of horse-racing, golf,
sailing and shooting, was 'well out of it!'

In *Pepita*, Vita claimed to be surprised that Lionel was not driven
mad – at least didn't appear to be – by her mother's eccentricities,
'her consistent unpunctuality, the extraordinary disorder of her
bedroom, the endless fuss over insignificant matters, the vindictive
grievances, the storms . . .'; indeed, by an obsession with fresh air so
intense that, wrapped in furs and with a hot-water bottle in her lap,

she took to having her meals brought to her out-of-doors on a tray, even when it was snowing. Vita made much of the 'Spanish' characteristics of her mother. 'Although on one side of her lineage,' she wrote, Victoria 'had the opulent Sackvilles aligned behind her, on the other she had all that rapscallion Spanish background'. It was this side that was responsible for that ruthless, capricious, tyrannical streak in her mother of which Vita was always in awe.

A more sympathetic portrait of Lady Sackville in her prime emerges in Violet Keppel's autobiography:

> There was much about her mother I was at a loss to account for. Her vivacity, effervescence, like new wine in an old bottle? She was a woman of about fifty. In her too-fleshy face, classical features sought to escape from the encroaching fat. An admirable mouth, of a pure and cruel design, held good. It was obvious that she had been beautiful. Her voluminous, ambiguous body was upholstered, rather than dressed, in what appeared to be an assortment of pattens, lace, brocades, velvets, taffetas. Shopping lists were pinned to her bosom. She kept up a flow of flattering, sprightly conversation, not unlike the patter of a conjuror, intent on keeping your mind off the trick he is about to perform. Like the conjuror, she fascinated you, more especially as these monologues were uttered in a youthful, high-stepping voice, with a strong French accent.

Ever since the turn of the century, Lionel had been engaged in a string of extramarital affairs, the latest and most long-lasting of these being with a singer called Olive Rubens. By 1912 Olive and her husband Walter were frequent visitors to Knole (and also close friends of Victoria, although she was later to complain how she had objected to Olive's 'scale-singing that went on for hours in the Court, when I was still in bed').

Letters from Victoria to her daughter often refer to the strained domestic circumstances, and to Lionel's growing neglect of – and increasing off-handedness with – his wife. On 9 October 1912, 'Dada was frightfully silent at lunchtime, so I read the M. Post . . .'; a week later, on 16 October, she wrote: 'I am so glad I came back yesterday from London instead of hanging about unnecessarily – Dada had a happy dinner there & I felt I was not wanted & it was wise to come back ... Things are not getting on very well in that quarter ... he does not understand my nature at all ... So there is a dead lock and I am doing little or nothing to change things, as I have tried and failed three times.'

The family was also short of money. At around £13,000, the income from the estate was by now perhaps a third of what was needed to support an establishment such as Knole. Old Lionel had died a relatively poor man. During his life, he had had the Knole income and his pension from the Foreign Office. And in death, all he left were life insurance policies worth a total of £7,100 to his children, his wardrobe, a few personal effects ('and you know how few they were', his nephew Lionel wrote to Seery), some tools bought for the estate during his lifetime out of income, and a bank overdraft of £1,000. 'Oh, what a mess poor O'Mann made of everything,' his daughter wrote to Seery, 'but I do forgive him as you know. It is rather dreadful not to provide for his children properly, and to leave it to me to do, alas! Those three allowances [to Amalia, Max and Flora] and the interest due on the trial money cripple us dreadfully and alas, it all comes thro' poor O'Mann's fault.'

Victoria tried to make some money through her interior decorating shop, Speall's, in South Audley Street, Mayfair. The shop, which sold lampshades and knick-knacks, became quite a feature of family life. In the letters that Vita wrote once – and sometimes twice – a day from her foreign trips, there are many reference to commissions she might undertake for Speall's ('a piece of pale-green marble for a hanging lamp ... it costs 20 lire') or an idea for Speall's ('why don't you make loose covers for telephone directories?'). The shop, however, generated nowhere near enough extra income to make any impact on the estate's debts.

Where Victoria excelled was in her ability to mix business with pleasure, or more particularly, to accept money and gifts from admirers. 'Never refuse a good offer, my child,' she told Vita; 'I have refused many good offers in my life [this was probably an exaggeration], and always regretted it.' She was good, for example, at helping her husband to sell heirlooms from Knole in order to restore the family fortunes. In 1911, she met the seventy-four-year-old American businessman John Pierpont Morgan as he was buying the portrait of *Miss Linley and Her Brother* by Gainsborough for £36,000. Morgan was persuaded to buy the tapestries of the *Seven Deadly Sins* at Knole for £65,000. On 20 July he visited Knole to inspect his acquisitions, and then attended a big dinner in the Great Hall on 30 July. 'He has a wonderful personality,' wrote Victoria; 'I have not met anyone as attractive.' The following year J. P. Morgan declared his love for Victoria, but that is as far as the relationship went.

Victoria's most significant admirer, though, was Seery, who swiftly became a firm favourite of all the family. When Seery came to know of the Sackvilles' financial difficulties (and Victoria was careful from early on in their friendship, which had begun in the late 1890s, to keep him fully informed of these), he helped, first by loans and then by converting the loans into gifts. It was a tempestuous relationship – more an *amitié amoureuse* than a full-blown affair – and Victoria was, in turn, charming and then tiresomely capricious, wildly extravagant in her fondness and then utterly grasping. In a letter dated 13 July 1910, Victoria complained to Vita how 'horrid' Seery was being and how 'economical with his motor car and every thing else. I have even got to pay for the Illustrated Papers, and all my stamps now!' Even before they knew of his will, Seery's family were already referring to the Sackvilles as 'The Locusts'.

The correspondence between Victoria and Seery is a chronicle of petty squabbles. 'You are a very tiresome old thing,' begins a typical letter from Seery in 1911. Victoria, on the other hand, always believed that she was in the right. As she explained in a letter to Vita, dated 12 January 1912: 'I have behaved like an Angel, and he like a demon. I look upon the whole thing as hopeless – I simply have not got the strength to fight that endless battle, and for a doubtful result.' The doubtful result she was referring to was the money that Seery would leave. According to Victoria, Seery threatened to cut her out of his will on an almost daily basis. Lionel was more circumspect. In her diary in 1914, Victoria recalled the 'many unpleasantnesses' she had had with her 'dear old Seery', but 'Lionel advises me to be very diplomatic and put up with his humour. He says I must think of the future.'

Victoria was at Speall's on 17 January 1912, waiting for Seery to take her out to lunch, when she got a telephone call saying that he had collapsed and died at Hertford House. Seery left Victoria £150,000 and the contents of his house in Paris. Although she was allowed to spend the income from the £150,000, rather than any capital, there were no such restrictions on the works of art (valued for insurance purposes at £350,000), which Seery had expected her to keep at Knole. She was furious that the executors of the Scott estate would not allow her to take dealers round Seery's house in rue Lafitte, inviting offers for the pieces of furniture before they were legally hers.

Although the larger part of his fortune of £1,180,000 was to be divided between his brothers and sisters, the Scott family contested Seery's will. They claimed that Lady Sackville had exercised 'undue influence' over Seery in his declining years in order to alienate his affections, and fortune, from his rightful heirs.

The case came to court on 24 June and occupied eight days over the next fortnight, ending on 7 July. Two of Britain's most outstanding barristers of the day represented the parties: F. E. Smith, later Lord Birkenhead, for the Scott family, and Sir Edward Carson for the Sackvilles. Victoria had even written to Smith on 19 June, five days before the case opened: 'I can't believe that you would let yourself be mixed up in this painful affair when you and I meet among our friends in society and I meet your wife often too.'

The case was almost a society event. The ladies on the wooden benches of the public gallery – including Mrs Asquith and Clementine Churchill – certainly dressed as if for one, and brought cushions and picnic hampers so that they did not have to abandon their seats during the lunch breaks. F. E. Smith's opening address lasted nine hours, during the course of which he painted a picture of a mercenary woman who, bit by bit, had weaned Sir John Scott from the members of his family by disparaging them to him. He claimed 'in the first place, and this is as undue influence, that Lord and Lady Sackville secured such an ascendancy over Sir John Scott by modes and to such an extent, which I will describe to you, that his mind in these matters ceased to be his own mind and became in fact Lady Sackville's mind.' She had ordered his servants about, advised him not to appoint his favourite younger brother Walter as his private secretary, rearranged the furniture in the family house in Connaught Place, borrowed their carriages and their cook, insinuated 'herself into the position of the mistress of the house', invited her own friends to Seery's dinner parties to 'make them more lively' and, when King Edward came to lunch in rue Lafitte and Victoria acted as hostess, had told the Scott sisters to eat in a hotel. 'Within a few short months,' F. E. Smith concluded, 'these sisters could not call their brother's home their own.'

It was alleged that, in addition to the will, Victoria had obtained almost £84,000 from Seery over a ten-year period – including a sum of £38,600 to pay off a mortgage on Knole that had been raised to pay the costs of the 1910 litigation. But it was more than that. During the 'pendency of the claim', Lionel had been allowed to apply Knole rents for the upkeep of the property but had not been allowed to take them as personal expenditure; Seery, it emerged, had effectively been paying the daily expenses of the family, including the running costs of a motor car, as well as the legal expenses. Seery even paid Lionel £17,000 to buy the house at 34 Hill Street, Mayfair, and to do it up, with Lionel then making it over to his wife. Much of the evidence in court consisted of a detailed breakdown, cheque by cheque, of how much Seery had handed over: £125 here, £42 8s. 6d. there; £4,800 for presents, £9,000 to the second Lord Sackville (Lionel's uncle); £5,000 for 'buying back Knole silver' and so on. There had been a steady financial subsidy to Knole and the Sackvilles.

At the heart of the Scott case was the question of a draft codicil found in Sir John's house after his death, which revoked most of the legacies made to Victoria, leaving her only £30,000. It showed at least that Seery had considered changing his will. Letters from Victoria to Seery appear to accept that he had considered this at some point, although there does seem to have been a rapprochement by the time of his death. Much of the evidence for the existence of a codicil came from a mysterious witness called Major Arbuthnot who claimed that, arriving early for dinner at Connaught Place in July 1911, he had spotted Victoria and Vita going through the drawers of Seery's desk – searching, it was inferred, for the codicil. Sir Edward Carson was to argue that the idea of mother and daughter rifling through the drawers was irrelevant – there was no proof that any documents were missing – and that, in any case, Vita had been ill in bed at Hill Street that day.

Carson argued that Sir John was 'a man of sound mind', a 'free agent', not the 'miserable, cringing creature dominated over by Lord and Lady Sackville'. He claimed that Sir John had the interests of Knole estate very much at heart, which is why he had given money to Lionel. 'As will be proved to you,' Carson continued, 'he became extremely anxious that the Knole collection should not be broken up. He found the Sackvilles there under very trying circumstances; they were not rich people; they do not profess to have been rich people. They were rich to this extent, that they had got treasures . . . but they prefer to preserve these things.' They were 'wholly, or almost wholly, without the means of keeping up the station in life to which they belong'. Victoria, in the witness box, confirmed that the money she and Lionel had received was for Knole, and that they did not really benefit: 'I was not the gainer at all.'

During the case, considerable doubt was cast on the morals of the Sackville family. Victoria was accused of having attempted to seduce Seery's youngest brother, Walter, and Lionel was quizzed about his rounds of golf or trips to Paris with his ladyfriend, Lady Constance Hatch, 'a stringy, wispy French-music-hall Englishwoman with whom Dada was for years most inexplicably in love', according to Vita. The trips to the Vaudeville, to the Folies Bergères, Versailles and Fontainebleau with Lady Connie were all detailed, while Victoria and Seery would shop and sightsee together. The jurors were asked by F. E. Smith to picture these odd couples in order to put the whole affair into some context: 'It is very important,' he said, 'in order that you should reconstruct as far as you can, what must be pronounced a remarkable and unusual ménage.'

The press made much of the case, as they had done with the legitimacy case three years earlier. 'The Million-pound Lawsuit', they called it. Victoria was called to the stand, dressed in blue, to match her eyes, with a feather boa and a big hat with an ostrich feather. She spent two half days and one whole day in the witness box, and F. E. Smith admitted afterwards that he had never had to cross-examine a witness who gave him more trouble. When asked a tricky question, she might reply: 'You don't seem to realise, Mr Smith, that Knole is bigger than Hampton Court.' Victoria unsettled Smith with her evasive replies and teased him about their social familiarity. When questioned about her dealings with Walter, she used her knuckles, swathed in elegant yellow gloves, to give an absurd imitation of him waddling stoutly on his knees across the room as he declared his love for her and tried to embrace her knees. 'It was the most ridiculous thing I have ever seen,' she claimed.

She dazzled the jurors – and her adoring daughter – with a combination of put-downs and pathos, bursting into tears when a letter from an indiscreet friend was produced as evidence against her. One day she won a commendation from the judge, when she claimed that she had come to court against doctor's orders after being ill in the night. 'The doctor says I am on the verge of a nervous breakdown,' she told the court, 'and I hope I shall get through today.' It was a bravura performance. Vita was among those called to give evidence, which she delivered in a clear, firm voice. The press, adopting her affectionately as 'Kidlet', one of her family nicknames, loved her.

On 7 July 1913, the case ended in victory and vindication for Victoria. In his summing up, the judge, Sir Samuel Evans, observed that 'Lady Sackville is a lady of high mettle – very high mettle indeed.' He explained how 'undue influence', of which Lord and Lady Sackville were accused, must involve coercion; and directed the jury not to find Lady Sackville guilty of fraud, with which she was also accused. The jury took just twelve minutes to find in Lady Sackville's favour on both counts. The long and the short of it was probably, as the *Pall Mall Gazette* observed, that 'Sir John was ready to give, and Lady Sackville scrupled not to receive.' After the case had finished, the Alhambra put on a popular musical revue based upon it, compounding the irony that a family noted for its reserve was temporarily once again the most notorious family in the country.

Victoria immediately gave full rein to her extravagance – but not before she had fired off a letter to F. E. Smith: 'Before the case I was mistaken and thought you were a gentleman. Since then I have discovered more and more that you are a CAD.' In his summing up, the judge had observed to the jurors that they would 'probably come to the conclusion, assuming that both parties are honest for this purpose ... that it was never intended by Sir John Scott that the beautiful objects of art which he and others had collected were going to be dispersed and sold ... He said in one of his letters that he had found a kindred spirit [Victoria] to whom he could confide his fine things.' How wrong such a conclusion would prove.

Victoria immediately sold Seery's works of art for £270,000 to the French art dealer Jacques Seligmann (some of them are now part of the Frick Collection in New York). She bought a Rolls-Royce for £1,450, and a £2,000 necklace, spotted in a jeweller's shop in Bond Street, for Vita. Although she provided the money to buy Lionel's yacht *Sumurun* (for which, incidentally, she complained that he only thanked her once), she was secretly pleased to have the power not to promise her husband a fixed income, because she did not think she 'should approve of the way he'd spend it'.

The shopping was some distraction from the bitterness she felt at her husband's affair with Olive Rubens. Olive was kind, gentle and cheerful – the opposite, temperamentally, of Victoria – and Lionel, appreciating the affection, had soon installed her with her complaisant husband Walter in a flat at Knole. Walter, who suffered from tuberculosis, was 'a bit of a bounder and low bred', according to Harold Nicolson.

Victoria, too, had begun to go her own way. There is, for example, an envelope in a trunk at Sissinghurst on which is scrawled: 'This is to be given to Vita at my death' and a date, 19 August 1913. Inside are letters from William Waldorf Astor written between July and October 1913 – the months leading up to Vita's wedding (she and Harold had announced their engagement in July) and a time when

Victoria was particularly vulnerable. Astor was sixty-five years old in 1913, a tremendously successful businessman: 'a big man, with singular capacity for silence and for silent action', according to the anonymous friend who wrote to *The Times* when he died. He had acquired two houses in England: Cliveden and Hever Castle, ten miles from Knole.

In one of the first of his letters, dated 8 July, he congratulated Victoria on the result of the case. But others reveal a sentimental side. On 20 July, writing from Hever Castle, he told her how happy he was, after her visit to Hever, and begged: 'for anything I may have said or done amiss in that splendid hour's excitement I entreat your forgiveness ... That momentous Saturday was the psychological hour which you & I have unconsciously waited. Its remembrance delights me, for what wonderful things awaken at the meeting of the hands. A woman in the flower of her prime – like yourself – needs a romantic attachment.' On 24 July, he asked her to accept £10,000 in Bank of England notes to buy garden ornaments for her Hampstead garden. On the 29th, signing himself Will and writing from Marienbad from where he was sending her up to three letters a day, he conceded: 'As you rightly say it is cruel & wicked to give pain to another ['I meant Lionel' added in pencil], but this could only happen if our game had been stupidly played.' He then went on to vouch for the discretion of his butler-valet Foley and proposed his property on the Embankment as an ideal trysting place. Victoria declined the invitation, but decided to meet him in Interlaken in August, chaperoned by Vita and Harold, although as she explained it would have to be 'a picnic without refreshments'.

The highlight of 1913 was Vita's wedding on 1 October. The wedding presents – more than 600 of them – were displayed in the Great Hall, including emeralds and diamonds given to Vita by her mother, and an amethyst and diamond ring sent by Violet. Hundreds of guests attended the reception, including four duchesses and all the jurymen from the Scott case; but there was only room for members of the family in the chapel, which was decorated with lilies from the greenhouses.

It was a beautiful day, and the sun streamed through the south-facing chapel windows. The bishop of Rochester conducted the ceremony. Walter Rubens played the organ, and his wife, Olive, 'in a very smart gown of chestnut-red velvet trimmed with skunk', sang an aria from Gounod's *Redemption*. Vita, who was given away by her father, wore a wedding dress of cloth of gold brocade and a veil of Irish lace which her mother had worn at the coronation of the Czar in 1896. The two bridesmaids were Rosamund Grosvenor and Gwen Nicolson (the first until recently her lover and the latter, Harold's sister, eventually to become so). Harold's eldest brother, Freddy, in the uniform of the 15th Hussars, was best man. Lady Sackville – possibly to everyone's relief, given the fact that she was on the verge of a nervous breakdown – stayed in her bed.

The night before the wedding, Vita had written a poem – 'To Knole':

> *I left thee in the crowds and in the light,*
> *And if I laughed or sorrowed none could tell.*
> *They could not know our true and deep farewell*
> *Was spoken in the long preceding night.*

In August 1914, Lionel received a telephone call during dinner, asking him to join his regiment, the West Kent Yeomanry. He left for the war – at first to a camp near Canterbury in East Kent, and then to fight in the Dardanelles, Palestine and France. In *Pepita*, Vita recalled his parting words to his wife. 'I wondered even then whether he intended any irony as he came up to my mother and spoke those familiar words which had so often irritated her in the past, "Well dear, I am afraid I must be going now." I do not think so; he was not a man to carry any irony in his soul . . . A quick kiss; and the headlights of his motor rushed him away into the darkness across the park.'

After their wedding, Vita and Harold continued to spend a great deal of time at Knole, particularly in the weeks around Christmas and New Year. They were still very much a young couple, domi-nated by their parents – the 'grown-ups' – and by a place, Knole.

It was at Knole that Vita had her first child. She went into labour the day after the declaration of war. As Harold waited in the early morning outside the main door at Knole for the doctor to arrive, he could hear the troop trains rattling through Sevenoaks station, taking the British Expeditionary Force to France and the killing fields of Flanders. On the morning of 6 August, two days after the outbreak of war, Vita gave birth to a son, Benedict.

The baby's christening led to one of many rows between mother and daughter. Without consulting anyone – let alone the newborn's parents – Victoria asked Astor to be a godfather to Ben. Lionel was angry, finding the approach inappropriate and self-seeking ('what would the world say!', he asked), and Victoria wrote to Astor withdrawing the invitation. Astor graciously conceded 'the force & correctness of Lord Sackville's view & fully agree that the matter shall go no further'. Nevertheless, the chosen godparents were a motley crew: the godmothers comprising Olive, Rosamund, and Violet – 'at her own sarcastic request'; the godfathers: Kenneth Campbell, a family friend who Vita claimed had once attempted to rape her, and Baron Bildt, an old flame from Lady Sackville's Washington days with whom she had, more recently, been in love.

Victoria did not like the Great War, and wrote to Lord Kitchener about it to complain: 'I think perhaps you do not realise, my dear Lord K, that we employ five carpenters and four painters and two blacksmiths and two footmen, and you are taking them all from us!' When her letter to the Field Marshal failed to make an impression, she tried the Chancellor of the Exchequer, Andrew Bonar Law, instead. She explained that it was extremely difficult to maintain Knole, 'which is much more a national property than a private possession', particularly in view of the recent rises in income tax and death duties, and asked for some concessions. 'Can you help me to save it? I should love to show you any time you could come down and see for yourself how fair and patriotic my intense request is.' A little postscript added: 'I live here alone and in the strictest economy.' Bonar Law sent a polite reply, concluding that it would be 'impossible to modify the income tax system at the present time'.

According to a letter to *Country Life* in 1915, 'all the men on the Knole estate under fifty joined the army in August, 1914'. As a result, much of Knole was shut up, cared for by a skeleton staff. Stubbs, the head gardener, had orders from Lady Sackville to neglect the flowers, to force vegetables, and to turn the lawn and Green Court into hay – and to just 'keep the greenhouse from freezing'. The Great Hall became a hospital ward for the wounded, with tastefully decorated lockers and a reading lamp over each bed.

Lionel's letters from the war remained unrelentingly good-humoured in tone. He wrote about the smell given off when a stray bullet hits a corpse in no-man's-land, but he also described the joys of quail shooting in the desert or bathing in the Suez Canal. There were many references to members of the estate staff, who were serving with him in the West Kent Yeomanry, but there were even more to Olive. Within a month of the outbreak of war, Lionel was arranging for her to sing in a concert near Canterbury for his troops: 'The concert was a great success last night,' he wrote to Vita. 'Tell Olive that they loved her singing because it is true.' He would occasionally recruit Vita as a go-between, asking her to put a penny stamp on the 'enclosed' and send it to Olive, or to 'get me something nice for Olive for Xmas – say for about £5 or £6 and I will send you the money when I hear from you'. Whenever home on leave, Lionel would try to spend as much time as he could with Olive. He would read aloud to her in the Library where he had once read to Victoria. In her diary entry for 19 November 1917, Victoria wrote: 'I went back to Knole and found Olive there. L. had altered the Library greatly. I had a sad shock when I got to his room, as my two portraits, when I was two and twenty-three, which had been hanging there since 1889, had been put out of sight.' She also discovered that when Lionel was home on leave, he even had his breakfast alone with Olive in the Rubens' flat at Knole.

Victoria's letters, scrawled chaotically on the back of old circulars, tell of her love, her pain at her estrangement from Lionel, and her anger. 'We seem to be worse strangers than ever,' she complained; 'I hardly see Lionel . . . He is always in a hurry or comes into the room, looks out of the window, taps with his finger and says nothing,

looks bored and says goodbye. Poor, poor Lionel and poor me.' On
9 May 1916, Victoria wrote to Vita during one such visit:

> Dada generally cuts me short when I tell him anything, as he is
> almost mute with me, by saying: you have already written this, or
> you have already told me all this . . . I have never had a more dread-
> ful week, my child. It is really hopeless. He had absolutely nothing
> to say when we were alone; I had to make frantic efforts to keep
> going . . . When you are bored with someone, or a person has got on
> your nerves, nothing but tremendous will can do good; he has not
> got it in him to make the effort successfully. And I do not feel angry.
> I simply notice the hopelessness of everything in my married life.

There is a sad story alluded to in one of Victoria's letters to Vita, in
which she describes seeing an expensively mounted Turkish shell
on display in Olive's house. She knew immediately that this had
been a gift from Lionel to his mistress, and there had been no such
gift for his wife.

Victoria contented herself, after Seery's death, with a string of
distinguished male admirers. The most long-lasting of these attach-
ments was with the architect Sir Edwin Lutyens. Victoria met
Lutyens on 24 June 1916 in Lady Cunard's box at Covent Garden
for a performance of Verdi's *Otello*. She was fifty-four, large-
bosomed, with a complexion that was still beautiful, and a French
accent; the great architect was forty-seven. A month later he visited
Knole, and as Victoria showed him around they could hear the guns
from France.

Soon 'MacSack' and 'McNed', as they called each other, were
seeing a lot of each other and corresponding in a private language
laden with baby talk. He'd begin a letter 'Oh my gorgeous MacSack'
and sign himself 'Your velly vellumy McNeddie'. Victoria commissioned him to design some alterations at Hill Street and also some
minor works and rearrangements at Knole. By 1918, Lutyens was
spending almost every weekend at Knole and remodelling 39, 40
and 40a Sussex Square, Brighton, knocking the three into one, as a
holiday home for Victoria. She filled them with seven van-loads of

furniture from Knole and spent more and more time there. Their relationship was close and complex enough to be described as a love affair, and Lutyens's daughter Mary thought it was. Nigel Nicolson, her grandson, was of the opinion that, in middle age at least, Victoria was repelled by the idea of sex. Indeed, Victoria complained in her diary whenever Lutyens became 'lully' – a private word invented in 1917 after a visit to Lullingstone where 'something happened'.

Vita wrote a rather sanitised account of her parents' separation in *Pepita*, ascribing the final disruption to her father's return from war stronger and more decisive, a man who wanted to assert his authority on Knole's affairs – which had previously been very much Victoria's domain. 'For the first time in his life,' wrote Vita, 'he had really found himself as a man among men, away from the sapping feminine influence.'

But the truer and simpler reason for the separation was Victoria's increasing unhappiness about Olive's presence and influence. The woman, who had at first been a family friend and confidante of Victoria, was metamorphosing into the 'snake in the grass' described by Victoria in her *Book of Reminiscences*. In a letter to Vita, Harold described a particularly bitter row between his parents-in-law at Christmas 1918, concluding: 'Poor B.M.! ['Bonne Maman', the family name for Lady Sackville] Poor Dada! [Lionel] How happy each could be without the other! . . . I have the impression that Dada wants to make Knole more or less impossible for B.M. Perhaps I am wrong, but I feel that he has come to the conclusion that it is only by being rather cruel that he can beat her. I think he is right, of course, because if he is nice to her, she will only take advantage of it.'

Harold had spotted that quiet ruthlessness which Lionel concealed beneath his gentle reserve. Victoria was very upset when Lionel took Olive to the christening of my father, Hugh, in Brighton in March 1919, despite her specific request not to 'as she is not a relation . . . and they know how much I mind the Aunts' gossiping'.

Matters came to a head when Victoria returned from London on 5 April 1919:

I arrived about 6.00 and went around the garden calling for Lionel . . . I was amazed to see under one of the tulip trees, O. and L. in each other's arms and kissing!! Just like any soldier and his girl in the Park. I got away as quick as I could and tore to the sycamore seat. They must have seen me . . . And that occupation was not much in accord with their stating both to me that their friendship was purely platonic. I spoke very much to the point and when I had done, I said I would not allude to the matter again, but they must really try to behave more decently & carefully & show me some respect . . . They looked like whipped dogs.

The following month, during the weekend of 17 May, Lionel told Victoria that he had invited the Rubens to stay for 'a day or two' in the family apartments at Knole, at which Victoria threatened to leave and went upstairs to pack. Vita spent a 'miserable weekend' carrying messages back and forth between her parents, including this rather chilly one from her father to Victoria: 'I still think that you are making a great mistake in going away, but as it is your decision and choice I will say no more about it, except that if, in course of time, you feel like coming back, the door will not be entirely closed to you. I cannot take the whole blame for what has happened but I am sorry for the pain which you have been caused.'

This was not enough to appease Victoria, who was longing to be begged to stay. She wrote in her diary:

He ought to consider his wife's wishes in her own home, where she has done so much & where I was absolute mistress for twenty years, till Papa died . . . I am really too unhappy here since the evil day that he fell in love with Olive . . . Oh! The misery and humiliation of these six years! I love Knole & the possession of the finest place in England. It was so uncomfortable & different when I went there in 1889 & I have made it so comfy and brought it back to healthy life like if it had been a sick child. But I am so unhappy with L. & his systematic treatment of me, that I had better go.

She felt that she had 'slaved away at this place' for nothing – another victim of a monstrous inheritance.

Lutyens was staying at Knole the weekend that Victoria left. She gave him a lift back to London on Sunday afternoon. 'I did not tell him everything during our drive to London,' she wrote in her diary, 'so as not to distress him. But he sees that I cannot stay at Knole any longer. He was so nice and friendly about it all. He suggested all sorts of charming plans to distract my attention.'

But these charming plans would often founder, as the couple fell out – over money or over artistic direction. Part of the problem, as she acknowledged, was that 'even if I had to work with Michelangelo, I would prefer to do my own jobs, according to my inspiration'.

Victoria moved out of Knole for good, exasperated, hurt and humiliated. Her letters from the 1920s veer wildly between vituperation and affection. There's one particularly poignant one to Vita, in which she describes

> a dreadfully sad afternoon at Knole of which I took final farewell. I don't think I shall ever go there again. I was stupid enough to feel a *serrement de coeur* when I passed through the dining room, to see one solitary place. But then I remembered, as a palliative, all the méchancetes and deep words I had received and I [moved] on to the old French Library . . . that part of the house where I had lived since 1889. Going through my clothes, was also very painful; finding the dress he proposed to me in, and my wedding dress and orange blossoms – Well! let us draw a veil over all this, child . . .

Many of these letters still feel terribly raw eighty years later. Victoria gets cross with Vita for appearing 'alongside of Mrs Rubens at the concert for the Estate people', and at Lionel for his bad treatment of her, both in the past and now when he is threatening to 'blackmail' her with 'so-called proofs' (presumably of her alleged infidelity) to force a divorce. By 1924, Lionel was considering naming Lutyens in a petition for divorce, as Victoria had refused Lionel's request for a divorce again and again: 'NO to that terrible and quite unnecessary humiliation of that snake in the grass in my place at Knole.' As so often in Knole's emotional history, there is a constant interplay of past and present. 'I don't see why one should always knock under, to other people,' wrote Victoria; 'I agree with Lady Anne [Clifford]. But I am not as exacting and cantankerous as she was. She had the luck of living in "spacious days" and yet I would hardly change with her.'

Life at Knole in the 1920s became increasingly erratic and, for a family noted for its reserve and restraint, surprisingly rackety and louche. Here were Lionel, Lord Sackville, living with his mistress, Olive, and – from time to time – her complicit husband Walter; and Vita about to embark on the most passionate affair of her life – with Violet Keppel.

Vita and Violet had been friends since childhood, but they became lovers in April 1918. In some ways, the couple were like naughty teenagers, keen to shock. The escapade that Vita described as her *'best* adventure' started in her London home. Here, one evening in the autumn of 1918, she put on men's clothes, before driving in a taxi to Hyde Park Corner. There she alighted as 'Julian', strolling around Mayfair, 'smoking a cigarette, buying a cigarette off a boy who called [her] "sir", and being accosted now and then by women'. 'The extraordinary thing was, how natural it all was for me,' wrote Vita. In Bond Street, she met Violet, and together they took a train to Orpington and booked into a lodging house for the night as man and wife. In the morning they took the train on to Sevenoaks and smuggled themselves into the stables at Knole, where they changed.

Between 1918 and 1920, Vita and Violet spent many months together – in Cornwall and the South of France. After Violet's marriage in June 1919, she and her husband, Denys Trefusis, honeymooned in France. Vita followed them there, staying at a small hotel in Versailles where she took Violet. It was a chilling insight into Vita's predatory and possessive nature, although she too was all-consumed by the relationship. Even as the affair was coming to an end, Harold wrote to his wife on 8 February 1921: 'I know that when you fall into V[iolet's]'s hands your will becomes like a jelly-fish addicted to cocaine.'

As well as Lionel and Olive, and Vita and Violet, the other unconventional presence at Knole was that of Vita's cousin, Eddy

Sackville-West. To his face Vita was always a loving friend, but privately – and perhaps rather inconsistently – she disapproved of her cousin Eddy's domestic arrangements and his taste in decoration. From the mid-1920s Eddy had rooms in the tower above the outer wicket at Knole. The rooms were approached from the Green Court by a stone spiral staircase, and overlooked the main entrance and the park on one side and the Green Court on the other. Painted on the walls were musical notations and signs of the zodiac, and just outside his bedroom door there still hangs a life mask made from a mould of wax which had been applied to his face as he breathed through a straw. It was here that Vita visited Eddy on her return from Tehran in 1926. 'Mincing in black velvet', was how she described him to Harold: 'I don't object to homosexuality, but I do hate decadence. And it is a nasty fungoid growth on Knole of all places . . . I don't think Dada likes it much.'

As Vita was finishing *Knole and the Sackvilles*, she had written to Eddy that, given the fact that the Sackvilles were 'nearly all stark staring mad . . . You and I have got a jolly sort of heredity to fight against'. If *Knole and the Sackvilles* was Vita's love letter to Knole, the other book that would for ever identify Vita with Knole was Virginia Woolf's novel *Orlando*.

Vita met Virginia Woolf at a dinner party in December 1922. Woolf was not initially impressed. 'Not to my severer taste,' she wrote in her diary: 'florid, moustached, parakeet coloured, with all the supple ease of the aristocracy, but not the wit of the artist. She writes fifteen pages a day – has finished another book – publishes with Heinemanns – knows everyone . . . why she writes which she does with complete competency and a pen of brass, is a puzzle to me.'

Despite Virginia's intellectual snobbery, Vita was being asked to write for the Woolfs' publishing company the Hogarth Press within days of their meeting; and, within a couple of years, they were very close friends. In her diary for Saturday, 5 July 1924, Virginia recorded her first visit to Knole:

Just back . . . from Knole, where indeed I was invited to lunch alone with his Lordship [Vita's father]. His lordship lives in the kernel of a vast nut. You perambulate miles of galleries; skip endless treasures – chairs that Shakespeare might have sat on – tapestries, pictures, floors made of the halves of oaks; & penetrate at length to a round shiny table with a cover laid for one . . . Knole is a conglomeration of buildings half as big as Cambridge I daresay . . . But the extremities & indeed the inward parts are gone dead. Ropes fence off half the rooms; the chairs & the pictures look preserved; life has left them.

Over the next few years Virginia became a regular visitor to Knole, staying there once – in 1927. The arrangement of the visit was the subject of much correspondence. Lionel was clearly only just master of his own house, as his mistress and his daughter vied for control. Vita wrote to Virginia on 15 January 1927 – a couple of days before the visit – 'You've no idea of the intrigues that have been going on here to ensure your getting the room I wanted you to have. How I have shamelessly lied, tucked Olive away in a room she never has, bundled her clothes out, bribed the housekeeper, suborned the housemaids.'

After her stay, Virginia described Knole as having

too little conscious beauty for my taste: smallish rooms looking on to buildings: no views: yet one or two things remain: Vita stalking in her Turkish dress, attended by small boys, down the gallery, wafting them on like some tall sailing ship – a sort of covey of noble English life: dogs walloping, children crowding, all very free & stately: & [a] cart bringing wood in to be sawn by the great circular saw . . . How do you see that? I asked Vita. She said she saw it as something that had gone on for hundreds of years. They had brought wood in from the Park to replenish the great fires like this for centuries & her ancestresses had walked so on the snow with their great dogs bounding by them. All the centuries seemed lit up, the past expressive, articulate; not dumb & forgotten; but a crowd of people stood behind, not dead at all . . .

On the same visit, Virginia had described Lionel as 'the figure of an English nobleman, decayed, dignified, smoothed, effete'. In

the years between Vita's wedding and his death, her father, like her
grandfather before him – and many Sackvilles before and since –
had gradually retreated from the world, turning away from the
emotional intensity of life at Knole. In early January 1928, he came
down with influenza, which was followed by pericarditis – an
inflammation of the heart – and he was in considerable pain. Thomas
Horder, doctor to several members of the Royal Family, was sent
for, and Harold returned from Berlin. Olive, Vita and Harold spent
much of the time, day and night, in Lionel's sitting room so as to
be close to the dying man. On the 27th, Horder broke it to them
that there was no hope of recovery, and a little after midnight on
the 28th he died.

His body was placed in a lead coffin in the chapel at Knole. 'I wish
you could see it,' Vita wrote to Virginia Woolf. 'It is very beautiful
and quite unreal.' Harold wrote an appreciation of his father-in-law
for *The Times*. He was a shy, modest, retiring, and humorous man,
wrote Harold; and more cultivated than he made himself out to be.
He had been vice chairman of the Kent County Council, chairman
of the Kent Territorial Army Association, a county magistrate and
deputy lieutenant, and formerly lieutenant colonel with the West
Kent Yeomanry. But, according to Harold, he loved Knole above
all things, and regarded it as his sacred trust, spending nearly all he
possessed on its maintenance, and the minimum on himself.

Virginia was perhaps more perspicacious when she described him
the previous summer as a

worn man, inheriting noble nose & chin which he has not put much
into himself; a straight, young-looking man, save that his face has the
lacklustre of a weak man whose life has proved too much for him.
No longer does he struggle much for happiness, I imagine; accepts
resignedly; & goes to Maidstone almost daily, as part of the routine
of his nobility. He plays golf; he plays tennis. He thinks Bernard
Darwin [golf correspondent of *The Times* and *Country Life*] must
be a man of surpassing brain power. We sat together under a vast
goat skin coat of Vita's, watching them play, I found him smooth
and ambling as a blood horse, but obliterated, obfusc, with his great

Sackville eyes drooping & his face all clouded with red and brown. One figured a screw or other tool whose worms & edges have been rubbed smooth, so that though they shine, plaid silver, they no longer grip.

There is nothing like a death to expose the fault lines in a family, let alone one as dysfunctional as the Sackvilles had become. Since leaving Knole in 1919, Victoria had attempted every now and then to be magnanimous about her husband. But Lionel's death precipitated an outburst of anger. Vita and Olive had been nursing the dying Lionel, and it was Vita who bore the full force of her mother's humiliation and fury. Discouraged by the Nicolsons, Victoria did not attend the funeral on 31 January (nor, due to her delicate position, did Olive); and she soon fell out with Harold and Vita, writing in her diary: 'Vita has treated me abominably in the last few years.' And: 'I had loved her so. I have finished with that monster of ingratitude.' It was around this time that Victoria started referring to her daughter as 'the Vipa' (rather than 'the Vita').

Virginia Woolf was a source of great consolation to Vita in the months following her father's death. On 12 February she wrote to Eddy: 'Vita seems better and had answered about three hundred letters [about her father] but I'm afraid it is a dismal affair for her, and your aunt's [Lady Sackville's] behaviour could only be tolerated in an Elizabethan play. That she may take a dagger to her own throat or drink broken glass is rather my hope, I think.'

One of the most dramatic scenes was enacted in the offices of the family solicitors, Pemberton's. As Vita described in a letter to Harold on 18 April 1928, she was surprised to meet Victoria in a 'towering rage' at the solicitors (Victoria had learnt of her daughter's appointment to discuss her father's will and had come to confront her): ' "Give me your pearls!" screamed B.M., "twelve of them belong to me, and I wish to see how many you have changed, you thief." . . . Then the scene began in real earnest. Darling, never, never Have I heard such floods of the vilest abuse, aimed at both Pemberton and me. She was like a mad woman, screaming Thief and Liar, and shaking her fist till I thought she was going to hit me . . . Then she started abusing Dada, at which I simply walked out of the room.'

This was simply one incident in a series of strange delusions and schemes. In March, Victoria had written to Knole's new owner, her brother-in-law Charles, asking whether she could rent the house for a couple of years; and in the summer, she started a rumour that Vita intended to divorce Harold in order to marry Eddy and thereby gain possession of Knole.

Although Vita was effectively a Sackville twice over – her parents had been first cousins and her grandfathers brothers – she did not inherit Knole. The title and the house passed to her father's younger brother, Charles, who at that point held a sinecure as Lieutenant Governor of Guernsey and Alderney, and then to her cousin Eddy. 'Knole,' she later wrote, 'is denied to me for ever, through a "technical fault over which we have no control", as they say on the radio.' Inextricably linked with the loss of her father, then, was the loss of Knole, the place she loved with what she described as an 'atavistic passion', an intensity that transcended her love for any person, Harold included.

On 11 February 1928, Virginia Woolf had written in her diary: 'Lord Sackville is dead & lies at Withyham & I passed Knole with Vita yesterday & had to look away from the vast masterless house, without a flag. This is what she minds most. When she left the house behind the old cart horses, she went for ever, she said, after a complete rule for three days.'

In the days before handing over the house to her uncle Charlie, now the 4th Lord Sackville, Vita had been sole mistress of Knole, arranging the funeral and giving all the orders. These days came to mean a lot to her, as she recalled in a letter to her son Ben at Eton. The way she overcame what she saw as the 'Sackville weakness' of withdrawal had to 'do with Grandpapa's death, and the three or four days in which I had to rule Knole and make every decision'.

She hardly set foot in the house again for thirty years, apart from a trip to collect her father's elk hound, Canute, and to sort through her father's personal belongings, after which she wrote: 'Knole was looking particularly lovely, outside, in the sunshine; but gloomy inside, as all the blinds were down and dust sheets like shrouds over everything, which I really prefer, as I didn't like everything looking just the same. Anyhow I feel as if I have now broken the ice of going there, though I shan't go there without some inevitable reason ever in future.'

The 'technical fault' to which Vita had referred – her gender – caused her much resentment. Charlie gave her a key to the garden, but years later it got lost. Charlie sent a replacement, but soured her pleasure somewhat by asking her not to lose it again and having the word 'Knole' rubbed from it. Vita had the word engraved back on. Vita stayed away from Knole, partly because she disliked Charlie's second wife, Anne. But she could still describe the house vividly from memory almost twenty years later, when the National Trust commissioned her to write the guidebook to the house; and she was still bound to the place by what Harold described as 'some sort of umbilical cord'.

There was, however, one major consolation for Vita's having been born a girl, for her exclusion from her inheritance, for her father's death earlier that year. On display in the Great Hall at Knole is a facsimile of the bound manuscript of Virginia Woolf's novel *Orlando*. The novel is dedicated to Vita Sackville-West and, in the words of her son, the late Nigel Nicolson, it is 'the longest and most charming love-letter in literature'.

A printed copy of the book arrived in a brown paper parcel from the Hogarth Press, followed a few days later by Virginia Woolf herself bearing the manuscript as a present. Vita wrote to Harold: 'I am in the middle of reading *Orlando*, in such a turmoil of excitement and confusion that I scarcely know where (or who) I am!' Vita was 'completely dazzled, bewitched, enchanted, under a spell . . . You made me cry with your passages about Knole, you wretch,' she wrote to Virginia. Virginia replied by telegram: 'Your biographer is infinitely relieved and happy.'

Vita is the eponymous hero or heroine (Orlando changes sex over the four centuries in which the novel is set), and Orlando's ancestral home is a house, like Knole, with a legendary 365 rooms. The pages are threaded through with specific references to Knole and its past and present incumbents: the head gardener Stubbs, Canute the dog, and so on. Harold features as Marmaduke Bontrop Shelmerdine, Esquire. Violet Keppel, now Trefusis, was the Russian Princess. 'She talked so enchantingly, so wittily, so wisely,' is how Virginia Woolf describes Princess Sasha in *Orlando*. In a letter to Vita, she wrote of Violet: 'I still remember her, like a fox cub, all scent and seduction.'

The book featured pictures purportedly of Orlando and the book's other characters. These consisted either of photographs of Vita or Angelica Bell, or of portraits from Knole which Vita and Virginia had chosen together on a visit to the house: the Archduchess Harriet is a portrait of Mary Curzon, 4th Countess of Dorset; Orlando as Ambassador is from a pastel portrait of Lionel, 1st Duke of Dorset, by Rosalba Carriera, and so on.

Orlando ends in the present day – indeed, on the novel's publication day, 11 October 1928, when Orlando returns to Knole to welcome a great Queen to the house. This was the year of Vita's father's death; and the novel allows Vita – as Orlando – to take possession in fantasy of the house that she had been denied in fact. As Harold described *Orlando* to Vita: it is a 'book in which you and Knole are identified for ever, a book which will perpetuate that identity into years when both you and I are dead'. Lady Sackville, on the other hand, stuck a photograph of Virginia Woolf into her copy of *Orlando* and captioned it: 'The awful face of a mad woman whose successful mad desire is to separate people who care for each other. I loathe this woman for having changed my Vita and taken her away from me.'

'Dear Eddy,' Vita had written to her cousin; 'Knole is now to you what it used to be to me; but I know you love it as much as I do.' Of course, he did not – and she knew it, fantasising that if neither Charlie nor Eddy wanted Knole, 'I would be quite ready to take it off their hands.' Her father's death brought some of her resentment of Eddy to the surface. She hoped that Eddy would be amused – but also 'annoyed' – by *Orlando*; Eddy's father, Charlie, certainly annoyed Vita by complaining about the reproduction of pictures from Knole in *Orlando* without his explicit permission.

Vita only used the key that uncle Charlie had given her to the garden at Knole once, and that was in 1928. On 16 May she wrote to Harold from Long Barn, their home three miles from Knole:

> I allowed myself a torture-treat tonight: I went up to Knole after dark and wandered about the garden. I have a master key, so could get in without being seen. It was a very queer and poignant experience: so queer and so poignant, that I should almost have fainted had I met anybody. I mean, I had the sensation of having the place so completely to myself, that I might have been the only person alive in the world – and not the world of today, mark you, but the world of at least 300 years ago. I might have been the ghost of Lady Anne Clifford.

Once again, the ghosts of the past were being invoked to convey a sense of present melancholy, and to bring to a close a twenty-year period that had begun and ended with a funeral – and with a house, shuttered and shrouded in dust sheets.

Chapter 11

'A disobliging new world' (1928–1946)

Charles Sackville-West, 4th Baron Sackville

Within days of Lionel's death, *Country Life* carried a leading article under the heading 'Such as Knole':

> Knole is one of a group of great and historic houses that are kept up by their owners as much for the benefit of the public as for themselves [it began, before citing Castle Howard, Chatsworth, Hardwick, Burghley and Penshurst]. The house is open most days of the week, and the park is always open to wander in wherever the visitor wishes. It is exceedingly unjust and short-sighted that one who inherits such a place should pay death duties on a house and park which is regarded even by him as national property. The logical course of retaliation for an owner would have been to develop the park at Knole as a suburban building site, to export the priceless furniture and pictures to America [which Lionel had, in fact, done to an extent] and to sell the materials of Knole to several millionaires. He would then have been a rich man, with no obligations to tenants, to the country or to the public.

The idea that houses such as Knole were as much part of a national as a personal heritage, and should therefore be relieved of death duties and local rates, was not new: Victoria had, of course, peddled it – with some success – to the Chancellor of the Exchequer in the 1890s, and partly as a result he had introduced the principle of exemption on artworks of national or historic interest. This, and several of the other issues outlined in the article, would continue to dominate the heritage debate into the twenty-first century.

The period between the end of the First World War and the beginning of the Second was particularly hard for the country house, as it was for the country as a whole. By the end of the First World War, income tax, land tax and rates accounted for around 30 per cent of the income of a landed estate, and the budget of 1919 raised death duties on the larger estates to almost 50 per cent. Between 1918 and 1921, some 7 million acres (around a quarter of England) was sold, causing *The Times* to complain that England was 'changing hands'; many houses were pulled down and their features – panelling, staircases, fireplaces and so on – sold off to builders and architectural scrap merchants.

In April 1921, Knole was advertised as being available for rent. 'Announcements of houses to be let furnished are among the commonplaces of life, but it is something exceptional and noteworthy when such an announcement is made in respect of one of the most celebrated stately homes in England. Yet this is the case of Knole, which, with, immediate possession, is to be let furnished for a term,' declared *Country Life*. The article went on to describe the house, its history and treasures. 'But though these are the chief glories of the house, Knole has its more prosaic rooms, adapting it as a place to live in as well as to look at; and with a family suite of sixteen bedrooms, eleven bathrooms, nine reception rooms and a billiard room, tennis lawns and a covered squash court, it has everything to make it a convenient country house of our own day no less than a splendid heritage from the centuries that have passed.'

Knole never was let (other major country houses, including Leeds Castle, Blickling Hall and Corsham Court, were on the market at the same time). But the very possibility is typical of a time when many owners believed that the country house was no longer viable, and an indication of just how precarious was the family's hold on Knole.

In the 1920s and early 1930s, periodicals such as *Country Life* were aware of the growing threats to the country house. They reacted in a nostalgic, escapist way, celebrating in their pages, as John Buchan and P. G. Wodehouse did in their novels, places that were creeper-clad, surrounded by emerald lawns, and bathed in a perpetually golden light. Just as the country-house poem of the seventeenth century had extolled liberal housekeeping and hospitality, one of the main arguments, put forward in the pages of *Country Life*, was that country houses such as Knole had always been open to the public, and that their owners had always been public benefactors (disregarding the fact that it was less than fifty years since owners such as Mortimer had closed their parks and homes to visitors). Knole managed to attract around 1,000 visitors a year between the wars, which was considerably more than many houses, but well below the figure of 10,000 in the 1870s and 3,000 before the First World War. Many of these visitors, however, noted the cheerlessness of the state rooms, and the dust.

Houses, and the idea of inheritance, played a crucial, and slightly obsessive, part in Vita Sackville-West's books and their titles. In *The Heir*, published in 1922, the reluctant inheritor of a Tudor house, Blackboys, is drawn into its spell. Blackboys was modelled on nearby Groombridge Place, but the descriptions could just as well have applied to Knole, with its long galleries, oak parlour and 'the upholstered depth of velvets and damasks, like ripe fruits, heavily fringed and tasselled; the plaster-work of the diapered ceilings; the fairy-tale background of the tapestry, and the reflection of the cloudy mirrors'. Vita's *Knole and the Sackvilles* was published in the same year as *The Heir*, and although an historical account of the house and the family who had owned it, its lyrical celebration of some of Knole's myths verges at times on the fictional – for which Vita was gently teased by Virginia Woolf in *Orlando*. Orlando's ancestral home is easily identifiable as Knole, as is Chevron, the stately home at the heart of Vita's novel *The Edwardians*, which was published in 1930, two years after she left Knole following her father's death.

Absence from the enchanted palace of her ancestors tended to make Vita's heart grow fonder and more fantastical. Chevron's rooms, like Knole's, include the Queen's Room, the Tapestry

Room, Little North, George III's; and the room described as 'Queen Elizabeth's Bedroom' – in which Sebastian, the young master of Chevron, attempts to seduce the local doctor's wife – is obviously the King's Room, where 'the great four-poster of silver and flamingo satin towered to the ceiling and the outlines of the famous silver furniture gleamed dimly in a ray of the moon'.

Knole was getting a lot of literary exposure in the 1920s and 1930s, providing the inspiration or backdrop to a series of novels, its rooms getting used time and time again like film sets for yet another scene in a different production. Vita's cousin, Eddy Sackville-West, was at it too. At least one of his novels is dominated by the brooding presence of an ancestral home. In *The Ruin*, which was published in 1931, Knole is portrayed as Vair, its rooms faithfully described and its treasures holding the family who lived there in a mystical 'victorious grasp'. 'The pictures – the countless pictures – the china, the carving, the silver, the gold, the furniture – all possessed a composite soul with which to rule their masters.'

This was the house that – unexpectedly for the second son of a sixth son – my great-uncle Charlie inherited in 1928. Major General Sir Charles Sackville-West, 4th Lord Sackville, was a professional soldier, who had served with distinction in India, in South Africa during the Boer War, and in the trenches of northern France and Flanders during the First World War. After retiring from the army, he was Lieutenant Governor of Guernsey and Alderney from 1925 until 1929, when he took up residence at Knole with his American second wife, Anne. Almost immediately, he was forced to sell family heirlooms, including tapestries depicting scenes from the Passion of Christ that had hung in the Chapel for hundreds of years and were now destined for the Museum of Fine Arts in Boston. Victoria, the Dowager Lady Sackville, did not miss the opportunity to snipe at the new owners, writing to Charlie's son, 'poor dear Eddy': 'You must be missing so many of our family pictures going to America. It is dreadful, especially for you. But what else can be done, except for Charlie and Anne to live with the strictest economy as my Father & I did when we got to Knole in 1888. We shut up everything & had such a simple, cheap wedding in 1890.'

The house parties of the pre-war years continued, however, and cocktails were served at Knole for the first time. Visitors' books, dating from the day Charlie and Anne arrived at Knole until the outbreak of the Second World War, chronicle a regular procession of guests, some for the weekend and others just for the day: politicians such as Stanley Baldwin, Winston Churchill, Austen Chamberlain and Anthony Eden; literary figures like Rebecca West and Compton Mackenzie; a smattering of royalty, from King George V and Queen Mary to the King and Queen of Siam; local bridge-playing friends; and members of the family – Eddy and his sister Diana, my father and uncle, Ben and Nigel Nicolson with their father Harold – although without Vita, who was still in mourning for the loss of Knole and, in any case, disliked Anne. In 1931 and 1932, two of the Sackvilles' most frequent guests were Mrs Wallis Simpson and 'the husband thereof', as she signed Ernest Simpson into the book. Their visits stopped abruptly in 1933, the year she began her affair with the future King Edward VIII.

Photographs of Charlie show a figure of great inter-war elegance: co-respondent shoes, and the distinctive yellow waistcoat that had earned him the nickname 'Tit-Willow' from his students at Sandhurst. In the 1940s, the diarist James Lees-Milne went to lunch at Knole and found him 'as exquisitely dressed as ever, in a blue tweed suit and canary-coloured waistcoat which, when his delicate build and abrupt movements were taken into account, brought to mind that domesticated bird. A gaunt pale blue nose upon a white face and a crest of white hair did not detract from the resemblance. A familiar gesture shared with Eddy was the appliance behind an almost transparent hand of a gleaming tooth-pick to a gleaming *ratelier.*'

The Second World War finally brought to an end this era of country-house living – just as the First World War had threatened to do. In June 1940 the writer James Pope-Hennessy described a visit to Knole in elegiac terms: 'We walked in the great dark gardens in the evening light with wide turf alleys and rhododendron flowers, and urns on pedestals; and the house and the elms; but there was only an illusion of peace and the previous tranquil world, and the whole ordered landscape seemed quivering with imminent destruction.' Eddy moved out of his 'ladylike apartments' at Knole, writing self-pityingly to his friend Jane Eyre: 'My only servant had a nervous breakdown, & that coincided with my father's desire to use my rooms for a friend of mine whom he wished to help run the place for him – a thing he very justifiably finds me to be incapable of doing . . . How dreadful everything is!'

Many of the house's more valuable contents were removed to a slate quarry in North Wales for safe keeping, accompanied in a lorry by Charlie's younger brother, Bertie, my grandfather. Eddy helped to pack up the silver at Knole in eleven huge containers and take it to safe storage to a bank in Torquay. It was just as well, because Knole was on 'Bomb Alley', between London and the Channel, where German bombers jettisoned any bombs they hadn't dropped on the capital before returning home. In September 1940, Charlie wrote to Eddy that they had been having 'a very bomby time at Knole', and the following month Eddy told Jane Eyre that the park was 'sown with bombs & crashed Junkers', adding fatalistically: 'How soon they will demolish the house is a matter for conjecture.'

The house was, in fact, slightly damaged by a flying bomb which landed in the park in February 1944. The windows of the west front were blown out but, as the diarist James Lees-Milne noted, 'the heraldic beasts on the gable finials turned round on their plinths and presented their backs to the outrage committed. What proud and noble behaviour!' Vita had not visited Knole since 1928, but she still felt any slight to the house most intensely. When she heard about the bomb, she wrote: 'I mind frightfully, frightfully. I always persuade myself that I have finally torn Knole out of my heart and then the moment anything touches it every nerve is à vif [alive] again. I cannot bear to think of Knole wounded, and me not there to look after it and be wounded with it. Those filthy Germans! Let us level every town in Germany to the ground! I shan't care. Oh Hadji [her nickname for her husband, Harold], I wish you were here. I feel hurt and heart-sick.'

As threatening to Knole as the war itself were the rising taxes. 'At this moment,' Charlie had written to his son in 1940, 'we are all under the influence of the budget . . . it is the end definitely for such houses as Knole. I do not see how anyone in any country will be able to buy objets d'art. The death duties on top of income and surtax will make it impossible to pay the wage bills & maintenance of the building, etc.' (In the budget of 1941, income tax at the top level was to rise to 19s. 6d. in the pound.) He feared that it would be the last summer 'in which flower gardens of any kind can be kept up'. Such fears were held by most country-house owners, for in the 1940s the country house, which now appears such a triumphant symbol of aristocratic survival, was slated for the scrap heap.

Many houses were requisitioned for government service or to help the war effort. Castle Howard, Longleat and the Vyne housed evacuated schools (girls' schools were considered the best tenants, then boys' schools). Some, like Corsham Court and Harewood, were transformed into military hospitals or convalescent homes; and Bletchley Park became an intelligence centre where secret German codes were decrypted. The worst fate to befall a country house was to be requisitioned by the army. Troops billeted at Blickling Hall in Norfolk broke the windows and forced the doors; and those at Eggington Hall in Derbyshire left the taps running, with the result that the ceilings collapsed and the house had to be demolished. Fortunately for Knole, Charlie, as an old soldier himself, knew all about the damage the army could do, and had the good sense to offer a wartime billet in the North Wing to the well-behaved Auctioneers' and Estate Agents' Institute. In 1945 the Institute presented Lord and Lady Sackville with a framed document, expressing a 'most cordial vote of thanks' for their hospitality during the six years of war.

There is a charming unpublished memoir of life at Knole in the 1930s and 1940s, written by the daughter of the head gardener Charlie Beavin. Margaret, whose family had lived and worked on the estate for more than 200 years, spent much of her childhood in the Gardener's Cottage. 'It was rather like living, during the summer months at least, in a huge bowl,' she writes; 'a cornucopia from which spilled fruit, vegetables, flowers and herbs.' The 5 acres of kitchen garden supplied food and cut flowers for the big house:

arum lilies, from one of four glasshouses, which were then arranged at Knole in narrow glass vases, five or six feet tall; violets from the cold frame, which adorned Lady Sackville's breakfast tray every morning, accompanied by a few large strawberries perhaps; carnations from one of over a hundred heavily scented varieties that were used as buttonholes for Lord Sackville and his guests.

A watercolour Margaret painted from memory of the Knole kitchen garden in the 1930s shows how the main body of the garden was divided into plots for growing vegetables: beds of asparagus, globe artichokes, carrots, sprouts, potatoes, peas, beetroot and cauliflowers. Between the plots were rows and rows of lavender bushes, from which the flowers were cut and taken in baskets to Knole. Grapes were transported there in boxes of wood shavings, covered with vine leaves; peaches and nectarines were tucked into boxes of tissue paper; and melons, half-wrapped in their own leaves, were laid in baskets half-filled with sphagnum moss. I, too, remember something of this lost domain from my earliest visits to the kitchen garden in the 1960s, when a handful of gardeners still produced vegetables for the big house. More recently, I came to love the Gardener's Cottage when I lived there before moving into Knole. There is a delicious melancholy about the place, secreted within its crumbling red-brick walls, with its dilapidated green-houses, and its vegetable beds now gone to seed and set aside.

Margaret Beavin's memoirs describe the final flourish of an old world that came to an end with the Second World War. During the Battle of Britain, which was conducted in the skies above Kent, her father took his turn as a fire-watcher at Knole, looking out for incendiary bombs, on the entrance tower, beside a notice stating: 'In the event of the Tower being hit by a bomb, descend by the rope.' Searchlights swept the night sky for targets; the ack-ack guns cracked, and the next day the ground would be covered with chaff, thin metal strips, dropped by the German bombers to confuse the radar systems. Walking her dog in the early morning, the young Margaret occasionally encountered a German parachutist dangling from the branches of a tree where he had got caught. She'd get close enough to see if the airman was alive or dead, before running off for help. If the airman was simply entangled, her father and the other gardeners might be able to get him down themselves before taking him indoors for a cup of tea and a cigarette, and awaiting the arrival of army personnel. Some of the German airmen were young, frightened, and fully expected to be shot. Margaret also recalled the rumble of lorries, massing in the army vehicle depot that stretched from the back of the kitchen garden to the top of River Hill, in preparation for the D-Day landings of 1944.

Since most of the younger men and women from the estate were called up or volunteered for armed service, every able-bodied person left had to give a hand, producing food for the war effort. My grandfather Bertie, Margaret remembers, presented himself promptly at the kitchen garden every afternoon, always wearing tweed plus-twos and heavy-duty boots, and dug furiously for the next three hours, oblivious – as a result of his deafness – to any air-raid warnings.

Bertie had moved into a flat overlooking the Stable Court in 1937, the year after his wife Eva had died, and lived there simply and ascetically until his own death in 1959. In contrast to the muted despair of Lady Anne Clifford's diaries, or the histrionics of Victoria's, Bertie's accounts of daily life at Knole during the war and after are reassuringly restrained, a model of Sackville reserve. So reticent are his diaries that it is never clear why he lived apart from his wife through most of his children's growing up and through his wife's long illness.

His diaries describe an unchanging routine of study (particularly Arabic), physical exercise, and help around the house – cataloguing the books in the Library, for example. On 15 October every year until 1958, the year before his death, he produced a timesheet. Of the 338 hours recorded in 1940, leaf sweeping accounted for 181 hours, hoeing swedes for 54 hours, and digging in the kitchen garden for 103 hours. In the following years of war, he added time spent help-ing to make camouflage nets. Thousands of pages are devoted to these activities, for many days a simple 'ditto' signifying an exact repeat of the previous day. It was a routine interrupted occasionally, but never disrupted, by an air-raid warning or by a bomb landing in the park. One of these bombs was responsible for my grandfather's only hole in one. According to my father, my grandfather was an appalling golfer – despite the fact that he played pretty much every day of his adult life. One day a bomb landed quite near to the tee he was playing off, and the explosion (rather than the sound, for he was stone deaf) shook him out of his habitual incompetence. The result: a hole in one.

Such events were, it seems, more earth shattering than any emotional upsets. On 9 July 1942, the entry read: 'Fine. Golf, camouflage work & hoeing as usual. At 5 p.m. got a message from War Office reporting Lionel [his son] as missing June 20th. Possibility (though to my mind slight) that he may be a prisoner' – which it later transpires he was. A similar sang-froid characterises his reactions to his daughter Betty's wedding and, later, her nervous breakdowns, the handover of the house to the National Trust, and the arrival of his grandchildren, including me. Into their respective seventies, Bertie played a silent round of golf with his elder brother Charlie most days. I imagine them rather like my father, Hugh, and my uncle, Lionel, two brothers who, a generation later, also in their seventies, would go to the Estate Office at Knole every morning. No one was quite sure what they did there, surrounded by old plans of the estate, trunks stuffed with title deeds, and drawers littered with ancient cheque stubs (as with the old keys, Sackvilles only very rarely threw anything away); but it certainly wasn't chat. 'Morning, Huffo [as Hugh was known in the family]'; 'Morning, Lionel' was the extent of their generally amiable, if distant, communication.

Vita was as pessimistic as her uncle Charlie about the future of the country house, writing in 1941 that, what with the war, war taxation and the present rate of death duties, 'it seems improbable that any family fortune will long suffice to retain such homes in private ownership . . . The only hope for these houses seems to be that they should pass into the good keeping of the National Trust.' This was a fate which, in the event, she only just came to accept for Knole, and which she would not contemplate for Sissinghurst. Charlie had, in fact, been in discussion with the National Trust since 1935 – and in particular with the Trust's Historic Buildings

Secretary, the diarist James Lees-Milne. These negotiations continued throughout the war.

As James Lees-Milne travelled the country for the National Trust, he was aware that he was witnessing the dying days of a way of life. Lunching with Charlie at Knole in August 1943 in the large oak-panelled dining room, he found Lord Sackville

> as courteous and charming as ever. We had venison liver from deer killed in the park [which gave Lees-Milne violent diarrhoea that evening]. In the afternoon we and the agent toured the house very rapidly in order for me to get some idea of the parts which the Trust would lease back to him. Most large houses upon acquaintance look smaller than at first they appeared. Not so Knole. It is a veritable rabbit warren. It turned out today that in our recent discussions we had all three overlooked the North Wing, which consists of fifteen bedrooms as well as reception rooms.

Negotiations were complicated for a number of reasons. First, an act of Parliament was needed for the National Trust to accept and own properties of outstanding architectural or historic interest, together with an endowment for their upkeep and maintenance; and there needed to be tax-exempt leaseback arrangements for the families involved. Separately, at Knole, an order in Chancery was going to be needed to break the family settlement, so that the transfer could take place.

But as well as legal reasons there were personal reasons for the delays. Eddy was keen on the idea to start with, but, according to Lees-Milne, he became 'suspicious of his father's motives' as the negotiations continued. Charlie and Eddy were slow to make up their minds, Eddy irritating Vita for being 'as floppy as an unstaked delphinium in a gale'. Captain Glasier, the Sackvilles' agent, was against any handover at all, and believed that Knole had better be split up for what it was worth. Together, Glasier and his assistant, Frank Mason, perfected 'a technique of infuriating procrastination', according to the accountant advising the National Trust, which worked in the family's favour. Furthermore, there was the worry that Charlie, who seemed particularly old and frail at the time, would die before any negotiations were completed.

Lees-Milne sympathised with Charlie's predicament: 'Was an irreversible handover of his great inheritance of over three and a half centuries going to be worth the candle? His misgivings were surely understandable for there was no precedent to go by, no previous case of an entailed property of similar importance having yet been handed over and a tenant-for-life emerging blissfully happy. When I heard from Eddy what the situation was I felt much sympathy for this charming, gentle, elegant and patrician old man who dreaded living on charity.' Such considerations presumably explained what Lees-Milne saw as Charlie's unpredictability: 'He [Lord Sackville] always received me in the most affectionate, fatherly manner and appeared perfectly frank. Yet I came to learn that he was, if not devious, suspicious and fearful of taking decisions. Although appearing to be master of his own mind and property he would dive for shelter behind his executors and agent at the slightest sign of trouble.'

Nevertheless, in 1946, the Sackville family finally handed the house over to the National Trust under the Country Houses Scheme, with an endowment, which was supplemented from the Trust's own resources, towards its maintenance. The family retained possession of the park and many of the contents of the house, and was granted a 200-year lease on various private apartments within the house. There's a cartoon in *Punch*, from 1947 – the year that Knole opened again to visitors under new ownership. It's of a father and son of the post-war period, a time when country-house owners felt that private ownership was becoming more of a burden than a privilege. 'This is my last warning, Charles,' says the father; 'if you do not mend your ways I shall leave the estate to you instead of to the National Trust.'

By today's standards, the terms of the handover favoured the family. The National Trust acquired the liability of the crumbling fabric, while the family retained most of the assets, its priceless contents. This was principally because James Lees-Milne, who brokered the deal for the National Trust, was extremely sympathetic to the owner-donors. Writing in his diary after a glass of post-prandial port with Charlie and the trustees of the Knole Estate, he wrote: 'I believe we must always be frank with decent owners like Lord Sackville. My sympathies are always with them. In fact my loyalties are first to the houses, second to the donors, and third to the National Trust. I put the Trust last because it is neither a work of art nor a human being but an abstract thing, a convenience.'

Since then – and as a result of those priorities – the National Trust has occasionally been accused of providing retirement homes for 'distressed gentlefolk', of allowing the former owners of its properties to live a life of upholstered luxury, in a style to which they had for generations been too impecunious to grow accustomed.

The National Trust's publicity department would have liked an official handover, but Charlie was 'dead against it', according to James Lees-Milne. 'He did not see himself in the role of willing benefactor of the National Trust to be accorded grateful thanks on a public stage. He saw himself as the inheritor of a glorious palace the burden of which he had been forced by a disobliging new world to shift on to the shoulders of an alien organisation while retaining, as far as it were possible, the status granted him by the old world.' Charlie was irritated when people began to ring – prematurely – inquiring about the opening hours.

In 1946, on a visit to Knole, Lees-Milne described the 'piles of dust under the chairs from worm borings. The gesso furniture too is in a terrible state. All the picture labels want renewing; the silver furniture cleaning; the window mullions mending.' The furniture was in a shocking state of repair, and the best seventeenth-century carpets had silver-fish in them and were in just as neglected a condition as the furniture. When one of the expert craftsmen employed by the National Trust on the restoration met Lord Sackville and told him that 'the condition of the furniture is deplorable, caused by utter neglect', Lord Sackville bridled and James Lees-Milne had to soothe him.

Vita felt the handover very keenly. 'Of course I cannot pretend that I like it but I know that it is the only thing to be done,' she wrote to James Lees-Milne. She respected the National Trust – indeed, she was a founder member of its Gardens Committee in the late 1940s – but she didn't want it for Sissinghurst, as she wrote in her diary on 29 November 1954:

> H. said that Nigel had sounded him on whether I would ever consider giving Sissinghurst to the National Trust. I said, Never, never, never! *Au grand jamais, jamais.* Never, never, never! Not that hard little metal plate at my door! Nigel can do what he likes when I am dead, but so long as I live, no National Trust or any other foreign body shall have my darling. No, no. Over my corpse or my ashes, not otherwise. No, no. I felt myself flush with rage. It is bad enough to have lost my Knole, but they shan't take Sissinghurst from me. That at least is my own. *Il y a des choses qu'on peut pas supporter.* They shan't; they shan't; I won't. They can't make me. I won't. They can't make me. I never would.

Knole was probably the greatest love of Vita's life – deeper than her writing, deeper than her love for Harold. In 1937, as she was completing *Pepita*, the biography of her grandmother and her mother, and being brought ever closer to Knole, she had acknowledged how Knole had always got in the way of her relationship with her husband and also with her cousin. 'Knole has been an awful and deep block,' she wrote to Eddy; 'I suppose my love for Knole has gone deeper than anything else in my life. If only you had been my brother this block wouldn't have occurred, because I shouldn't have minded in the least if you had succeeded to Dada, in fact, I should have liked it. As it is, I do love you as though you were my brother, and even beyond that, perhaps because I never had a brother – and you are the nearest substitute I can get.'

Ten years later, she was commissioned by the National Trust to write the new guidebook to Knole. Because she had not been to Knole since the year of her father's death, she agreed to the commission so long as James Lees-Milne checked the location of all the furniture and pictures. However, her memory was such that he didn't recall raising a single question about the contents described in her text. The experience brought back much of her earlier unhappiness, as she wrote to Harold on 24 September 1947:

> I've done my proofs of the little guidebook I wrote for the National Trust on Knole. They bit. I am always fascinated, as you are, by the strange movements of the human heart. You see, I can write quite coldly and unmovedly a guidebook about Knole, and can also reread it in proof, and then suddenly it will bite, like rodent teeth closing on one's wrist, and I wake to the truth, 'This is my Knole, which I love more than anything in the world except Hadji', and then I can't bear to go on reading my own short little bare guide book about my Knole which has been given over to someone else, not us. Oh, Hadji, it's silly to mind, I know, but I do mind. I can't quite understand why I should care so dreadfully about Knole, but I do. I can't get it out of my system. Why should stones and rooms and shapes of courtyards matter so poignantly? I wish you were here. I know you would understand. But nobody really feels Knole as I do. Nobody really does.

The surrender of Knole to the National Trust in 1946 guaranteed its survival, and for this I admire Charlie and am grateful to him. Here was a deeply conservative man who went against three and a half centuries of family history, who agonised over the decision to hand his glorious inheritance to an alien organisation, but when forced to do so by that 'disobliging new world', did so with grace. Although he had told James Lees-Milne that no Sackville after Eddy would live at Knole, his forward thinking has prolonged the Sackville family's residence at Knole well beyond that.

Eve Rogers, a friend of Charlie and Anne's from nearby Riverhill House, remembers an evening at Knole shortly after the war. She and her husband had been asked to dinner – black tie, evening dress and jewels, Anne had insisted – and there were just three couples present, the Rogers, the Sackvilles and some American friends of Anne's. After dinner, they moved to the Colonnade, the light from its wall sconces reflected in the silver-framed mirrors, and the seventeenth-century furniture casting shadows that deepened the perspective of the trompe-l'oeil wall arches and niches. The gramophone was turned on. Anne, who had a gammy hip, stuttered around the room, slightly out of step, with David Rogers; Charlie, in his late seventies, foxtrotted with the young Mrs Rogers; and the American couple sat the dancing out, looking on, bemused. This is how I like to think of Charlie, a veteran of the Boer War and the trenches of northern France, a dapper, diminutive major general, tripping the light fantastic in what is the most beautiful room in the whole of Knole.

Although this was 1946, there was a *fin de siècle* feel, and I wonder whether Charlie, that early-twentieth-century cavalier, ever felt any of the same regret felt 300 years earlier by Edward Sackville, 4th Earl of Dorset, after Knole had been sequestrated by Parliament: 'I am neither Thomas Earle of Dorset Lord High Treasurer of England nor Richard Earle of Dorsett . . . nor Edward Earle of Dorsett L[ord] Chamberlayne not longe agoe to the Kinge, but a poore unsuccessfull Cavalier . . .'.

Chapter 12

Under New Ownership (1946–)

Knole and the National Trust

In 1947 the first priority for the National Trust at Knole was to give the place a good spring clean. This job fell to just two people: Knole's first National Trust guides, Mrs MacLean and Barbara Tate – who had come to Knole as a housemaid in 1930s and, with the exception of the war years, would live in the house until her death in 2006. They spent the first three months of 1947 cleaning the rooms and their contents, in preparation for the opening. It was a monumental task. On their hands and knees, from dawn to dusk, during one of the coldest winters of the twentieth century, when the house was 'like a refrigerator' according to James Lees-Milne, the two of them scrubbed away the years of wartime neglect in the unlit, unheated rooms. They did not even have the necessary cleaning equipment and had to beg and borrow brushes, dusters and mops from friends, or salvage them from jumble sales.

On 3 April 1947, Knole was opened to the public by its new owners, one of nineteen new National Trust houses, including Blickling and Cotehele, shown for the first time that year. 'The silver in the King's Room [was] all cleaned and shining as though awaiting its royal visitor,' wrote James Lees-Milne. Such was the publicity surrounding the great event that there were more than 1,000 visitors over Easter and a further 2,000 over the spring holidays several weeks later. The popularity of the house, when it opened, rather took the National Trust by surprise. The two guides could barely cope with the crowds, and there were inevitable delays and bottlenecks in a house not designed for mass tourism. Some visitors, disgruntled by the queues, whiled away the waiting time by scratching their names on the gatehouse door. The staff got tired and complained about the lack of tips.

Towards the end of the first season, James Lees-Milne wrote to his assistant, Robin Fedden: 'There must be something wrong at Knole. A great number of grumbles from visitors this year at having to wait hours and then ill manners of the wicket-gate people. When we were there everything seemed to work very smoothly, but I suspect the dragoness at the gate, and that extraordinary *gauleiter* figure with a walking-stick, are probably extremely dictatorial with the public – at least they frightened us to death.' Fedden agreed that 'the pre-Trust inhabitants of Knole still feel, and sometimes show, that they are doing the public a great favour in admitting them to My Lord's house at all'. For the National Trust, this was part of a more general problem of houses where the donor's staff continued to work both for the old master and the new, giving rise to tensions that can still surface to this day.

The National Trust had undertaken to retain the family maintenance staff of up to twelve men, including their agent Frank Mason who remained an employee of both organisations, but gave his first employer, Lord Sackville, his primary allegiance. As a result, the family maintained a fair degree of autonomy in the management of the house. This arrangement continued until the 1980s, my father succeeding Frank Mason as agent both for the family and the National Trust; it worked principally because my father was the most accommodating and fair-minded of men.

Despite the initial teething troubles, tours of the house were soon streamlined, and a massive programme of repairs, restoration and conservation begun. Hardly a stone was left untouched. Over the past fifty years, the National Trust has spent more than £3 million on the house and its contents, and government grants worth millions more have been spent on the stonework, roofs and leadwork. Some 75 per cent of the brick chimneys have been rebuilt, many of the windows including the oriel window in Bourchier's Tower replaced, and several of the façades including that of the Great Hall refaced. One project alone – the restoration of the King's Bed, with its myriad gold threads – cost £250,000, lasted thirteen years and employed a total of 140 volunteer needlewomen.

Between 1945 and 1955 hundreds of country houses in England were demolished, at the rate of something like one a week at its peak in 1955. Others became schools or hotels, or were acquired by local authorities as repositories for museum collections. Knole, on the other hand, as a result of its acquisition by the National Trust, is probably in better condition now than it has ever been in the past 150 years or so. And it has been spared the commercialisation adopted as a survival strategy by other aristocratic families. Lord Montagu was photographed on his hands and knees before Beaulieu opened to the public in 1952, with the caption: 'It's enough to bring a Peer to his knees.' The Duke of Bedford hosted nudist congresses in the park at Woburn (which opened in 1954), did the twist on Australian TV, and joined Lord Montagu to sing a duet of Noël Coward's 'The Stately Homes of England' on BBC's *Tonight* programme. I can't imagine my great-uncle Charlie, in his yellow waistcoat, introducing lions to the deer park at Knole (as at Longleat, which opened in 1952) or indulging in any of the kind of capers which can be associated with the stately home business.

The debate about spending public money on private houses because they were part of 'the national heritage' intensified in the post-war period. The question was generally resolved by a simple trade-off: public funds, in the form of grants and tax concessions, in exchange for greater public access. In 1950 a report into the preservation 'of houses of outstanding historical or architectural interest' recommended that, in exchange for access, grants be awarded for repair and maintenance under the auspices of Historic Buildings Councils. It was government grants from this source that funded the first programme of repair works at Knole in 1954.

The other development which enabled the stately home to rise, phoenix-like, from the ashes of the 1940s and 'to impose itself as the very quintessence of Englishness' was the growth of the cult of the country house. Two exhibitions were partly responsible for this – and Knole featured in both of them. The first, 'The Destruction of the English Country House', was held at the Victoria and Albert Museum in 1974, and presented the country house, and its owner too, as an endangered species. The introduction to the book accompanying the exhibition was written by the historian Roy Strong and began with an 'Evocation of Knole' from *Orlando* ('The great wings of silence beat up and down the empty house'), and it ended with the now-familiar argument: 'Country house owners are the hereditary custodians of what was one of the most vital forces of cultural creation in our history. They deserve consideration and justice as much as any other groups within our society as they struggle to preserve and share with us the creative richness of our heritage.' Other writers echoed these sentiments. What had begun as an elegy turned into a polemic against the new capital taxes proposed by the government and a special plea for further exemptions for 'heritage assets'.

The second exhibition, 'The Treasure Houses of Britain', was held at the National Gallery of Art in Washington in 1985–86. Knole was represented by some richly decorated silver furniture from the King's Room, which took pride of place in a Jacobean long gallery, one of seventeen rooms specially recreated for the exhibition. 'Treasure Houses' was really the apotheosis of the cult of the country house, but some critics were more cynical. They argued that the celebration of the country house was an attempt by the aristocracy to safeguard its inheritance by reinventing itself as the live-in guardian of the national heritage.

Although Knole itself had been handed to the National Trust in 1946, there was still the question of what to do with the rest of the estate, including many of the contents in the house. Charlie's son Eddy was, in the words of my uncle Lionel, considered to be 'an unmarrying man', and in any case had never cared that much for Knole. Novelist, critic and all-round aesthete, Eddy and his major-general father had a relatively distant relationship – possibly as a result of Charlie's treatment of his first wife, Maud – 'my poor afflicted mother!', as Eddy described her. My uncle Lionel found the letters that Charlie wrote to Maud flaunting his infidelities so distasteful that he burned them. Maud died, aged forty-seven, in 1920 in Paris, and in 1924 Charlie married an American called Anne Bigelow. 'Cannot contemplate it at all,' wrote Eddy; 'I hope they will be happy – the only excuse for such a *mésalliance* in these times when the aristocracy cannot afford them.' Eddy disliked Anne intensely, although Charlie adored his second wife, if no one else did, and aged fifty-three his philandering appears to have come to an end on his second marriage.

The portrait of Eddy by Graham Sutherland which hangs at Knole is, as his cousin Benedict Nicolson described, a 'magnificent image of controlled distress'. Throughout his life, this exceptionally talented man had periods of deep depression, as well as generally frail health, suffering like his mother and sister from telangiectasia, an hereditary disorder of the blood vessels that causes frequent haemorrhaging, in particular nose bleeds. But he also suffered from hypochondria, his bathroom stuffed with medicaments and his place at the dining table ringed with tiny snuff boxes filled with pills. In Nancy Mitford's novel *The Pursuit of Love*, he appears as Uncle Davey: 'Davey gave a series of little sniffs. This usually denoted that his nose was about to bleed, pints of valuable red and white corpuscles so assiduously filled with vitamins would be wasted, his resistance still further lowered.'

Eddy dreaded the responsibility of ownership and, in any case, would have been quite incapable of managing Knole. He could barely manage his own affairs, and into his early fifties was still financially dependent on an allowance from his father, who was in his early eighties – a dependence which further strained relations between father and son. My uncle Lionel was increasingly 'recognised as the future incumbent of Knole'. A scheme was needed which, in Lionel's words, would 'divest [Eddy] of Knole responsibilities' but give him 'sufficient funds (which meant a lot) to live on'.

As part of a major rearrangement of the Knole estate in the early 1950s, Charlie sold his reversionary interest in Knole for a capital sum that would enable him to live there for his lifetime (and holiday for several of the winter months in the United States, the Caribbean or the South of France) and to provide for Anne if he predeceased her. In March 1955, the estate was disentailed. Eddy received £200,000 for surrendering his interest in Knole, which made him a rich man and enabled him to buy a house in Ireland the following year. 'Ireland suits my temperament,' he told the *Daily Mail*; 'I prefer it to that big place in Kent . . . Here I can farm a few acres and entertain a few friends. That is all I ask from life.' It was the first home that he had owned, and he decorated it with style, swathing the drawing room in maroon flock wallpaper with huge white roses, and painting the library a Prussian blue that set off the orange floor-to-ceiling bookcases. The maids he dressed in red uniforms and he, too, took to wearing a red dinner jacket.

Under the terms of the new discretionary trust, my uncle Lionel was to bypass Eddy and become heir to Knole. For Christmas 1954, Charlie sent his son 'the usual small and dull present', accompanied by a teasing reference to Eddy's imminent wealth: 'I suppose next year you will be sending me a cheque.' Eddy continued, nevertheless, to ask for the loan of furniture from Knole (which irritated his father and involved Lionel as a trustee of the new trust). Charlie agreed, long-sufferingly, so long as the trustees had no objection, but concluded his typewritten, dictated letter: 'I am a very old man and do hope this will not develop into an acrimonious correspondence.'

Lionel was put in the invidious position of mediating between Eddy, Charlie and the other trustees. It soon became clear that several members of the family had objected to the size of Eddy's payout – a fact of which Eddy, who had not been party to the negotiations, was unaware. Even though he acknowledged that the value of the furniture requested was negligible in relation to the scale of the overall settlement, Lionel pointed out to Eddy in November 1955 that the principles were important. 'And the trouble is that family agreement over the court settlement was arrived at with such difficulty that the subject of Knole and the things that belong there is liable to arouse great family bitterness . . .' Lionel went on to propose the loan of a number of items.

Anne died in 1961. 'She was an unloved woman,' wrote Harold Nicolson, but 'her death simplifies many things – jointures, legacies and turning her out of Knole', had she survived her husband. Vita had resented what she saw as Anne's offhand attitude to Knole, which, according to James Lees-Milne, Anne regarded 'as a sort of antiquated white elephant without the American mod cons'.

Anne's death encouraged Vita to visit Knole again after an absence of thirty years. 'It is like the light beginning to appear at the end of a long black tunnel of exile. I have minded it all so much,' she wrote. She had lunch with her uncle Charlie in March 1961, and then visited Knole again in May and July, when she and Harold found the house 'more lovely than ever'. She was also reassured by the fact that she liked Lionel and his wife Jacobine, who were doing up an apartment in a wing of the house, where they moved with their five daughters in 1961, and 'didn't mind talking to him about Knole, because he loves and understands it as I do, and Eddy doesn't'.

On Charlie's death in May 1962, Eddy became the 5th Lord Sackville, the first peer in four successions since the title had been created in 1876 to succeed his father. It is a further irony that, in an inheritance governed by male primogeniture, the only instance of a direct father-to-son Sackville succession in the past 200 years, and over the course of eight generations, involved a sixty-one-year-old bachelor who opted to be bought out of any rights to Knole. In 1964, the year before his death, Eddy wrote: 'Living at Knole now is (to me, at any rate) extremely disagreeable – particularly in summer, when it is all but impossible to walk outside the garden walls without stepping on a prone figure. It is like living in the middle of Hyde Park! However, my cousin Lionel luckily loves the house enough to put up with this (and other) features of the modern world, none of which I can abide.' On Eddy's death in 1965, my uncle Lionel became 6th Lord Sackville.

For a family home, there are surprisingly few eras, over the course of the past 400 years, when it seems as if Knole and its grounds were overrun by children. In the early seventeenth century, Lady Anne Clifford brought up two daughters at Knole. Half a century later, Richard Sackville, 5th Earl of Dorset, had thirteen children, of whom six reached maturity, their portraits, at play, giving this particular era at Knole a bounce and a bustle. In the eighteenth century there are a couple of periods, one at the beginning and one towards the end, when young families were living at Knole, but then hardly any during the nineteenth century, when – to continue the theme – the house was mostly owned and inhabited by elderly or childless couples. It was not until the 1890s that children – or, rather, a child, Vita – prowled the long galleries once again and set up dens in the garden; after which there was another long wait until the 1960s.

In 1967 my father and mother moved with their five children into another wing at Knole, thereby conclusively disproving Charlie's prediction, as reported to James Lees-Milne more than sixty years ago, that no Sackville after Eddy would live at Knole. The 1960s at Knole seem, certainly in retrospect and in the golden light of child-hood reminiscence, a younger and more optimistic era than the ones which preceded it, with two families and ten children, living side by side in separate apartments, in their stately, semi-detached home. It came to an end in 1971, with the early death of Jacobine, and a pall was cast upon the place. Lionel began to suffer from peri-odic bouts of depression, although, as James Lees-Milne noted on a visit to Knole in 1977, he had 'with age and tribulation acquired a distinction which reminded me of his cousin Eddy and his uncle Charlie'. Like many of his ancestors, including his uncle Lionel and his great-uncle Lionel, and many of his forebears before that, my uncle Lionel became more withdrawn, although there were still challenges to which he responded with dynamism and physical energy. It is largely due to my uncle Lionel, for example, that the park was replanted so successfully after the devastating storm of 16 October 1987, when 70 per cent of the trees in the park were lost.

Knole, too, inevitably became more introverted during the 1980s and 1990s. Gradually, it acquired the feel of an old people's home once again, dark, dusty and shuttered from the world. My uncle and his third wife were looked after, if that's the phrase, by an ageing, heavy-drinking housekeeper, a figure out of *Gormenghast*, who, as we discovered on taking over their apartment, had allowed large areas to sink beneath a semi-permanent skin of grease and grime.

Like my uncle, I am the beneficiary of male primogeniture: another example of an uncle–nephew succession. In July 1958, my mother had received a letter from her sister-in-law, Jacobine. 'All the family are absolutely delighted,' she read; 'I wish very much that you ... had been there to see the expression on his old face [my grandfather's] when he read the note announcing Robert's arrival – it was absolutely blissful. Uncle Charlie merely heaved a sigh of relief, and said in a tone of deep satisfaction, "So that's all right. What do you think we ought to do about it?" (Meaning, I suppose, ringing bells, running up flags, roasting oxes whole in the park for the cheering inhabitants of Sevenoaks, etc.) In fact, you've given a great deal of happiness already, and it is nice to know that this family will be carried on.' In a postscript, Jacobine went on to describe a visit to Sissinghurst the day before, during which Vita had run up the Sackville family flag on the tower in honour of the new arrival.

My aunt Jacobine's warm-hearted letter of congratulations to my mother on my birth did not dwell on the ironies of the situation. It was particularly generous in view of the fact that she had, the previous year, given birth to the third of her five daughters. Vita, too, was acutely aware of what my birth might mean for the various characters mentioned in the letter. Her reaction, as each of these girls was born, was one of mounting disbelief and sympathy, in contrast to her enthusiasm at my birth, the son of a younger son. For although the principle of male primogeniture had conspired against her inheriting Knole, the house which inhabited her soul in a way that no person ever did, Vita was enough of a conservative to fly the flag in other circumstances.

For the whole period of this story (or at least until the twentieth century), it has been an assumption of the British aristocracy that primogeniture has preserved places such as Knole and their collections intact. Without it, the argument goes, estates would long ago have been broken up, as they have been throughout most of Europe, their collections dispersed and sold, the houses at their heart abandoned and demolished. Knole has, indeed, survived intact, although the combination of primogeniture and an extraordinarily convoluted sequence of wills and name changes in the nineteenth century has preserved no more than a fiction of continuous ownership.

There is an idea that a place such as Knole can become slightly soulless without some reference to the people who have lived, or still live, there; that the owner's dog, the child's bicycle propped against an ancient drainpipe, the family photos on display, the occasional glimpse of an eccentric aristocrat (my uncle Lionel, for example, who in his jeans and tweed cap, was often mistaken for a gardener or a gamekeeper) are central to the spirit of the place, to a sense of living history. But is this simply wishful thinking on the part of a beneficiary – me – of a system that is manifestly unfair? Does anyone really care about the survival at places such as Knole of a connection with the family who have lived there for hundreds of years? And, if so, does that justify the fact that one child – a boy – should be favoured at the expense of the girls?

It is possible to trace back what might have happened, at any generation, if the oldest child, rather than the oldest boy, had inherited. Going back a hundred years – and discounting the claims of the 2nd Lord Sackville's five illegitimate children – Vita would have inherited Knole from her father; her son Ben would have inherited on her death, and Ben's daughter, Vanessa Nicolson, would now be living at Knole. Going back almost fifty years, my aunt Betty would have inherited Knole from Eddy or his sister Diana, and on her death my cousin Henry Barlow would have succeeded. Going back less than a decade, my cousin Teresa would have succeeded on my uncle Lionel's death.

None of this happened. My father died in 2001, and my uncle Lionel three years later. Just as Lionel, approaching fifty, had taken over from his uncle Charlie who died aged ninety-one, I was forty-five when I succeeded Lionel, who also died aged ninety-one. Because my uncle had himself been a beneficiary of the system – or, rather, lottery – that is primogeniture, and was, moreover, a deeply conservative man, he had come to accept, I think, the idea of my succession. I was spared, for example, the more meritocratic system introduced at Burghley, where family members are invited to apply for and are then interviewed for the post of custodian.

Whenever summoned by my uncle Lionel to discuss some aspect of Knole – and he issued these invitations increasingly in his last years – I would always experience some trepidation as I peered round his sitting-room door, and through the haze of smoke that engulfed him. 'If there's one thing I would like you to do when you take over . . .', he would say as he sucked noisily on his pipe. My heart would sink as I imagined the impossible posthumous promises that he might be going to ask me to make: take his third wife into our home at Knole after his death; compensate his daughters, my cousins, for their disinheritance in a way that I could never guarantee; undertake never to change the design of the garden or the decoration of a particular room? I should have known better, for his concerns were generally material rather than personal; and latterly, at least, he always treated me – and the predicament of the inheritance – with great grace and generosity. 'If there's one thing I would like you to do when you take over . . .,' he would continue, 'it is to install smaller baths. I hear that they now make these very cheap – and small – baths, so much better than those great cast-iron baths we have here that cost a fortune to fill.'

Before considering the baths, though, we did spend a lot of time thinking about whether we wanted to move from the Gardener's Cottage in the park, where we had been very happy and self-contained, into the big house itself. The fact that my wife and I talked long and hard about this decision might seem rather churlish – for who wouldn't jump at the chance to live in one of the greatest houses in Britain? But there are some compromises that have to be made for the pleasure and privilege of living at Knole.

The crucial compromise of living at Knole is one of privacy. We share the house with the National Trust, with their staff and volunteers, and with the 80,000 visitors who come here every year. It is less the sound of muffled feet and hushed voices wafting down the stairs from the show rooms that we have to come to terms with, but, rather, the fear of being overheard ourselves, through the connecting walls.

Our youngest child, Edie, felt this lack of privacy most acutely – with all the highly developed sense of fair play of a five-year-old. 'It's just not fair!' she complained with outrage, as she came back from school one Monday. One of her classmates had visited Knole that weekend: 'It's just not fair! That Abbi came to my house on Saturday. I can't just go to hers like that – without even asking.'

But we decided that the pleasures of life at Knole were more likely to outweigh the compromises. We chose to give it a go, although we have promised ourselves that we'll move out in our seventies, before the house becomes just too big for us. This time span more or less coincides with the one suggested by John Cornforth in *The Country Houses of England 1948–1998*: the ideal time for an owner to be 'in the saddle', he wrote, seems to be a quarter of a century, from the age of about forty to sixty-five.

John Cornforth was also responsible for the phrase that most aptly captures the spirit of Knole: 'Knole is a house with a special mystery about it', before going on to describe the King's Bed: 'a combination of rich patterns and mellow colours, whites that have gone grey with time, and gilding that smoulders rather than sparkles.' Part of the reason that Knole smoulders rather than sparkles is that, although the house has undergone a refurbishment of sorts every fifty to a hundred years or so since Thomas Sackville's major remodelling four centuries ago, most of these generational refurbs – ours included – have focused on the suite of rooms along the south front. So huge is the rest of the house that large areas have been inhabited only intermittently over the centuries. The state apartments, on the first floor, with their wonderful interiors, have been left mercifully untouched. Much of the furniture there, with its fragile upholstery, has remained under dust sheets in darkened rooms for long periods of time; and it is precisely this which accounts for its miraculous survival, for the state of the textiles which, as Eddy remembered of the bed hangings in the Spangle Bedroom, retained 'unfaded, deep in their inner folds, the richness of their original pomegranate red'.

In approaching our refurbishment of Knole, we have tried to negotiate this delicate balance between the beauty of benign neglect and the demands of responsible ownership, between preserving, on the one hand, the magic of a place where you can still make discoveries and, on the other, not allowing it to fall into decay. Such discoveries have included the Boulle cabinet that stood, throughout my childhood, on one side of an attic gallery, its pieces of tortoise-shell and brass marquetry slowly flaking onto the floor. The cabinet was very nearly consigned to a skip during a periodic clear-out of the attics in the 1980s, but was rescued instead (and went on to sell for over £1 million at Christies').

Another discovery – also of a mercenary, rather than an emotional, nature – was a painting of what appeared to be a couple of nymphs, attributed to a follower of Domenichino. It had hung for as long as anyone could remember in a particularly damp, and derelict, spare bedroom. Reidentified as being by Ludovico Carracci, it was put up for auction at Christies' and after three minutes of brisk bidding, sold for £6.5 million. Those three minutes paid for our recent refurbishment several times over, and effectively endowed family investment in Knole for another generation. It is an example of how the value of a house's art collection, originally no more than an ornament funded by the estate's landed backing, has in many cases in the twenty-first century outstripped the value of the land itself. The art, which had once been an extravagance, a drain on the estate's finances, was now underpinning them.

Our first challenge was the possibly intractable one of adapting a Jacobean palace for twenty-first-century domestic living, of carving a home in the midst of so many historical and architectural constraints. As a Grade I listed building, owned by the National Trust, whatever we did would have to be approved by our land-lords, the National Trust, by the local conservation officer, and by English Heritage; and whatever we did would cost money.

We appointed a conservation architect, Martin Stancliffe, who had worked on many great houses in the United Kingdom and Ireland, and is currently Surveyor to the Fabric of St Paul's Cathedral. Could you create a kitchen for us? we asked him. Oh, and while you're about it, could you do something about the light-ing throughout: it's awfully dark and gloomy? We had only one overriding request: we didn't want a total makeover, for anything to look too new or shiny. We wanted our refurbishment to smoulder, not sparkle, to be true to the spirit of Knole.

One of my co-trustees at the time suggested what it might cost: a quarter or perhaps half a million at a pinch. Martin got the hang of the house in a couple of days of wandering around, and watching the light fall in different rooms at different times of day. He understood far better, at the end of those two days, how different parts of the house connected than I did after years of familiarity. He also realised that our architectural problems were more fundamental than a new kitchen and better lighting; and that our financial exposure would be considerably more fundamental than half a million pounds.

We had noticed in our first few days of camping at Knole – long before the building works started – that at night all the lights in the windows surrounding the Pheasant Court, one of Knole's seven courtyards, were ours; and realised, therefore, that the courtyard was central to our accommodation. As it was, the courtyard was a rather dank space that divided our living space rather than united it. Martin made the Pheasant Court integral to our apartment, a completely private place which opened off the kitchen and where we could eat outside. The kitchen – which had been our starting point, our first requirement – had begun life as a draughty passage in Archbishop Bourchier's Palace, connecting the Great Hall with his private chapel. In the 1960s, this passage had been converted into a narrow kitchen but, by knocking through a sixteenth-century wall – the greatest challenge when it came to getting the necessary listed building consents – we could turn a dingy corridor-kitchen into a bright and open room.

One of the biggest architectural problems at Knole has always been the location of the staircases. Despite its alleged fifty-two staircases, very few of them lead where you want, as Horace Walpole had noted when he visited the house in 1752: 'There is never a good staircase.' By turning a stair in the French Library and exposing a window that had previously been obscured, Martin fused our apartment together, connecting upstairs and downstairs in the way that staircases should, and flooded it with light. Undoing generations of bodging by estate carpenters, Martin removed a warren of partition walls on the second floor, revealing the original mid-fifteenth-century rafters of Bourchier's Great Chamber, and demolished a brick-built 1930s lean-to in the Water Court, which is effectively our front door, to show the original stone arch. The result is more spacious, lighter and far closer to its architectural original.

Over the course of the building works, we have learnt a lot – not just about building, painting and decorating, but also about working with the National Trust. One of the questions I get asked most frequently is this: 'How *do* you get on with the National Trust?' It's always asked in a concerned, conspiratorial tone, and it always seeks out, and anticipates, the answer 'terribly badly'. My answer, as I explain how well we have begun to get on, often comes as rather a disappointment.

The relationship between the resident family and the National Trust, as in all its houses, is potentially tricky. Knole is a hybrid, where landlord and tenant live side by side, their respective interests and ownerships frequently overlapping. At Knole, the delicate balance of power between the family and the National Trust has encouraged both parties to work together. The National Trust owns the house itself, the garden and a small portion of the park. The family has 140 years of a lease left on large areas of the house, owns 90 per cent of the park, much of the collection in the show rooms and all of the collection in the private rooms. If both parties fell out, it would be a disaster for the house and the collection.

What we both realised a few years ago was that a window of opportunity had opened between the generations: a moment when our need for a refurbishment coincided with the National Trust's desire to celebrate Knole a little more, to give it the prominence it deserved, to unlock the potential of this great treasure house. For this to happen, both parties needed to invest in a shared vision. The National Trust has provided advice and made a financial contribution towards our works; and we, in turn, have granted greater public access, which will enable investment in other areas of the house. At the moment, just fifteen or so of Knole's '365' rooms are open to visitors, plus a couple of courtyards and staircases. By making more of the house accessible – particularly those parts that could add a whole new dimension to a visit – Knole will become easier to understand and appreciate.

The handover of Knole to the National Trust more than two generations ago was the start of a new story, and a story that will, with time, become just as central to the spirit of the place as Knole and the Sackvilles. This new story will come to involve more characters or, as the National Trust would say, more stakeholders: not just the family, but the staff who work there, the volunteers, and the visitors. All these people with competing claims to the place will doubtless nurture new generations of myths. That's one of the reasons I've written this book – to stake a pre-emptive claim to the myth of the place, to make my facts and fictions the ones that prevail. Vita Sackville-West attempted something similar in *Knole and the Sackvilles*; a guide will do it every time he or she takes a group around the house. In an age, when Knole is as much a public as a private place, this book is my stamp of territoriality, my equivalent of Thomas Sackville's initials on the drainpipes.

But only a small signature, because as Orlando muses in Virginia Woolf's novel about Knole: 'Here have lived, for more centuries than I can count, the obscure generations of my own obscure family. Not one of these Richards, Johns, Annes, Elizabeths has left a token of himself behind, yet all, working together with their spades and their needles, their love-making and their child-bearing have left this.' Woolf's lover, Vita Sackville-West, to whom *Orlando* was dedicated, particularly liked this passage, and so do I – capturing, as it does, the essence of the house in which I, too, was brought up, and in which I now live, and the family of which I am a member.

Select Bibliography

Archives

Centre for Kentish Studies, Maidstone, Sackville Mss, U269
Cumbria Record Office, Carlisle, Hothfield Mss (for Lady Anne Clifford)
East Sussex Record Office, Lewes, De La Warr Papers
Hatfield House, Hertfordshire, Cecil family papers
Lilly Library, Indiana University, Bloomington, Indiana, Diaries of Victoria, Lady Sackville
The National Archives, Kew, Thomas Sackville's will (PRO, PROB 11/113)

Unpublished sources

Colvin and Moggridge, *The Restoration of Knole Park: A Report for the Trustees of the Knole Estate,* 1989
Dixon, Philip, *A Report on the Works of 2007–08*
Knole Conservation Management Plan, commissioned by the National Trust from Oxford Archaeology, June 2007
Knole Park: Landscape Conservation Management Plan, commissioned by Knole Estates from Elise Percifull/Historic Landscape Management, May 2009
Simmons, Margaret, 'Apricot Days: A Memoir'
Smith, David L., 'The Political Career of Edward Sackville, 4th Earl of Dorset (1590–1652)', unpublished PhD dissertation, University of Cambridge, 1990

Stewart, Linda, 'Across the Miry Vale', unpublished Diploma dissertation, Portsmouth Polytechnic, 1992

Ward, Ian, 'The English Peerage, 1649–60', unpublished PhD dissertation, University of Cambridge, 1989

Published sources

Abbot, George, *A Sermon preached at Westminster, May 26, 1608, at the Funerall Solemnities of the right honorable Thomas, earle of Dorset* (London, 1608)

Abell, Henry Francis, *Kent and the Great Civil War* (Ashford, 1901)

Airs, Malcolm, *The Tudor and Jacobean Country House* (Bramley Books, 1998)

Alsop, Susan Mary, *Lady Sackville* (Doubleday, 1978)

'An Account of the Disturbances at Knole, with Letters and Press Opinions on the Subject' (privately published, Scarborough, 1884)

Aubrey, John, *Brief Lives*, ed. Andrew Clark (Clarendon Press, 1898)

Bacquet, Paul, *Un comtemporain d'Elisabeth I: Thomas Sackville: L'homme et l'oeuvre* (Geneva, 1966)

Bateman, John, *The Great Landowners of Great Britain and Ireland* (Leicester University Press, 1971)

Beauclerk, Charles, *Nell Gwyn: a Biography* (Macmillan, 2005)

Beckett, J. V., *The Aristocracy in England, 1660–1914* (Blackwell, 1986)

Berlin, Normand, *Thomas Sackville* (Twayne, 1975)

Birkenhead, Frederick, Earl of, *F. E.: The Life of F. E. Smith, 1st Earl of Birkenhead* (Eyre & Spottiswoode, 1959)

Birley, Derek, *A Social History of English Cricket* (Aurum Press, 1999)

Brady, J. H., *The Visitor's Guide to Knole* (Sevenoaks, 1839)

Brewer, John, *The Pleasures of the Imagination* (HarperCollins, 1997)

Bridgman, John, *An Historical and Topographical Sketch of Knole, in Kent* (London, 1817)

Campbell, John, *F. E. Smith, 1st Earl of Birkenhead* (Cape, 1983)

Cannadine, David, *Aspects of Aristocracy: Grandeur and Decline in Modern Britain* (Yale University Press, 1994)

——— *The Pleasures of the Past* (Collins, 1989)

——— *The Decline and Fall of the British Aristocracy* (Yale University Press, 1990)

Clifford, Anne, Lady, *The Diaries of Lady Anne Clifford*, ed. D. J. H. Clifford (Alan Sutton, 1990)

————*The Diary of the Lady Anne Clifford*, ed. Vita Sackville-West (William Heinemann, 1923)

Cokayne, G. E., *The Complete Peerage of England, Scotland, Ireland, Great Britain and the United Kingdom* (London, 1910–98)

Coke, Mary, Lady, *The Letters and Journals of Lady Mary Coke*, ed. J. A. Home (Kingsmead Reprints, 1970)

Coleman, John, 'Reynolds at Knole', *Apollo*, cxliii, April 1996, pp. 24–30

Collins, Arthur, *The Peerage of England* (New York, 1970, reprint of 1812 edition)

Colvin, H. M., ed., *The History of the King's Works* (HMSO, 1963–82)

Cornforth, John, *The Country Houses of England, 1948–98* (Constable, 1998)

————'Glow of Gold Brocade', *Country Life*, 6 August 1987, pp. 64–65

Coventry, George, *Memoirs of Lord Viscount Sackville*, 1825

Cowles, Virginia, *The Astors: The Story of a Transatlantic Family* (Weidenfeld & Nicolson, 1979)

Cramsie, John, 'Commercial Projects and the Fiscal Policy of James VI and I', *The Historical Journal*, 43, 2 (2000)

De-la-Noy, Michael, *Eddy: The Life of Edward Sackville-West* (Arcadia, 1999)

De La Warr, Anne, *The Sackville Chapel* (English Life Publications, 1993)

Derby, Edward Henry Stanley, Earl of, *A Selection from the Diaries of Edward Henry Stanley, 15th Earl of Derby (1826–93) between September 1869 and March 1878*, ed. John Vincent (Royal Historical Society, 1994)

———— *The Diaries of Edward Henry Stanley, 15th Earl of Derby (1826–93) between 1878 and 1893*, ed. John Vincent (Leopard's Head Press, 2003)

Devonshire, Georgiana, Duchess of, *Extracts from the correspondence of Georgiana, Duchess of Devonshire*, ed. Earl of Bessborough (John Murray, 1955)

Dodington, George Bubb, *The Political Journal of George Bubb Dodington*, ed. John Carswell and Lewis Arnold Dralle (Clarendon Press, 1965)

Drury, Martin, 'A Diplomat's Prize', *Country Life*, 3 October 1991, pp. 54–55

Dryden, John, *Dramatic Poesy and Other Essays* (Dent, 1950)

————*Essays of John Dryden*, ed. W. P. Ker (Clarendon Press, 1900)

Edgeworth, Maria, *Letters from England, 1813–44*, ed. Christina Colvin (Clarendon Press, 1971)

Einberg, Elizabeth, *Gainsborough's Giovanni Baccelli* (Tate Gallery, 1976)

Eliot, Karen, *Dancing Lives* (University of Illinois Press, 2007)

Everitt, Alan, *The Community of Kent and the Great Rebellion, 1640–1660* (Leicester University Press, 1966)

Farington, Joseph, *The Diary of Joseph Farington*, ed. Kenneth Garlick and Angus Macintyre (Yale University Press, 1978–98)

Fitzmaurice, Edmond, Lord, *Life of William, Earl of Shelburne* (London, 1875–76)

Foreman, Amanda, *Georgiana: Duchess of Devonshire* (HarperCollins, 1998)

Fowler, Alastair, *The Country House Poem* (Edinburgh University Press, 1994)

Fraser, Antonia, *The Weaker Vessel: Woman's Lot in Seventeenth-Century England* (Weidenfeld & Nicolson, 1984)

Friedman, Alice, *House and Household in Elizabethan England* (University of Chicago Press, 1989)

Girouard, Mark, *Life in the English Country House* (Yale University Press, 1978)

——*Robert Smythson and the Elizabethan Country House* (Yale University Press, 1983)

Glendinning, Victoria, *Vita: The Life of Vita Sackville-West* (Weidenfeld & Nicolson, 1983)

Guest, I., 'Italian Lady at Knole', *Ballet Annual*, 1957, No. 11

Harris, Brice, *Charles Sackville, 6th Earl of Dorset, Patron and Poet of the Restoration* (University of Illinois Press, 1940)

Hearn, Karen, *Talking Peace 1604: The Somerset House Conference Paintings*, Gilbert Collection (Somerset House, 2004)

Hill, L. M., 'Sir Julius Caesar's Journal of Salisbury's first 2 months and 20 days as Lord Treasurer, 1608', *Bulletin of the Institute of Historical Research*, Vol. XLV (1972), pp. 311–27

Historical Manuscripts Commission, *Report on the Manuscripts of Mrs Stopford Sackville of Drayton House, Northamptonshire* (HMSO, 1904–10)

——*Report on the Sackville Mss*, by Professor Newton (HMSO, 1938)

Holmes, Martin, *Proud Northern Lady* (Phillimore, 1984)

Howard, Maurice, *The Building of Elizabethan and Jacobean England* (Yale University Press, 2007)

Hunt, Tristram, *The English Civil War at First Hand* (Weidenfeld & Nicolson, 2002)

Ingamells, John, *A Dictionary of British and Irish Travellers, 1701–1800: Compiled from the Brinsley Ford Archive* (Paul Mellon Centre, 1997)

Jackson-Stops, Gervase, 'Purchases and Perquisites: The 6th Earl of Dorset's Furniture at Knole', *Country Life*, June 1977

Jullian, Philippe and John Phillips, *Violet Trefusis: Life and Letters* (Hamilton, 1976)

Killingray, David, 'Rights, "Riot" and Ritual: The Knole Park Access Dispute, Sevenoaks, Kent, 1883-85', *Rural History*, 5 (1994), pp. 63–79

Klein, Lisa M., 'Lady Anne Clifford as Mother and Matriarch', *Journal of Family History*, Vol. 26, No. 1, January 2001, pp. 18–38

Lees-Milne, James, *Diaries: Ancestral Voices, 1942–43* (Michael Russell, 2003)

—— *Diaries: Prophesying Peace, 1944–45* (Michael Russell, 2003)

—— *Diaries: Caves of Ice, 1946–47* (Chatto & Windus, 1983)

—— *Diaries: Midway on the Waves, 1948–49* (Faber, 1985)

——*Diaries: 1942–1954; 1971–1983*, ed. Michael Bloch (John Murray, 2006–07)

——*Harold Nicolson* (Chatto & Windus, 1980–81)

——*People and Places: Country House Donors and the National Trust* (John Murray, 1992)

Lutyens, Mary, *Edwin Lutyens* (John Murray, 1980)

McClung, William A., *The Country House in English Renaissance Poetry* (University of California Press, 1977)

McIntyre, Ian, *Joshua Reynolds: The Life and Times of the First President of the Royal Academy* (Allen Lane, 2003)

Mackesy, Piers, *The Coward of Minden: The Affair of Lord George Sackville* (Allen Lane, 1979)

——*The War for America, 1775–1783* (Longman, 1964)

Major, John, *More Than a Game: The Story of Cricket's Early Years* (HarperCollins, 2007)

Mandler, Peter, *The Fall and Rise of the Stately Home* (Yale University Press, 1997)

Marlow, Louis, *Sackville of Drayton* (Home and Van Thal, 1948)

Musson, Jeremy, *Up and Down Stairs: The History of the Country House Servant* (John Murray, 2009)

Nash, Joseph, *Descriptions of the Plates of the Mansions of England in the Olden Time* (London, 1849)

Nicolson, Adam, *Earls of Paradise* (HarperPress, 2007)

——*Sissinghurst: An Unfinished Story* (HarperPress, 2008)

Nicolson, Harold, *Diaries and Letters*, 3 vols, 1930–62, ed. Nigel Nicolson (Collins, 1966–68)

——*Harold Nicolson Diaries and Letters, 1907–1964*, ed. Nigel Nicolson (Weidenfeld & Nicolson, 2004)

Nicolson, Nigel, *Portrait of a Marriage* (Weidenfeld & Nicolson, 1973)

Peck, Linda Levy, *Court Patronage and Corruption in Early Stuart England* (Routledge, 1991)

——*Northampton: Patronage and Policy at the Court of James I* (Allen & Unwin, 1982)

Pepys, Samuel, *The Diary of Samuel Pepys: A New and Complete Transcription*, ed. Robert Latham and William Matthews (Bell, 1970–83)

Phillips, C. J., *History of the Sackville Family* (Cassell, 1929)

Pinto, Vivian de Sola, *Enthusisast in Wit: A Portrait of John Wilmot, Earl of Rochester* (Routledge & Kegan Paul, 1962)

Postle, Martin, *Angels and Urchins: The Fancy Picture in 18th-century British Art* (Draig Publications, 1998)

——*Sir Joshua Reynolds: The Subject Pictures* (Cambridge University Press, 1995)

Postle, Martin, ed., *Joshua Reynolds: The Creation of Celebrity* (Tate Publishing, 2005)

Prestwich, Menna, 'English Politics and Administration, 1603–1625', in *The Reign of James VI and I*, ed. Alan G. R. Smith (St Martin's Press, 1973)

Prior, Matthew, *Poems on Several Occasions*, ed. A. R. Waller (Cambridge University Press, 1905)

Prophecies delivered by a descendant from the Oracle of Delphos (Dublin, 1791)

Proud Northern Lady: Lady Anne Clifford, 1590–1676 (Abbot Hall Art Gallery, 1990)

Purkiss, Diane, *The English Civil War: A People's History* (HarperPress, 2006)

Redford, Bruce, *Dilettanti: The Antic and the Antique in Eighteenth-century England* (J. Paul Getty Museum, 2008)

Ridley, Jane, *The Architect and His Wife: A Life of Edwin Lutyens* (Chatto & Windus, 2002)

Rowell, Christopher, 'The King's Bed and its Furniture at Knole', *Apollo*, clx, no. 513 (November 2004), pp. 58–65

Russell, Francis, 'Picture Hanging at Knole in 1799', *Apollo*, cxxix, no. 325 (March 1989), pp. 168–72

Russell, George William, Lord, *Lord William Russell and His Wife, 1815–1846*, ed. Georgiana Blakiston (John Murray, 1972)

Sackville-West, Edward, 'Fear in Fancy Dress', in *Little Innocents*, ed. Alan Pryce-Jones (Cobden-Sanderson, 1932)

———'Sketches for an Autobiography', in *Orion: A Miscellany*, Vol. 3 (Nicholson & Watson, 1945–47)

Sackville-West, Robert, *Knole* (The National Trust, 1998)

Sackville-West, Vita, *The Edwardians* (Hogarth Press, 1930)

———*The Heir* (The Richards Press, 1949)

———*Knole and the Sackvilles* (William Heinemann, 1934)

———*The Letters of Vita Sackville-West to Virginia Woolf*, ed. Louise DeSalvo and Mitchell A. Leaska (Virago, 1992)

———*Pepita*, with an introduction by Alison Hennegan (Virago, 1986)

———'Shameful Reminiscences', in *Little Innocents*, ed. Alan Pryce-Jones (Cobden-Sanderson, 1932)

———*Vita and Harold: The Letters of Vita Sackville-West and Harold Nicolson*, ed. Nigel Nicolson (Weidenfeld & Nicolson, 1987)

Salisbury, Mary, Marchioness of, *A Great Lady's Friendships, Letters to Mary, Marchioness of Salisbury, Countess of Derby, 1862–1876*, ed. W. A. Gardner, Baroness Burghclere (Macmillan, 1933)

Samuel, Raphael, *Theatres of Memory: Past and Present in Contemporary Culture* (Verso, 1994)

Sharpe, Kevin, 'Image of Virtue: the Court and Household of Charles I, 1625–42', in *The English Court from the Wars of the Roses to the Civil War*, ed. David Starkey (Longman, 1987)

———*The Personal Rule of Charles I* (Yale University Press, 1992)

Smith, David L., 'Catholic, Anglican or Puritan? Edward Sackville, 4th Earl of Dorset and the Ambiguities of Religion in Early Stuart England', *Transactions of the Royal Historical Society*, s6, v2

———*Constitutional Royalism and the Search for Settlement, c.1640–1649* (Cambridge University Press, 1994)

———'The 4th Earl of Dorset and the Personal Rule of Charles I', *Journal of British Studies*, 30

———'The 4th Earl of Dorset and the Politics of the Sixteen-Twenties', *Historical Research*, 65

———'"The More Posed and Wise Advice": The 4th Earl of Dorset and the English Civil Wars', *Historical Journal*, 34

Somerset, Anne, *Unnatural Murder* (Weidenfeld & Nicolson, 1997)

Spence, Joseph, *Letters from the Grand Tour*, ed. Slava Klima (McGill-Queen's University Press, 1975)

Spence, Richard T., *Lady Anne Clifford* (Sutton, 1997)

Stone, Lawrence, *The Crisis of the Aristocracy, 1558–1641* (Clarendon Press, 1965)

————*Family and Fortune: Studies in Aristocratic Finance in the Sixteenth and Seventeenth Centuries* (Clarendon Press, 1973)

————*The Family, Sex and Marriage in England, 1500–1800* (Weidenfeld & Nicolson, 1977)

Stone, Lawrence, and Jeanne C. Fawtier Stone, *An Open Elite?: England 1540–1880* (Clarendon Press, 1984)

Strong, Roy, *William Larkin: Icons of Splendour* (Franco Maria Ricci, 1995)

Strong, Roy, et al., *The Destruction of the Country House, 1875–1975* (Thames & Hudson, 1974)

Summerson, John (ed.), *The Book of Architecture of John Thorpe in Sir John Soane's Museum* (Glasgow, 1966)

Sutton, C. N., *Historical Notes of Withyham, Hartfield and Ashdown Forest* (Tunbridge Wells, 1902)

Taylor, C., 'From Losses to Lawsuit: Patronage of the Italian Opera in London by Lord Middlesex, 1739–45', *Music and Letters*, no. 68 (1987), pp. 1–25

The Thomason Tracts, Reproduced from the collection of tracts in the British Museum (Scolar Press, 1968)

Tinniswood, Adrian, *The Polite Tourist: A History of Country House Visiting* (National Trust, 1998)

Tipping, Avray, 'Knole of the Dukes', *Country Life*, 8 June 1912

Trefusis, Violet, *Don't Look Round: Reminiscences* (Hutchinson, 1952)

————*Violet to Vita: The Letters of Violet Trefusis to Vita Sackville-West, 1910–21*, ed. Mitchell A. Leaska and John Phillips (Methuen, 1989)

Valentine, Alan, *Lord George Germain* (Clarendon Press, 1962)

Vivian, Frances, *A Life of Frederick, Prince of Wales, 1707–1751* (Edwin Mellen, 2006)

Walpole, Horace, *The Yale Edition of Horace Walpole's Correspondence*, ed. W. S. Lewis (Yale University Press, 1937–83)

————*The Letters of Horace Walpole*, ed. Paget Toynbee (Clarendon Press, 1903–05)

————*Memoirs of the Reign of George II*, ed. John Brooke (Yale University Press, 1985)

————*Memoirs of the Reign of George III*, ed. Derek Jarrett (Yale University Press, 2000)

Wells-Cole, Anthony, *Art and Decoration in Elizabethan and Jacobean England* (Yale University Press, 1997)

William Larkin and the 3rd Earl of Dorset: A Portrait in Focus (English Heritage, 1989)

Williamson, George, *Lady Anne Clifford* (Kendal, 1922)

Wood, Anthony A., *Athenae Oxonienses* (London, 1691)

Woolf, Leonard, *Downhill All the Way: An Autobiography of the Years 1919–1939* (Hogarth Press, 1975)

Woolf, Virginia, *The Diary of Virginia Woolf*, 5 vols, ed. Anne Olivier Bell (Hogarth Press, 1977–84)

—— *The Letters of Virginia Woolf*, 6 vols, ed. Nigel Nicolson with Joanne Trautmann (Hogarth Press, 1975–80)

—— *Orlando* (Penguin Books, 1993)

Worsley, Lucy, *Cavalier: A Tale of Chivalry, Passion and Great Houses* (Faber, 2007)

Wraxall, Nathaniel, *The Historical and Posthumous Memoirs of Sir Nathaniel Wraxall, 1772–1784*, ed. Henry B. Wheatley (Bickers & Son, 1884)

Zim, Rivkah, 'Dialogue and discretion: Thomas Sackville, Catherine de Medici, and the Anjou marriage proposal, 1571', *Historical Journal*, 40, 2 (1997), pp. 287–310

—— 'A poet in politics: Thomas Sackville, Lord Buckhurst and 1st Earl of Dorset (1536–1608)', *Historical Research*, vol. 79, no. 204

—— 'Religion and the Politic Counsellor: Thomas Sackville, 1536–1608', *English Historical Review*, Vol. CXXII, no. 498

Zim, Rivkah, and M. B. Parkes, ' "Sacvyles Old Age", a newly discovered poem by Thomas Sackville, Lord Buckhurst, Earl of Dorset (c. 1536–1608)', *Review of English Studies*, new ser., 40 (1989), pp. 1–25

Acknowledgements

It would not have been possible to write this book without the historical archives and collections in the United Kingdom and the United States. I am particularly grateful to Michael Carter and his colleagues at the Centre for Kentish Studies in Maidstone, Kent. I would also like to thank Robin Harcourt-Williams at Hatfield House; Christopher Whittick at the East Sussex Record Office in Lewes, Sussex; Brigitte Petit-Archambault in Paris; and the staffs of the London Library and the British Library. Special thanks to the Lilly Library at Indiana University, Bloomington, for awarding me an Everett Helm Visiting Fellowship to study the diaries of Victoria, Lady Sackville, and to the staff at the library for making my week in Bloomington so pleasant and productive.

It will be obvious from the bibliography how indebted I am to the scholarship and publications of others. But there are a number of people who have helped, at first hand, by reading and suggesting amendments to individual chapters. I take full responsibility, however, for any errors. I have enjoyed discussions with Ed Town and Alden Gregory, two research students writing PhDs on Knole's architectural history under the supervision of Maurice Howard. They have shared their findings with me and set me straight on sixteenth- and seventeenth-century Knole. Dr Rivkah Zim, of King's College, London, the world's leading authority on Thomas

Sackville, 1st Earl of Dorset, kindly read the first chapter; and Dr David Smith of Selwyn College, Cambridge, guided me through the third, on Edward Sackville, 4th Earl of Dorset. Anne, Countess De La Warr and her husband, William, Earl De La Warr, helped me unravel the twin histories of the Sackville inheritances in Kent and Sussex, and took me to the family vault at Withyham, where lie the coffins of more than thirteen generations of Sackvilles. Margaret Simmons has compared my description of life at Knole in the first half of the twentieth century with her memories of it; and Martin Drury, former Director-General of the National Trust, who has always had a particular affection for Knole and has known several generations of the Sackville family, commented on the last two chapters of this book.

I also want to thank friends who have read parts of this book, and in particular, Dr Chris Greenhalgh and Adam Nicolson. Adam, a distant cousin and one of my oldest and dearest friends, has been a generous critic, a supplier of encouragement and support – as well as of references to original documents. Above all, he is always happy to explore, in conversation, the further reaches of this slightly barmy, shared family heritage.

I am grateful to Caroline Michel, my literary agent, for believing that this story was worth publishing and then, with her colleague, the writer and editor Tim Binding, for helping me to give it a sharper focus. Michael Fishwick has been a superb and sensitive editor – I can't think of a single suggestion he has made with which I have disagreed – and his colleagues at Bloomsbury have nurtured the book through all stages of its development with great charm and efficiency.

Special thanks to those who have supported me, at work and at home, in this time-consuming, and occasionally obsessive, task: to Ellen Dupont and my colleagues at Toucan Books for putting up with my absences and distractions; to the trustees, agents and staff of Knole Estates, who make living at Knole such a pleasure; to the staff of the National Trust, who have been unfailingly help-ful in many aspects of my life, including providing information for this book; to my mother and next-door neighbour, Bridget

Sackville-West, who knows as much as anyone about Knole and its collection; and most of all to my own family, to my children Freya, Arthur and Edie, and to my wife Jane for her love and support.

Index

A NOTE ON THE AUTHOR

After studying History at Oxford University, Robert Sackville-West worked in publishing, in 1985 founding Toucan Books, which creates illustrated non-fiction books for an international market. He now combines that with chairing Knole Estates, the property and investment company which runs the Sackville family's interests at Knole. In 2008, he and his wife and three children moved into the house, which has been occupied by the Sackville family for four hundred years.

A NOTE ON THE TYPE

The text of this book is set in Linotype Stempel Garamond, a
version of Garamond adapted and first used by the Stempel foun-
dry in 1924. It's one of several versions of Garamond based on the
designs of Claude Garamond. It is thought that Garamond based
his font on Bembo, cut in 1495 by Francesco Griffo in collabora-
tion with the Italian printer Aldus Manutius. Garamond types
were first used in books printed in Paris around 1532. Many of the
present-day versions of this type are based on the *Typi Academiae*
of Jean Jannon cut in Sedan in 1615.

Claude Garamond was born in Paris in 1480. He learned how to
cut type from his father and by the age of fifteen he was able to
fashion steel punches the size of a pica with great precision. At the
age of sixty he was commissioned by King Francis I to design a
Greek alphabet, for this he was given the honourable title of royal
type founder. He died in 1561.